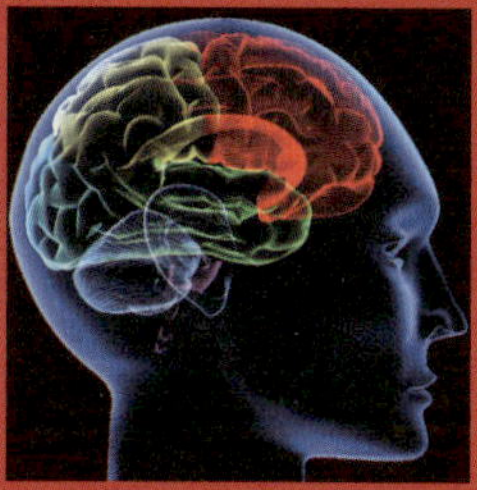

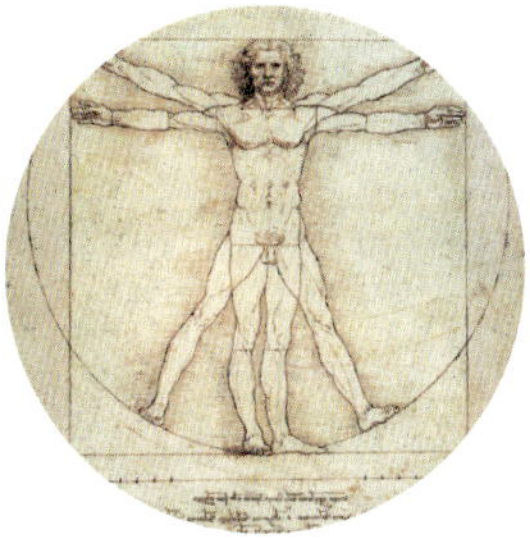

CHILDREN'S PHOTOGRAPHIC REFERENCE

ENCYCLOPEDIA OF EVERYTHING

This edition published by Parragon Books Ltd in 2013

Parragon Books Ltd
Chartist House
15–17 Trim Street
Bath BA1 1HA, UK
www.parragon.com

ISBN 978-1-4723-2443-6

Printed in China

CHILDREN'S PHOTOGRAPHIC REFERENCE

ENCYCLOPEDIA OF EVERYTHING

Parragon

Bath • New York • Singapore • Hong Kong • Cologne • Delhi
Melbourne • Amsterdam • Johannesburg • Shenzhen

CONTENTS

THE UNIVERSE AND PLANET EARTH

THE NATURAL WORLD

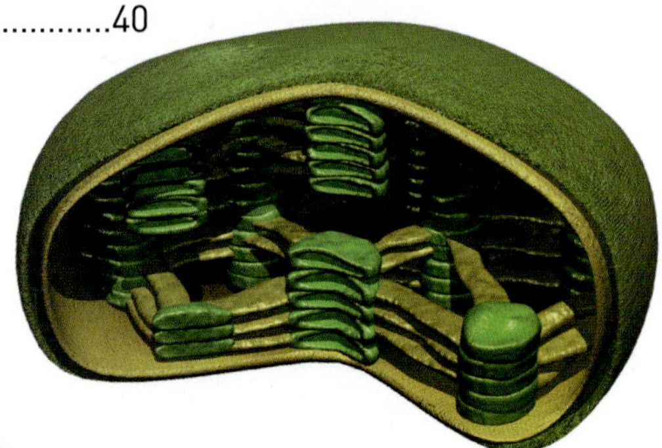

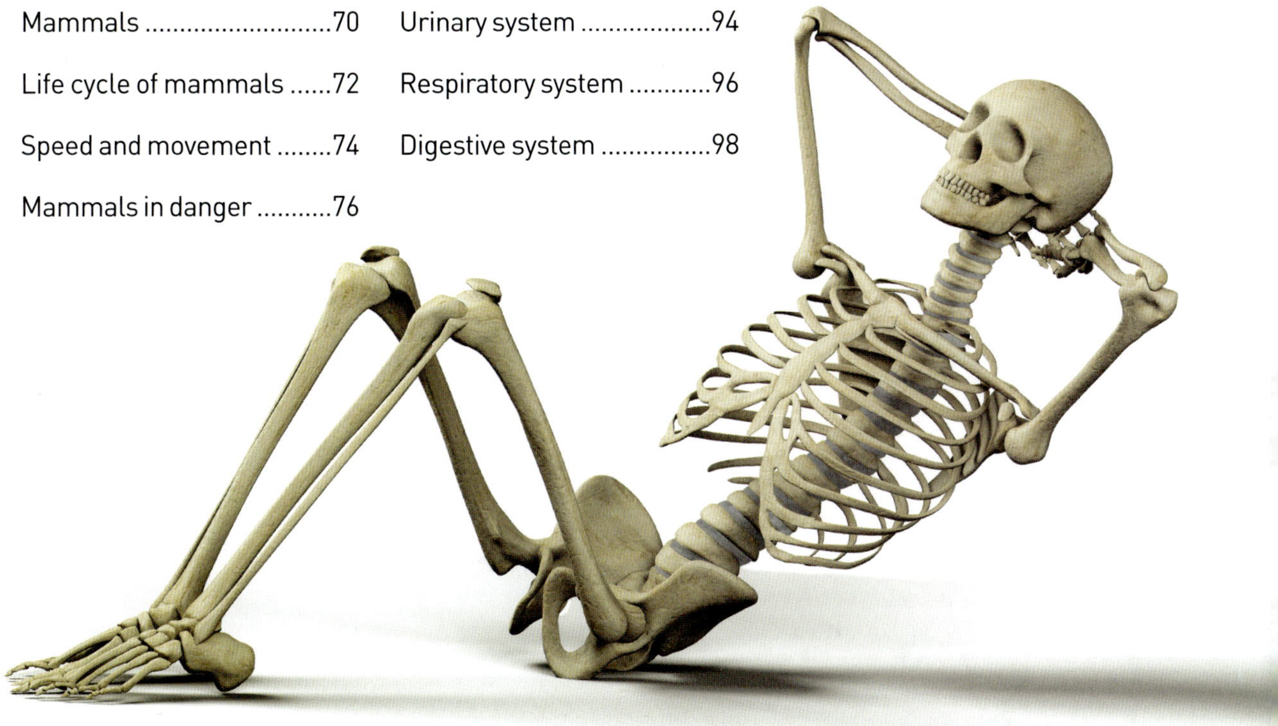

THE HUMAN BODY

HISTORY

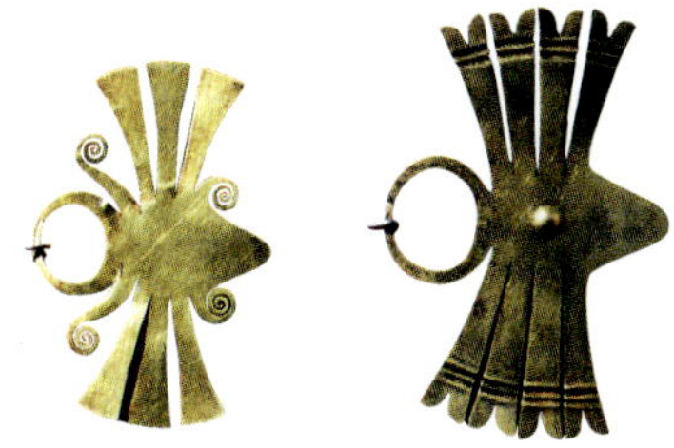

SCIENCE AND CULTURE

AIRBUS A380
A380

THE UNIVERSE AND PLANET EARTH

The Universe is an unimaginably huge place. It contains billions of galaxies, and each galaxy contains billions of stars. Around one of those stars, the Sun, orbits the planet Earth. Our planet is the only place in the Universe that we know contains life. Scientists are constantly discovering amazing new facts about the Universe. The one thing we know for sure is that there is still plenty that we have yet to find out.

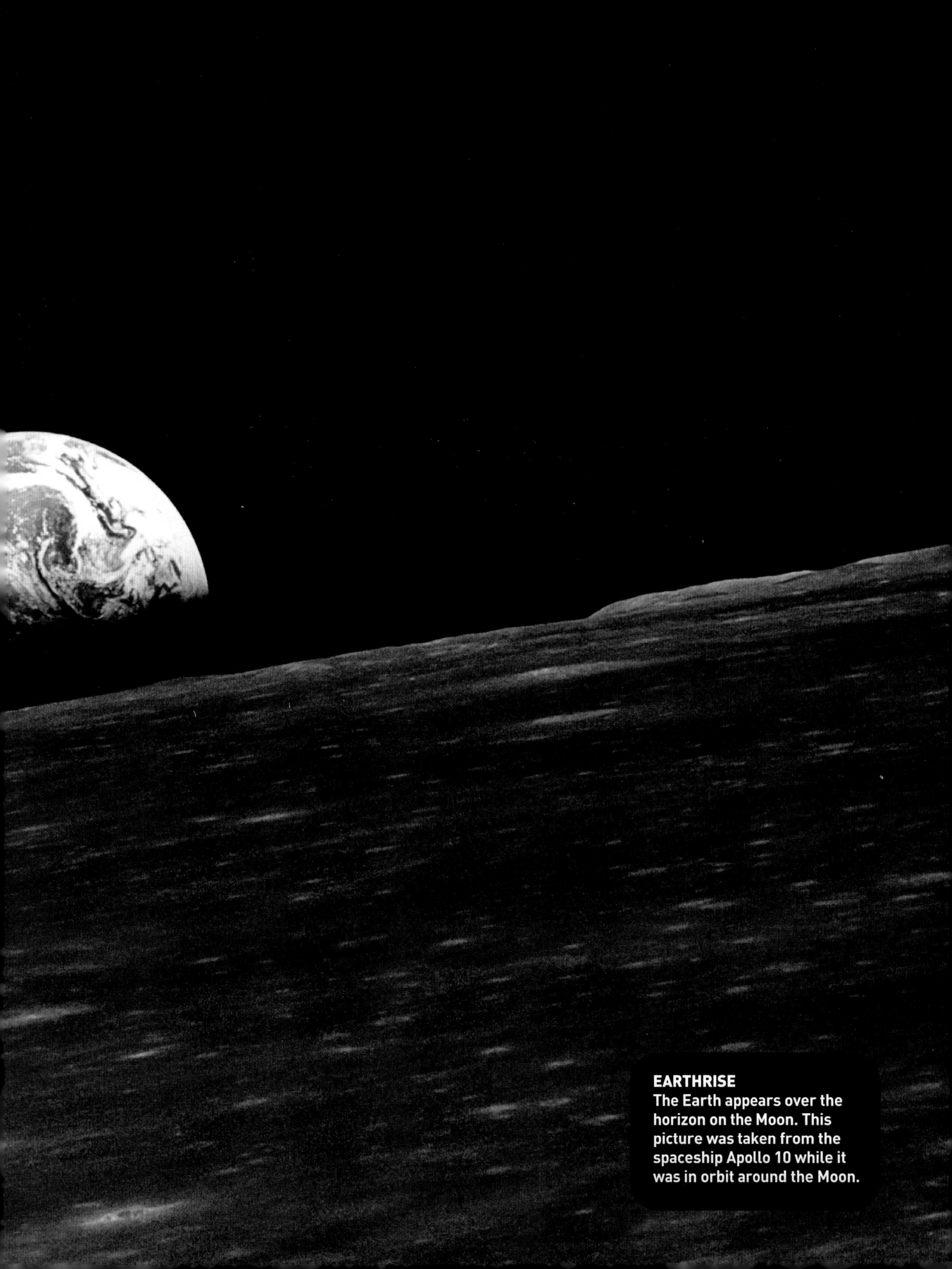

EARTHRISE
The Earth appears over the horizon on the Moon. This picture was taken from the spaceship Apollo 10 while it was in orbit around the Moon.

Our Universe

The Universe is all the matter, energy, space and time that exists. It is constantly expanding in all directions. The Universe contains things that we can see, such as galaxies, stars, planets, nebulae and comets, and things that we cannot see, such as dark matter. Throughout history, scientists have made many discoveries about our Universe, but much about it is still mysterious and unknown.

STAR
Stars are made of shining gas, which gives off light and heat. The hottest stars are a blue-white colour, while the coolest are orange, yellow or red.

PLANET
The planets are sphere-shaped bodies that do not give off their own light. They orbit stars.

4,000
The number of stars that can be seen by the naked eye.

SATELLITE
Satellites do not have their own light. They orbit planets. One planet may have many satellites.

LIGHT YEAR

A light year is a unit of length equal to the distance travelled by light in one year. Light years are used to measure the huge distances between stars, planets, satellites and other bodies in the Universe.

1 LIGHT YEAR = 9,461,000,000,000 km

DARK MATTER

Most of the material in space is a strange substance that we cannot see. Scientists call it dark matter. There is much more dark matter than visible matter in the Universe, but we know very little about it.

NEBULA
A nebula is a cloud of gases and dust that can produce dazzling light displays. Sometimes, new stars form from these clouds. The nebulae themselves have formed from the material left over when a star dies.

LOOK AT THE SKY

All the stars we see when we look at the night sky are part of our galaxy, the Milky Way.

GALAXY
The galaxies are large groups of stars, planets, gases and dust that are held together by gravity. There are billions of galaxies in the Universe, and the largest have as many as 100 trillion stars.

The Big Bang

For many years, most scientists believed that the Universe was probably infinite – meaning that it had no beginning and no end. Today, people believe that the Universe began with an explosion 13.7 billion years ago. This idea is called the Big Bang theory.

WHAT CAUSED THE BIG BANG?
This is a mystery that we still do not fully understand.

CHANGE

Ever since the Big Bang, the Universe has been changing. Today, it is filled with galaxies that may not always have existed. In the future, they may even disappear.

1

THE START
At the beginning of time and space, the Universe was a tiny, hot, dense spot.

2

THE EXPLOSION
The Universe grew extremely quickly in the first fraction of a second after the Big Bang. Larger particles of matter formed and clumps of gas also appeared.

BEST THEORY

Today, most scientists accept that the Big Bang is the best way to explain how the Universe formed. The Ukrainian astronomer George Gamow was one of the first people to develop this theory in the 1940s. For many years, it was a very controversial idea.

THEORIES

Theories are explanations of natural events that are made after looking at the evidence. A theory can never be completely proved, but more evidence can be gathered to support the theory so that it becomes the best explanation we have.

3

GALAXIES

In the first 1 billion years after the Big Bang, the first galaxies formed. The galaxies are made up of dust, gas, planets and billions of stars.

4

THE SOLAR SYSTEM

About 9 billion years after the Big Bang, the Solar System, containing our Earth, appeared.

125

BILLION

An estimate of the number of galaxies in the visible Universe. There may be many more.

The life cycle of stars

Stars are huge spheres of burning gas. We see them as lights in the sky, but in fact, they vary greatly in size, colour and heat. Most appear white but some are orange, red or blue. Stars do not burn forever. Large stars have more fuel and they burn it quickly. They last about 10 million years. Small stars may last for hundreds of billions of years.

BIG STARS

With a mass eight or more times greater than our Sun, these massive stars have a short life. When they come to the end of their lives, their centres collapse. This causes a huge explosion called a supernova, which can shine as brightly as a whole galaxy.

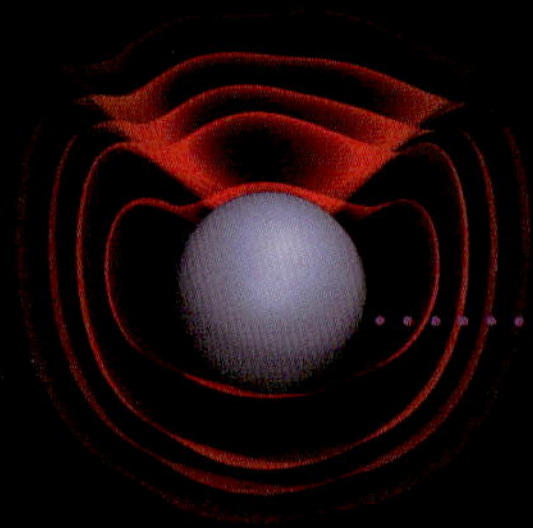

2 COLOUR
Massive stars are blue-white in colour.

3 RED GIANT
Near the end of their lives, all stars become red giants. They become bigger and their temperature drops.

1 STAR BIRTH
The force of gravity pulls the dust and gas together in clouds called nebulae. The material condenses, its temperature rises and it begins to shine. A star has been born.

2 COLOUR
Less massive stars are a pale red colour because their temperature is lower. Small stars, called red dwarfs, are the most common type of star in the Universe.

SMALL STARS

These less massive stars have a much longer life than the most massive stars, eventually turning into red giants after many billions of years.

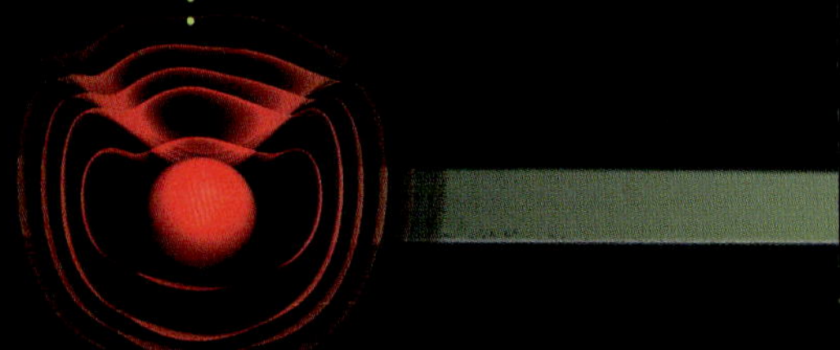

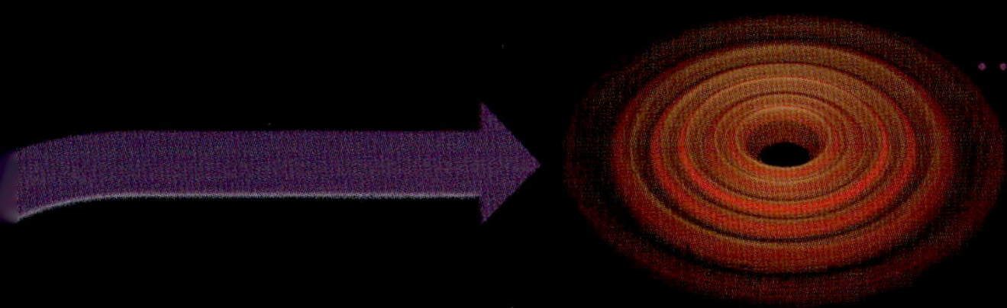

5 **BLACK HOLE**
After the explosion of a giant star, a huge black hole can develop. This is an area of space with an enormous gravitational force, from which light cannot escape.

4 **SUPERNOVA**
A supernova is a massive explosion that is caused when a star collapses at the end of its life.

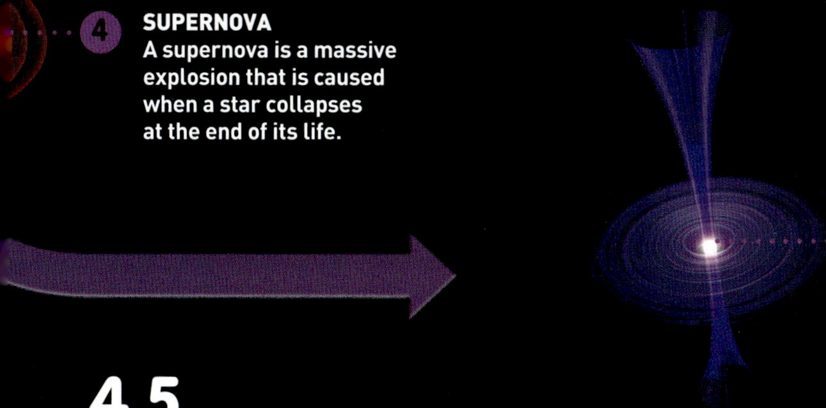

5 **NEUTRON STAR**
A supernova may leave behind a small, dense body called a neutron star.

4.5 BILLION YEARS
The age of the Sun.

3 **RED GIANT**
Like all stars, less massive stars become red giants. Their size increases and their temperature drops.

4 **NEBULA**
At the end of its life, the gases near the surface of the star start to drift off to form a cloud called a planetary nebula.

5 **WHITE DWARF**
After the star has shed its outer layers of gas, it leaves a white dwarf. This shines a bright white colour before it eventually goes out.

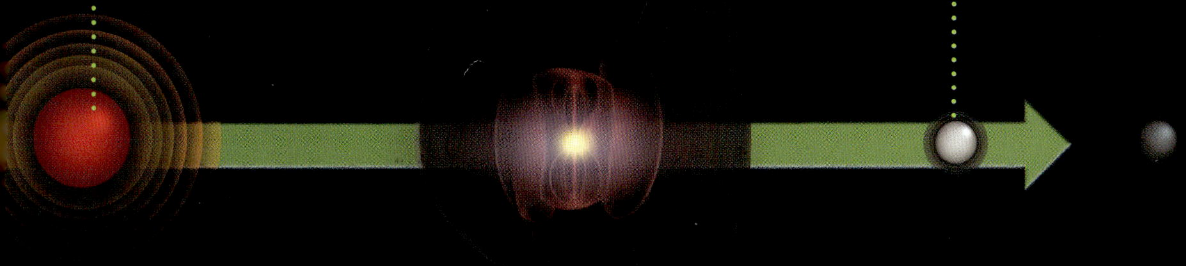

Galaxies

The galaxies are groups of moving stars, planets, gas and dust that are held together by the force of gravity. The first galaxies formed 200 million years after the Big Bang.

ONE GALAXY?

Until the start of the 20th century, it was believed that the Milky Way was the only galaxy.

GRAVITY

Every object in the Universe pulls every other object towards it with a force called gravity. The force is greater the larger the objects are and the closer together they are. Galaxies are held together by gravity.

MILKY WAY

The galaxy that contains the Earth is called the Milky Way. It is a spiral galaxy. We are situated in one of the spiral arms. The stars we see in the night sky are just a few of the billions of stars in the Milky Way.

KINDS OF GALAXY

ELLIPTICAL
These are sphere-shaped galaxies that are made up mostly of old stars. They contain very little dust or gas.

SPIRAL
Spiral galaxies are made up of old and new stars, which form a spiral shape like a slowly turning pinwheel.

IRREGULAR
Galaxies with no regular shape are called irregular. These galaxies contain a lot of new stars.

COLLIDING GALAXIES

Sometimes two spiral galaxies collide with each other. In time, these galaxies will join to form one irregular galaxy.

MORE THAN
100 BILLION
The number of stars in the Milky Way.

The Solar System

The Sun is the closest star to our planet. Eight planets orbit the Sun. Many smaller objects also orbit the Sun, including dwarf planets, asteroids and comets. The Sun and all the other bodies that orbit it, are together known as the Solar System.

RINGS
Saturn's rings are formed from small particles that are orbiting the planet.

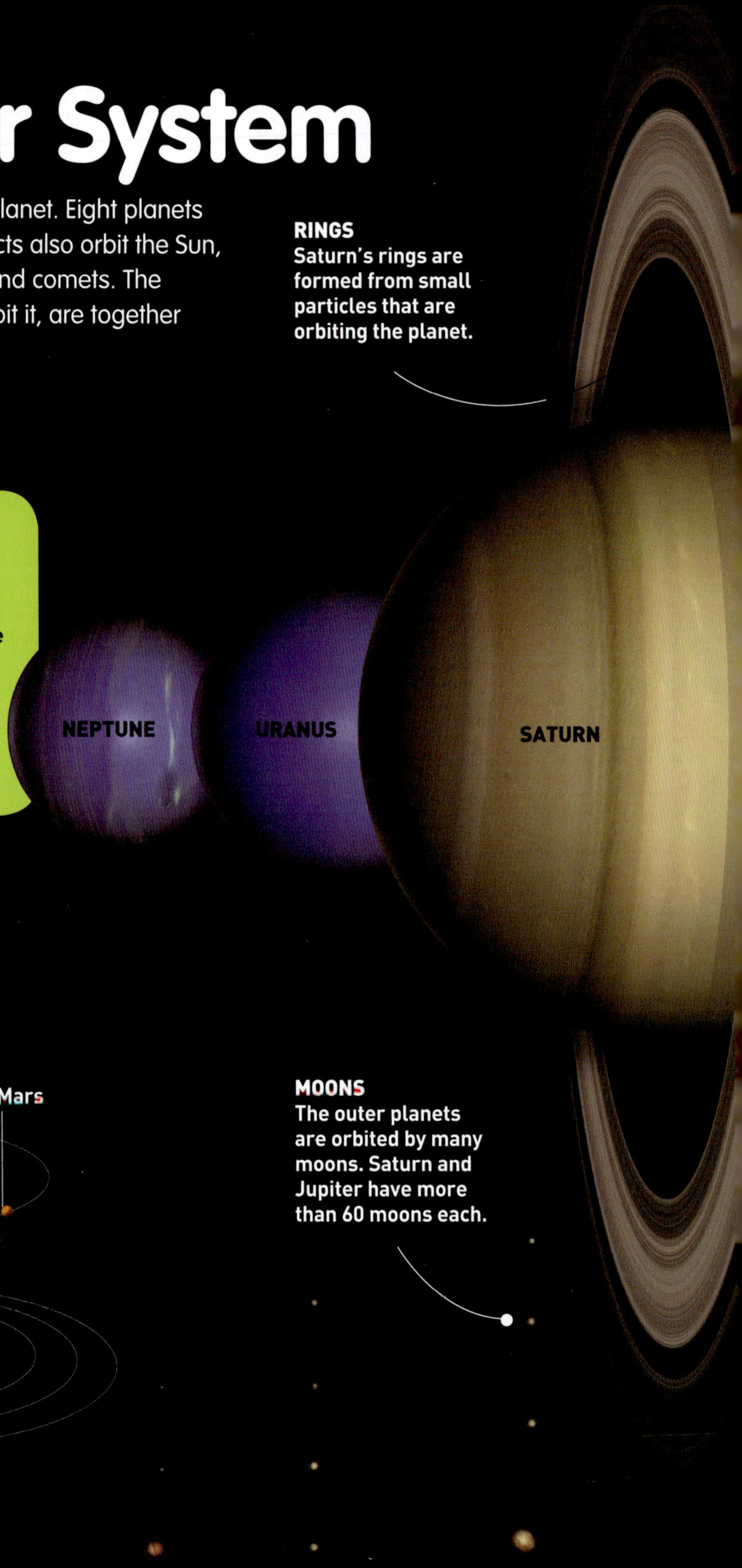

GAS GIANTS

The outer planets – Jupiter, Saturn, Uranus and Neptune – are enormous spheres made of mostly gas. These planets are known as gas giants and are very cold at their surfaces.

YEARS

The time it takes for a planet to complete one orbit of the Sun is the length of the planet's year. The further away a planet is from the Sun, the longer its year.

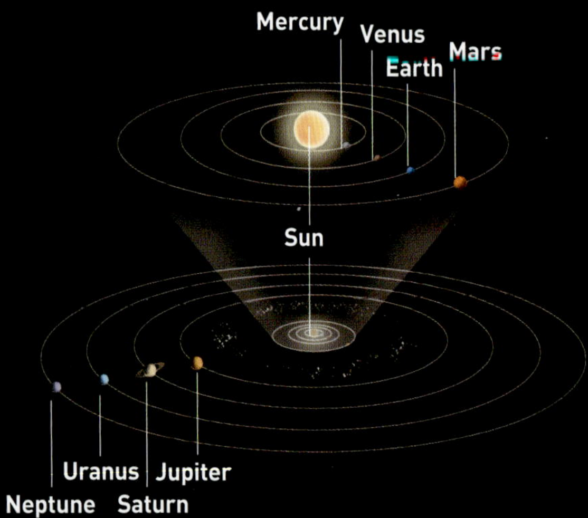

MOONS
The outer planets are orbited by many moons. Saturn and Jupiter have more than 60 moons each.

150
million km
The distance from the Sun to Earth.

ASTEROID BELT
This region of the Solar System contains millions of pieces of rock.

DAYS

Each planet rotates around its own axis. The time it takes to do one rotation is the length of the planet's day.

ROCKY PLANETS

Orbiting between the Sun and the asteroid belt are four smaller rocky planets. All except Mercury are surrounded by atmospheres. Mercury and Venus are very hot, while the surface of Mars is colder than Earth.

BIGGEST PLANET
Jupiter is the biggest of the eight planets. Its volume is more than 1,000 times greater than the Earth.

The Sun

The Sun is the only star in the Solar System. It is a medium-sized star that formed 4.5 billion years ago. It has about 5 billion years of life left. Its light and heat make life possible on our planet.

8.5 MINS

The time it takes for light to travel from the surface of the Sun to the Earth.

SHINING GASES

The Sun is made mostly of hydrogen (90 per cent) and helium (10 per cent). These two gases are very hot, making the Sun shine.

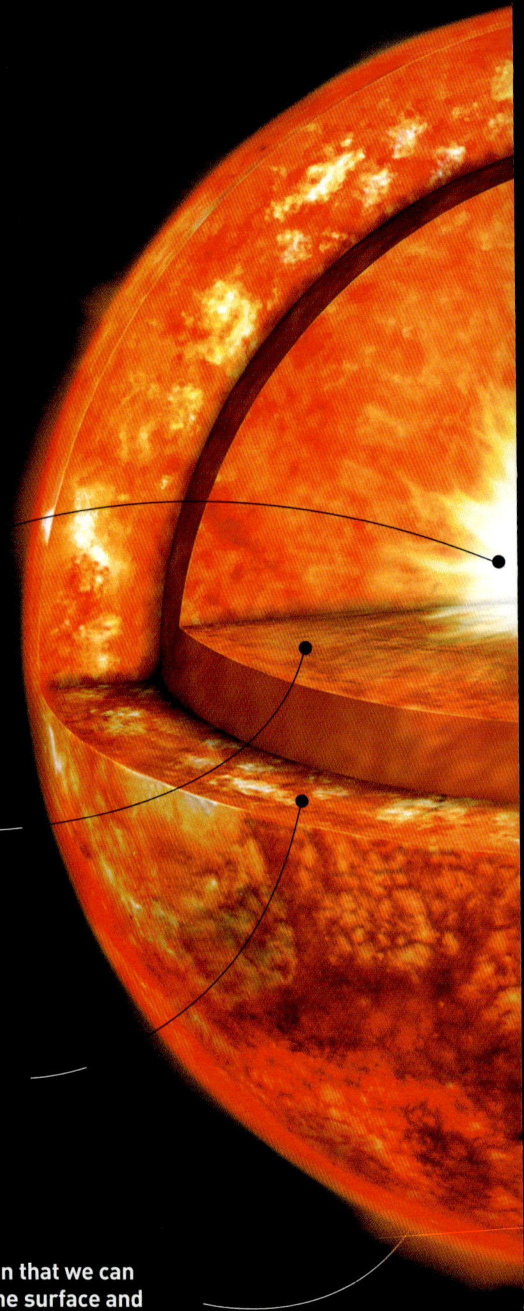

CORE
The Sun's core is 15 million °C.

RADIATION ZONE
Energy from the core passes through this zone.

CONVECTION ZONE
Energy is carried to the surface of the Sun in the convection zone.

PHOTOSPHERE
The part of the Sun that we can see, made up of the surface and

FACT FILE

Symbol	☉
Distance from the Earth	149.9 million km
Diameter	1,391,000 km
Temperature at surface	6,000 °C

SOLAR WIND

A continuous 'wind' of particles is given off in all directions by the Sun. Near the Earth, the solar wind has a speed of 450 kilometres per second. It causes weather events such as the northern lights and magnetic storms.

ECLIPSE

When the Moon passes between the Sun and the Earth, this causes a solar eclipse. It goes dark on Earth for a few minutes.

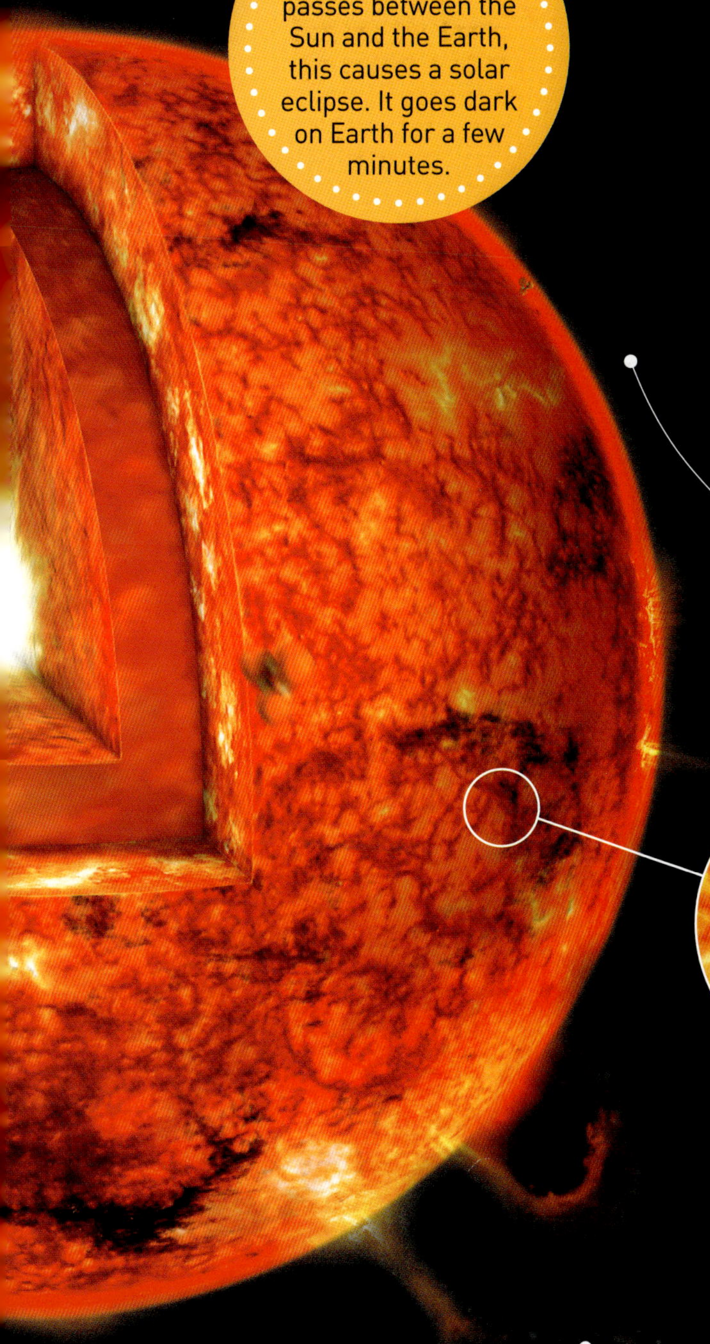

CORONA
The outer part of the atmosphere stretches many millions of kilometres into space. It is 2 million °C.

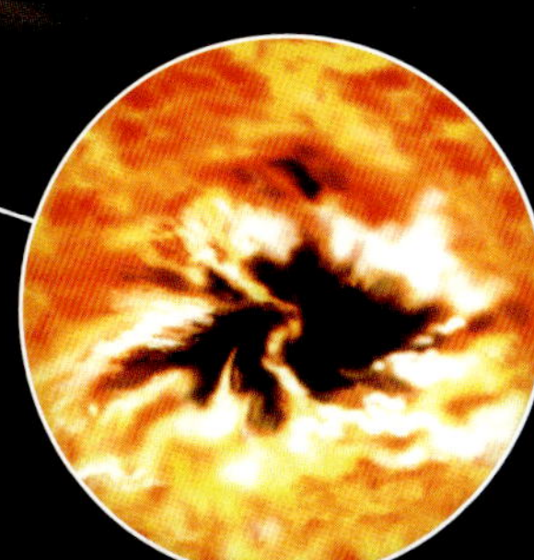

SUNSPOTS
Sunspots are darker areas on the Sun's surface where the gases are cooler.

FLARES
Flares are extremely powerful explosions on the surface of the Sun that throw up huge amounts of material into space.

The Earth

Our planet is the third closest to the Sun and the largest of the rocky planets. It is known as the Blue Planet because of the colour of the oceans that cover two-thirds of the surface. The Earth is the only planet where liquid water has been found on its surface.

WATER
Clouds form from water vapour in the air that has condensed back into liquid.

ATMOSPHERE
The atmosphere is made up of several gases, mainly nitrogen and oxygen.

SOUTH POLE

LIFE

The Earth is the only planet where life is known to exist. There are several reasons why life can exist on our planet: the presence of liquid water at the surface, temperatures that are neither too hot nor too cold, and a protective atmosphere. The Earth is also the only planet where there is water in all three states:

SOLID

Water freezes at 0 °C. At the poles, the coldest places on the planet, water is frozen.

LIQUID

A large part of the Earth's surface is covered in liquid water. Most of it is salt water.

GAS

Water exists in the air as water vapour. It condenses back into liquid to form clouds.

HUMAN ACTIVITY

Humans put harmful chemicals into the atmosphere when they burn coal, oil and gas.

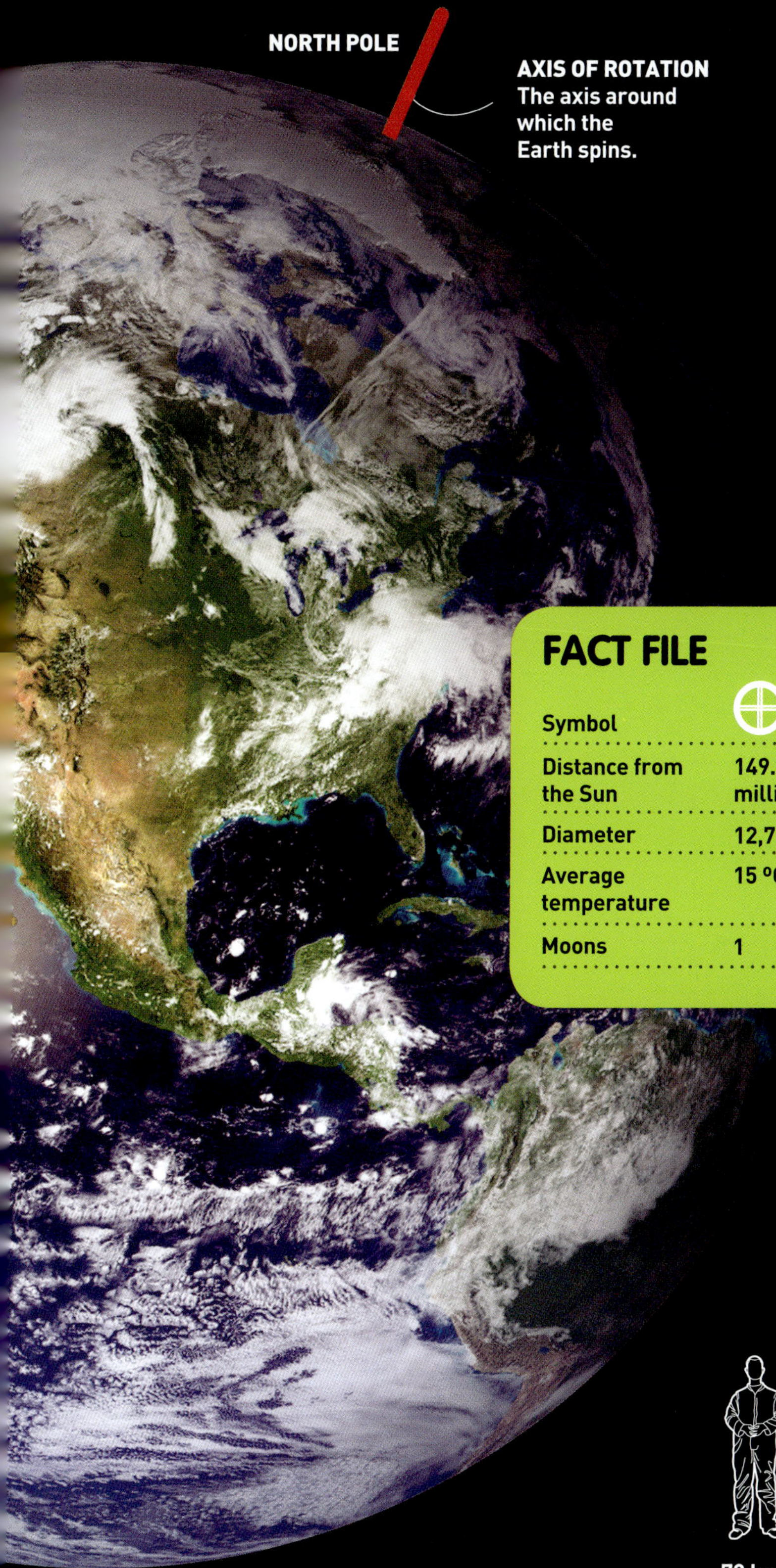

AXIS OF ROTATION
The axis around which the Earth spins.

STRUCTURE

The Earth is made up of different layers. The outermost layer is the atmosphere, which is made up of a mixture of gases. Under this is the surface, which is mostly covered in water. The surface is the top of a thin, solid crust. Under the crust is the mantle. At the centre is the solid core.

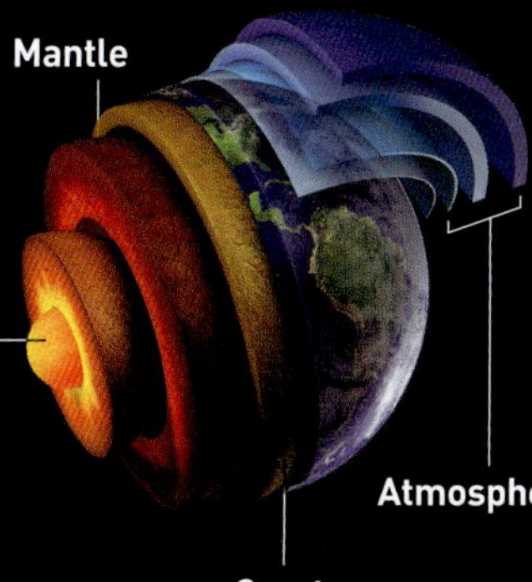

FACT FILE

Symbol	⊕
Distance from the Sun	149.9 million km
Diameter	12,756 km
Average temperature	15 ºC
Moons	1

3
The percentage of water on the surface of the Earth that is fresh water.

GRAVITY

We are held onto the surface of the Earth by the force of gravity. Gravity gives us our weight. The strength of a planet's gravitational pull depends on its size, and we would weigh different amounts on other planets or on the Moon. For example, the same person would weigh these amounts:

70 kg on Earth | 11 kg on Moon | 177 kg on Jupiter

The Earth's movements

Like all the planets in the Solar System, the Earth spins on its own axis and it also orbits the Sun. These two movements cause the difference between day and night and the changing of the seasons.

23.5°
The angle at which Earth is tilted.

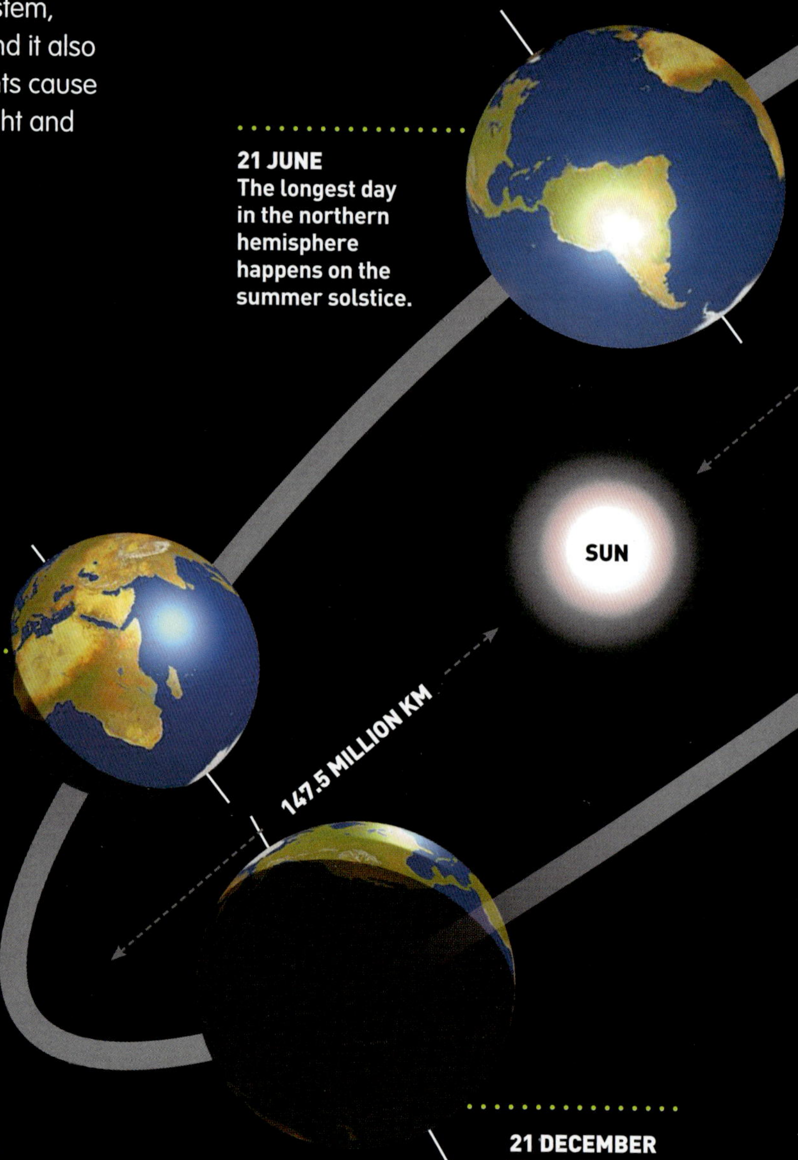

21 JUNE
The longest day in the northern hemisphere happens on the summer solstice.

YEARLY ORBIT

The Earth takes 365 days, 5 hours and 48 minutes to orbit the Sun. As the Earth spins on its tilted axis, the regions change throughout the year depending on their distance from the Sun. This is what causes the change of the seasons as well as the length of our days and nights.

21 SEPTEMBER
This is the autumn equinox in the northern hemisphere. Day and night are the same length – both 12 hours.

DAILY ROTATION

The Earth turns around its own axis each day. This movement causes day and night. It also makes the planet slightly flattened at the poles, and causes ocean currents.

PLEASE NOTE: FOR THE PURPOSES OF THIS DIAGRAM THE EARTH AND THE SUN ARE NOT SHOWN TO SCALE.

21 DECEMBER
This is the winter solstice in the northern hemisphere. It is the shortest day of the year.

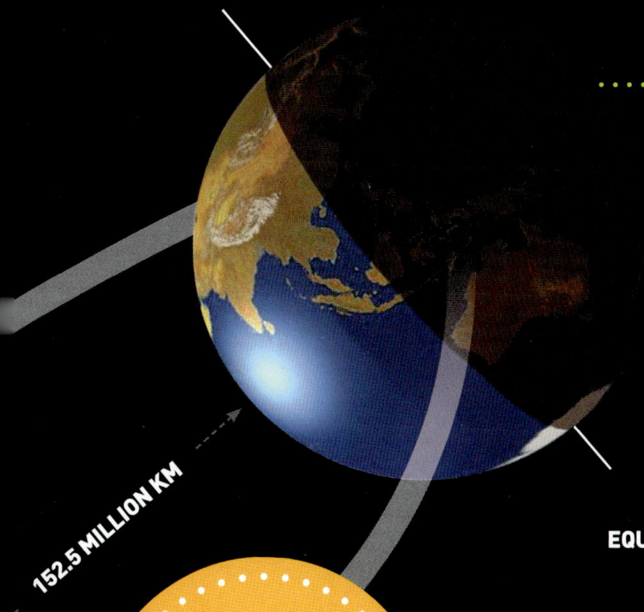

21 MARCH
This is the spring equinox in the northern hemisphere. Day and night are the same length.

LEAP YEAR

Every fourth year, the month of February has 29 days instead of 28. This is called a leap year.

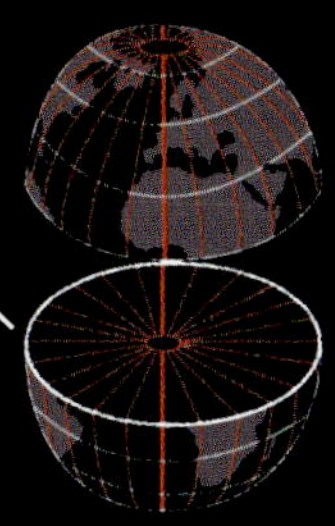

HEMISPHERES

The Earth is divided into two halves: the northern and southern hemispheres. The equator is the imaginary line that separates the two hemispheres. When it is summer in the north, it is winter in the south.

JET LAG
Long-distance flights can cause jet lag. This is because a change in time zones can upset our body's natural rhythm.

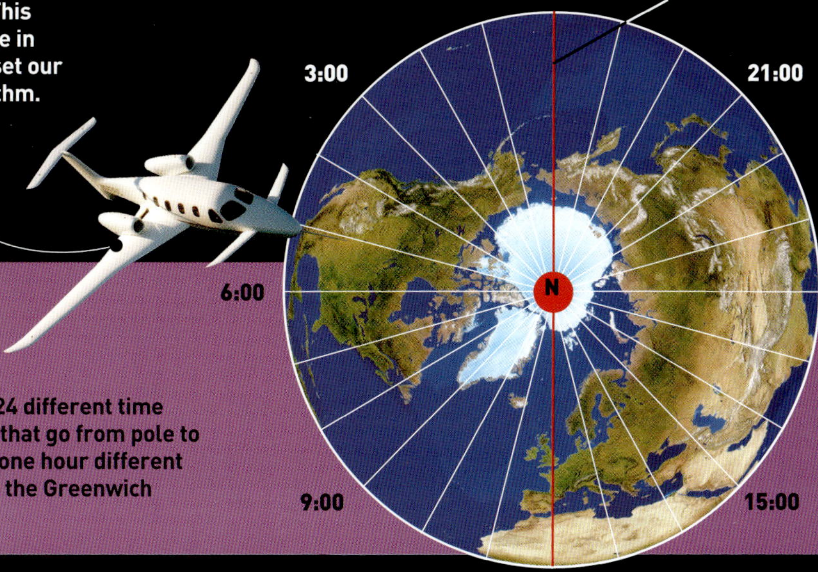

TIME ZONES

The Earth is divided into 24 different time zones by imaginery lines that go from pole to pole. Each zone's time is one hour different from its neighbours, with the Greenwich Meridian at the centre.

The Moon

The Moon is our planet's only natural satellite. It orbits the Earth with the same side always facing towards it. Seen from the Earth, the Moon changes shape depending on the light from the Sun that it reflects towards us.

FULL MOON

In myths and stories, a full moon, with its bright moonlit nights, was thought to cause strange happenings.

ORBIT

For each complete orbit, the Moon makes exactly one rotation. Because of this, the same side of the Moon always faces us.

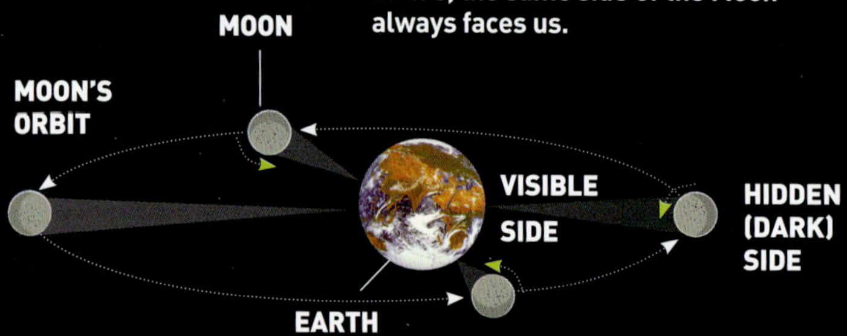

CRATERS
The Moon's surface is covered in craters caused by the impact of asteroids and comets.

SEAS
These areas appear dark to us. Despite their name, they are dry.

THE TIDES

The Moon's gravity pulls at the water in the Earth's oceans. This causes the tides. At the point where the Moon is directly overhead, its pull on the Earth's water is strongest, and the water rises to cause a high tide. There is also a high tide at the opposite side to this, where the Moon's pull is least strong. High tides happen about once every 12 hours.

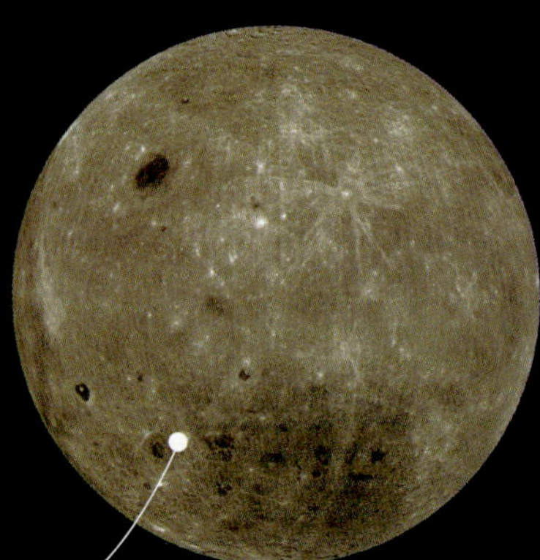

DARK SIDE
The dark side of the Moon cannot be seen from the Earth. It was first photographed by a Russian space probe in 1959.

29.5 DAYS

The average length of the Moon's orbit.

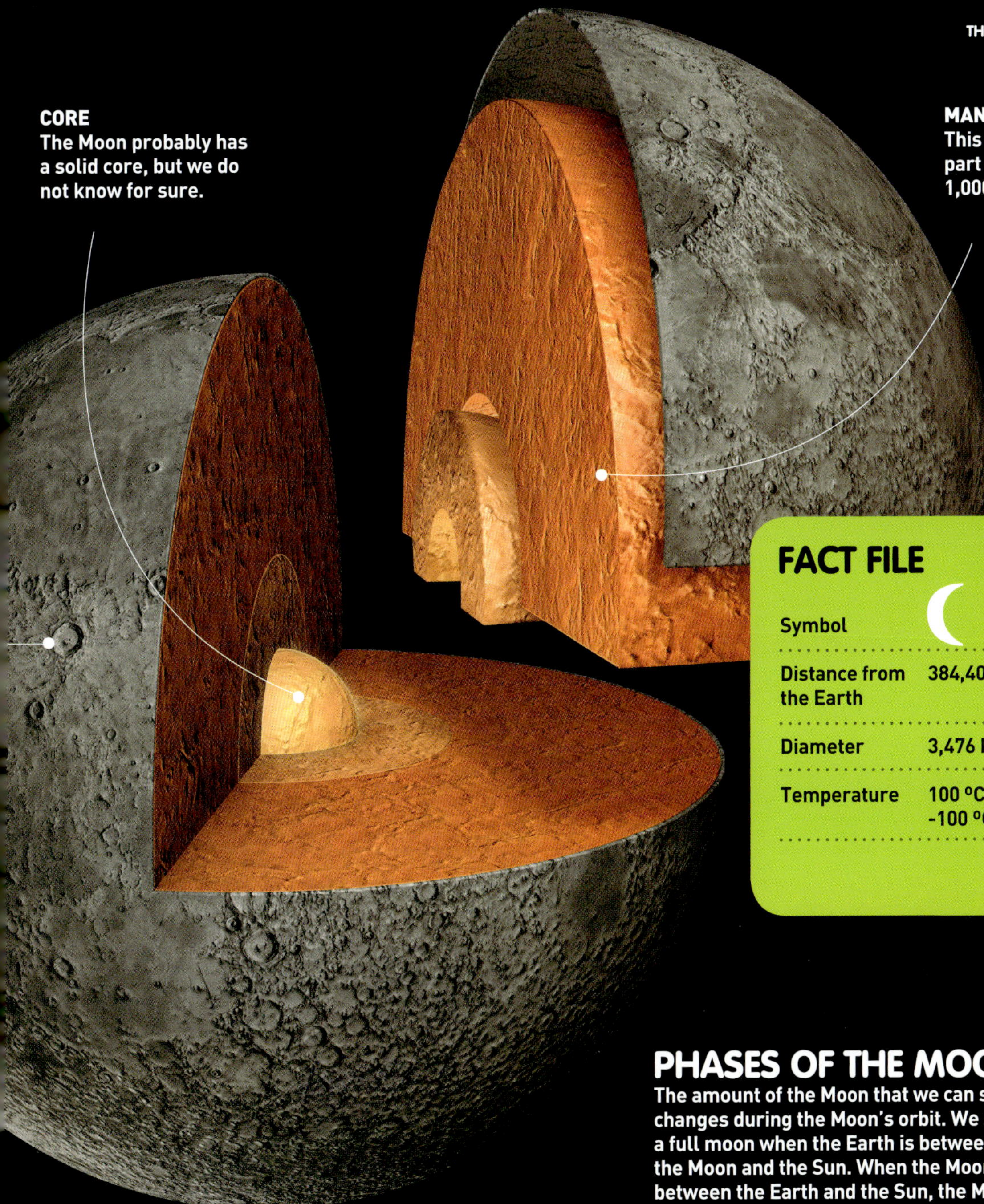

FACT FILE

Symbol	☾
Distance from the Earth	384,400 km
Diameter	3,476 km
Temperature	100 °C (day) -100 °C (night)

PHASES OF THE MOON

The amount of the Moon that we can see changes during the Moon's orbit. We see a full moon when the Earth is between the Moon and the Sun. When the Moon is between the Earth and the Sun, the Moon is entirely in shade. This is a new moon.

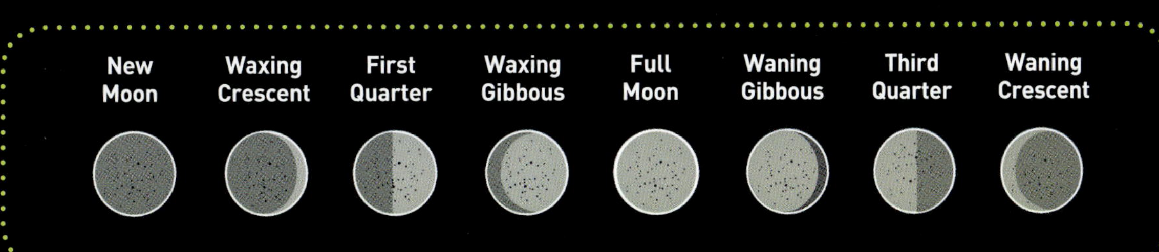

The early Earth

The Earth and the other planets in the Solar System first formed 4.6 billion years ago. At first, the Earth was a huge ball of burning rock, with no water or atmosphere. Over the course of millions of years, great changes took place. First the Earth's crust formed, then the atmosphere, the oceans, and finally the continents, as the Earth became the planet that we know today.

1

FORMATION
The Earth formed from a huge cloud of gas and dust.

2

COOLING
Little by little, the surface cooled to form a dry crust.

10

MOUNTAIN RANGES
The highest mountain ranges, such as the Alps, the Andes and the Himalayas, started to form about 60 million years ago.

9

THE FIRST CONTINENTS
Land started to appear 1.8 billion years ago. Little by little, it grew into a huge mass of land, which later broke up into the continents we know today.

4 BILLION YEARS

The age of the oldest rocks.

LIFE
When the atmosphere formed and liquid water appeared, the first life started to evolve.

3

ASTEROID AND COMET IMPACT
Without an atmosphere to protect it, the surface of the Earth was struck by the impact of asteroids and comets.

4

SUPERVOLCANOES
Burning material exploded through the crust in the form of huge volcanoes.

5

THE ATMOSPHERE
The gases given off by the volcanoes formed a layer around the planet.

6

THE FIRST RAIN
Volcanoes created water vapour, which condensed in the atmosphere to form clouds.

7

THE FIRST ICE AGE
About 2.4 billion years ago, the planet cooled enough for the surface to freeze.

8

THE SEAS AND OCEANS
As the crust cooled, liquid water built up on the surface to create oceans and seas.

Structure of the Earth

The Earth is very different under its surface. The rocky ground on which we live is only a thin crust. Underneath the crust is the mantle, made of solid and liquid rock, and in the centre is a hot metal core. The whole planet is surrounded by a layer of gases that form the atmosphere.

HOW FAR HAVE WE EXPLORED?

From the surface to the centre of the Earth it is more than 6000 km. So far, we have managed to explore 12 kilometres down.

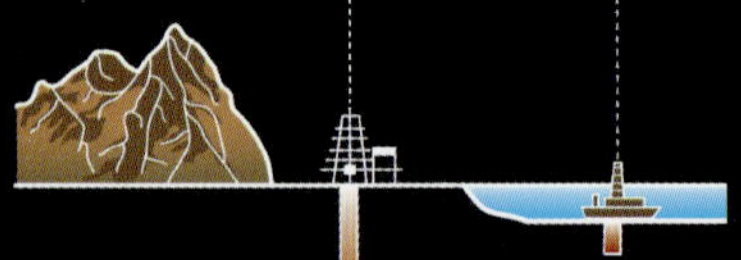

INNER CORE
The inner core is made of solid iron and nickle.

OUTER CORE
The outer core is made of molten iron and nickel.

OUTER MANTLE
The movement of the outer mantle causes earthquakes and volcanoes.

INNER MANTLE
Heavy rocks make up the mantle. They are at more than 1000 °C.

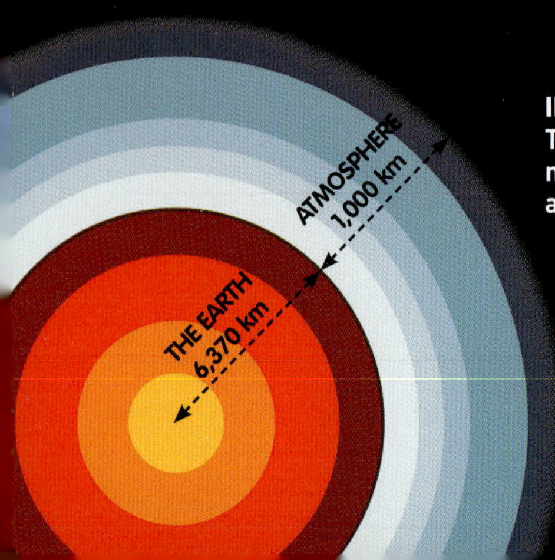

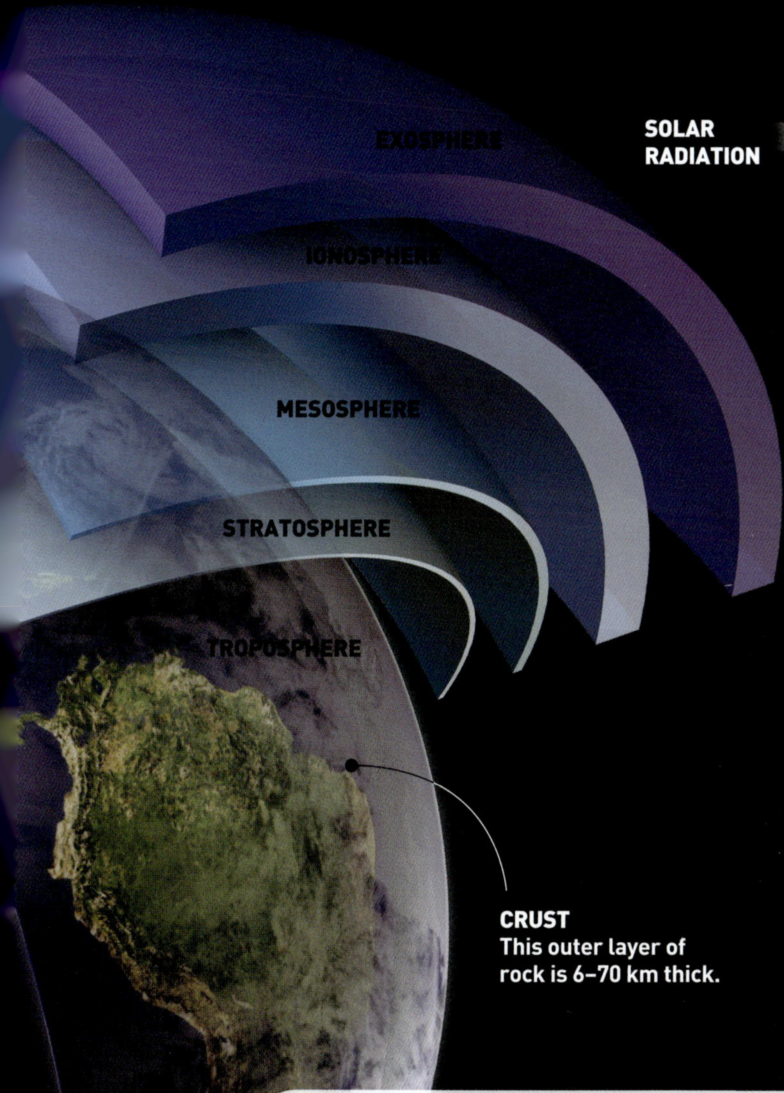

CRUST
This outer layer of rock is 6–70 km thick.

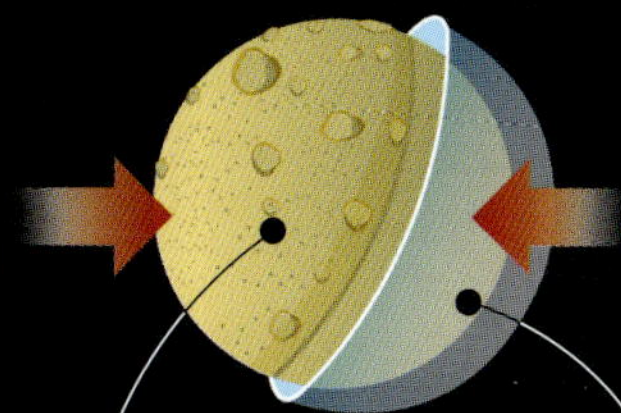

NO ATMOSPHERE
Life would be wiped out by the radiation and heat.

ATMOSPHERE
Filters the Sun's rays and distributes its heat.

THE ATMOSPHERE

The atmosphere is made up of a mixture of gases, mainly nitrogen and oxygen. It is divided into different layers depending on the amount of gases at each height. The atmosphere gives us the air we breathe and it protects us from the Sun's harmful rays.

HOT PLANET

The temperature of the Earth rises the closer you get to the centre.

THE HYDROSPHERE

The hydrosphere is the name for the liquid part of the Earth, including the oceans, lakes, rivers, groundwater and water in the atmosphere. Water covers more than two-thirds of the Earth's surface.

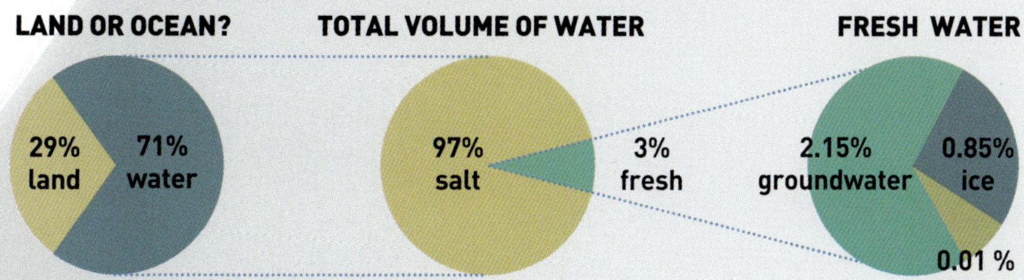

The continents

The Earth's crust is made up of parts that fit together like the pieces in a jigsaw puzzle. Called tectonic plates, they float on top of the semi-liquid mantle and are continually moving. The movements of the plates caused different continents to form millions of years ago, and even today, the continents are still on the move.

250 MILLION YEARS AGO
The Tethys Ocean slowly divided Pangea into two subcontinents: Laurasia and Gondwana. They joined together again to make a super-continent.

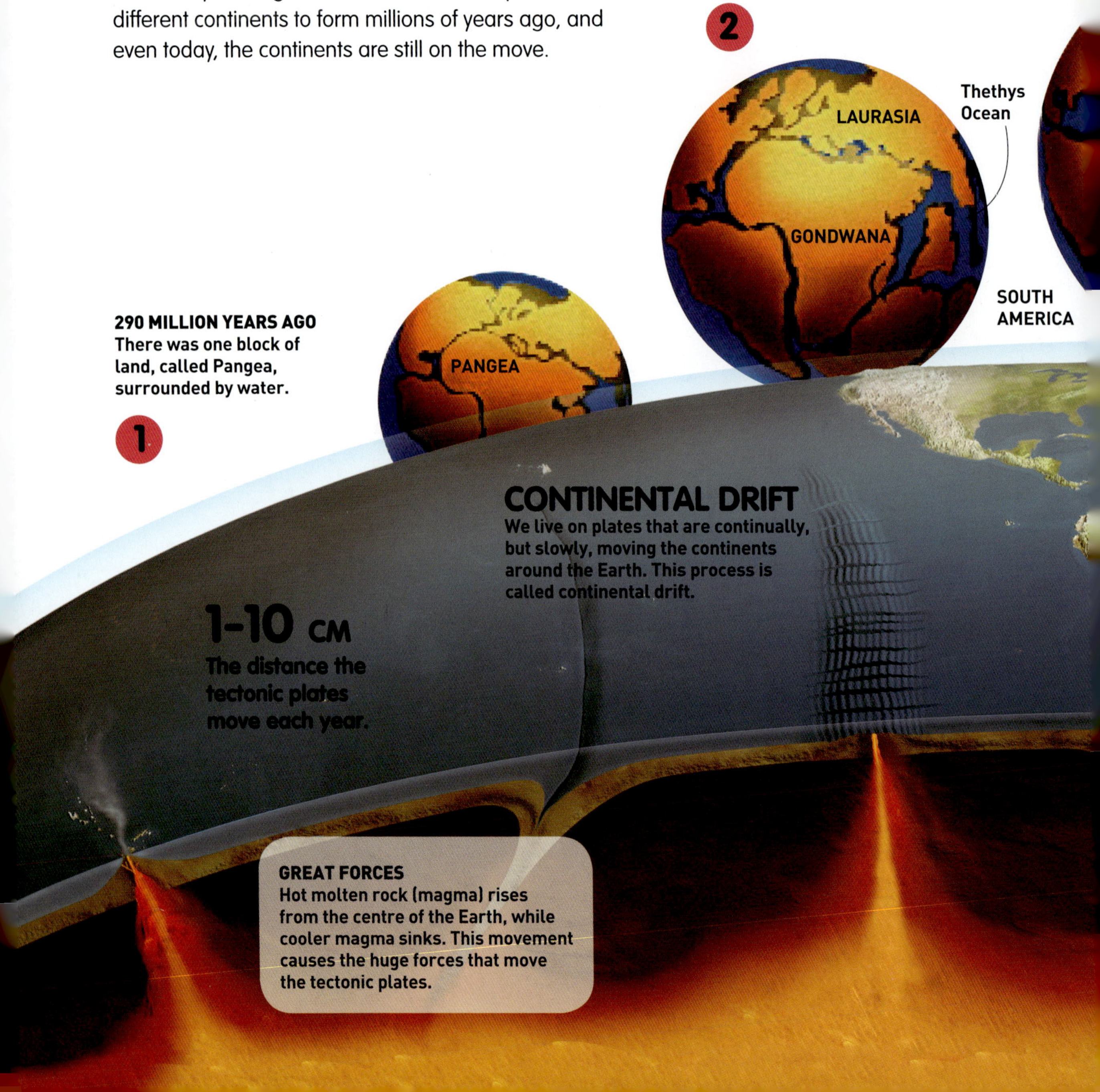

290 MILLION YEARS AGO
There was one block of land, called Pangea, surrounded by water.

CONTINENTAL DRIFT

We live on plates that are continually, but slowly, moving the continents around the Earth. This process is called continental drift.

1-10 CM

The distance the tectonic plates move each year.

GREAT FORCES
Hot molten rock (magma) rises from the centre of the Earth, while cooler magma sinks. This movement causes the huge forces that move the tectonic plates.

200 MILLION YEARS AGO
The North American and Antarctic plates separated. Africa and South America divided to create the Atlantic Ocean.

3

60 MILLION YEARS AGO
The shape of the continents was similar to the shape we have today. India collided with Asia, creating the Himalaya Mountains.

4

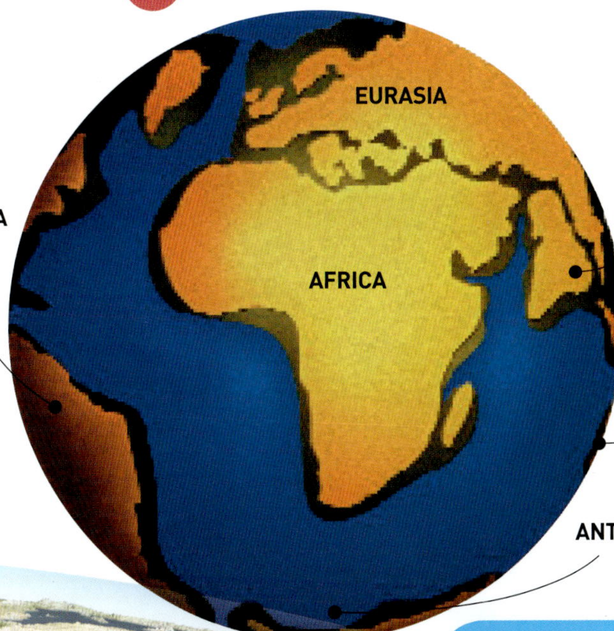

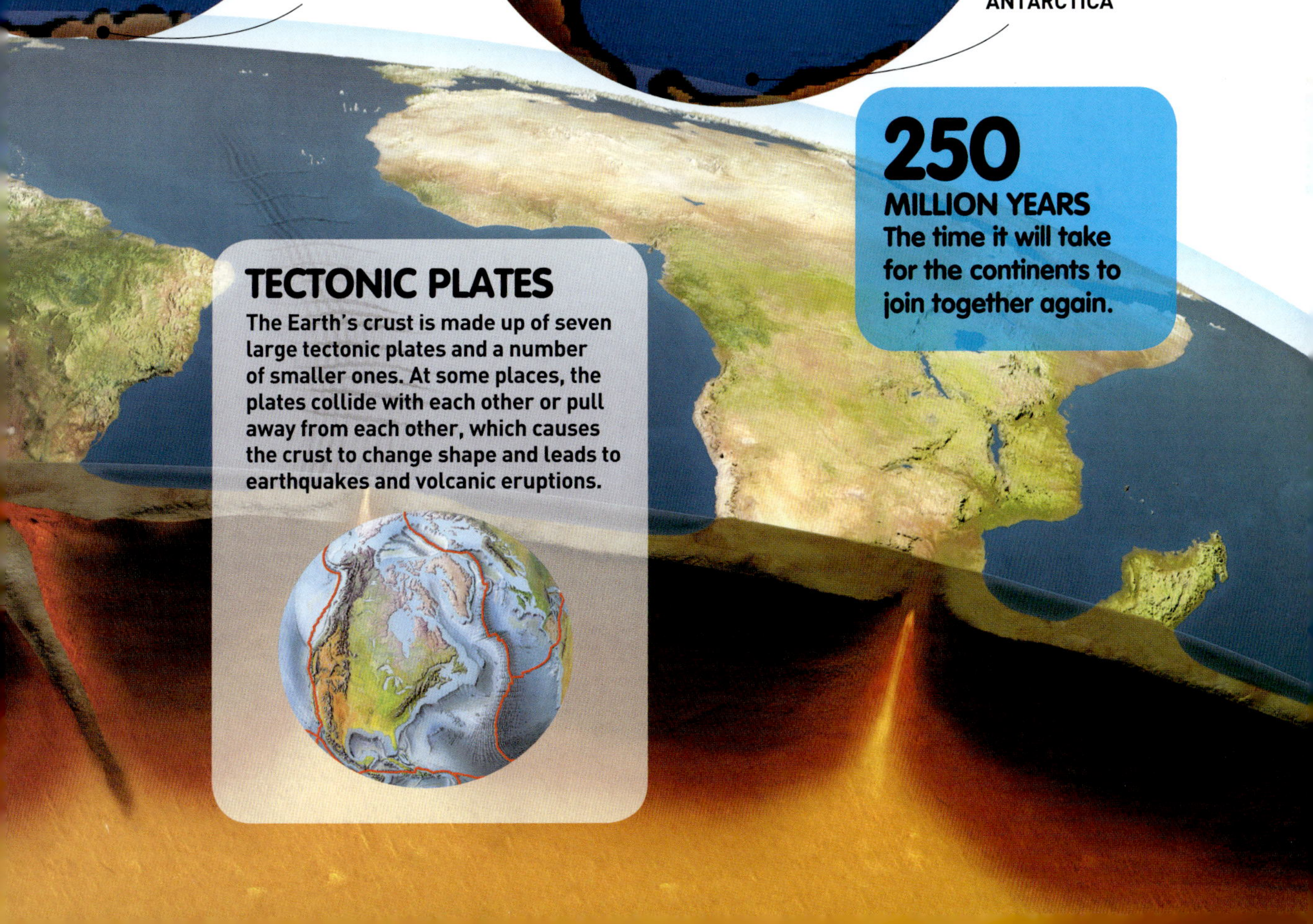

250
MILLION YEARS
The time it will take for the continents to join together again.

TECTONIC PLATES

The Earth's crust is made up of seven large tectonic plates and a number of smaller ones. At some places, the plates collide with each other or pull away from each other, which causes the crust to change shape and leads to earthquakes and volcanic eruptions.

The oceans and seas

For the last 4 billion years, a large part of the Earth has been covered in salt water, which surrounds the continents. The water forms large, deep oceans and smaller, more shallow seas. Underneath the waves, there are huge underwater mountain ranges and deep trenches.

THE FIVE OCEANS

Geographers divide the part of the planet covered by water into five oceans: Southern, Arctic, Atlantic, Indian and Pacific. The Pacific Ocean is the largest.

TYPES OF SEAS

	**INLAND**	Totally surrounded by land, such as the Caspian Sea.
	**COASTAL**	Shallow areas along the coast of the continents, such as the Argentine Sea.
	**CONTINENTAL**	Between land, but with a channel to the ocean, such as the Mediterranean Sea.

WATER PRESSURE

The pressure of the water becomes greater the deeper you go in the oceans. Because of this, humans need to travel in special submarines if they want to go down very deep.

36 grams

The amount of salt in every litre of water in the Atlantic Ocean.

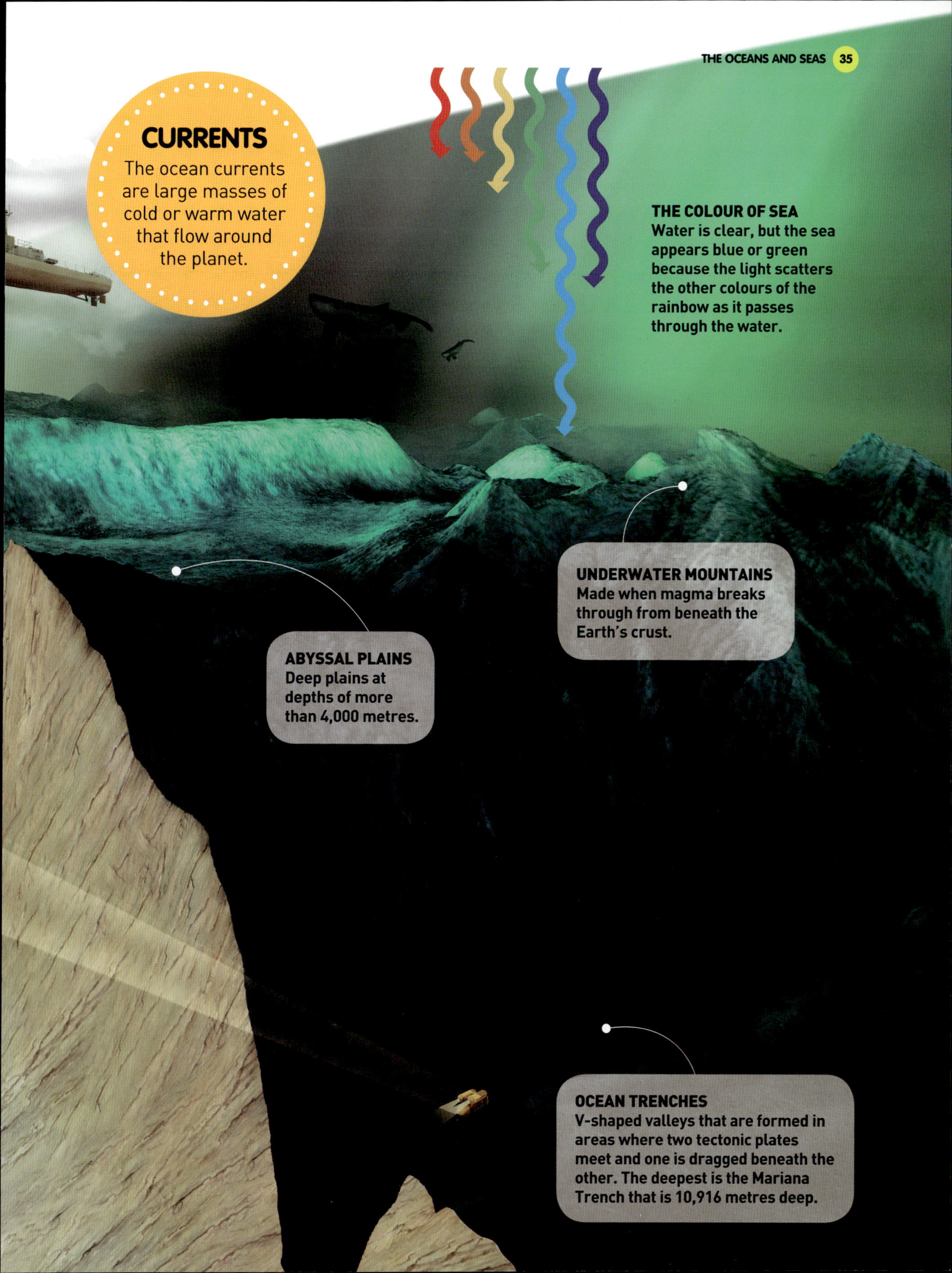

CURRENTS

The ocean currents are large masses of cold or warm water that flow around the planet.

THE COLOUR OF SEA
Water is clear, but the sea appears blue or green because the light scatters the other colours of the rainbow as it passes through the water.

UNDERWATER MOUNTAINS
Made when magma breaks through from beneath the Earth's crust.

ABYSSAL PLAINS
Deep plains at depths of more than 4,000 metres.

OCEAN TRENCHES
V-shaped valleys that are formed in areas where two tectonic plates meet and one is dragged beneath the other. The deepest is the Mariana Trench that is 10,916 metres deep.

The atmosphere

Our planet is surrounded and protected by a layer of air called the atmosphere. The atmosphere gives us the oxygen we breathe and protects us from the harmful rays of the Sun. The atmosphere can be divided into layers. Each layer has different mixes of gases, but only the layer closest to the ground can support life.

RADIATION

Only 51 per cent of the Sun's radiation reaches the surface. The rest is absorbed or reflected by the atmosphere.

GASES IN THE AIR

The air we breathe is a mixture of different gases. Most of the air is made up of nitrogen, followed by oxygen, which we need to stay alive.

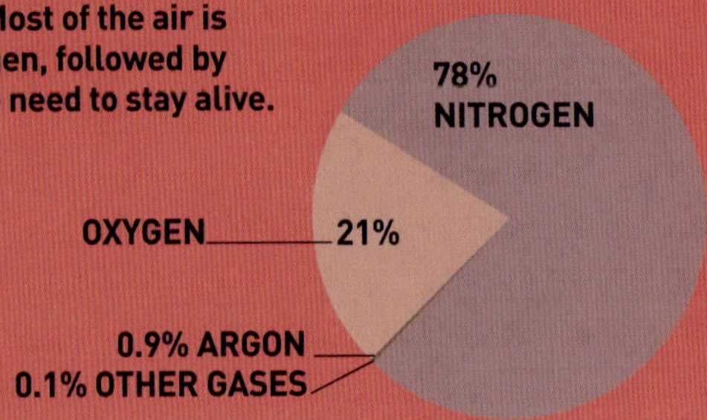

GREENHOUSE EFFECT

Many of the Sun's rays that reach the Earth are reflected back into space. Some of the gases in the atmosphere can trap this heat from disappearing into space. This is called the greenhouse effect, and keeps the planet warm enough for life.

-22 °C

This would be the average temperature on the Earth without the greenhouse effect.

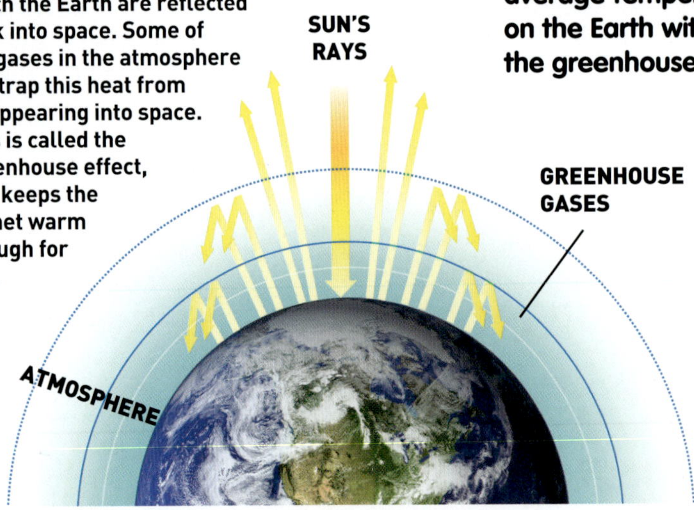

IONOSPHERE

In this layer, the temperature reaches 1500 °C. The air at this height is very thin.

AURORAS
These displays of light are caused by charged electrical particles from space that collide with gas atoms in the atmosphere.

TROPOSPHERE
Aircraft fly in the troposphere.

STRATOSPHERE

The stratosphere contains the ozone layer, which protects life on the Earth from the Sun's most dangerous rays.

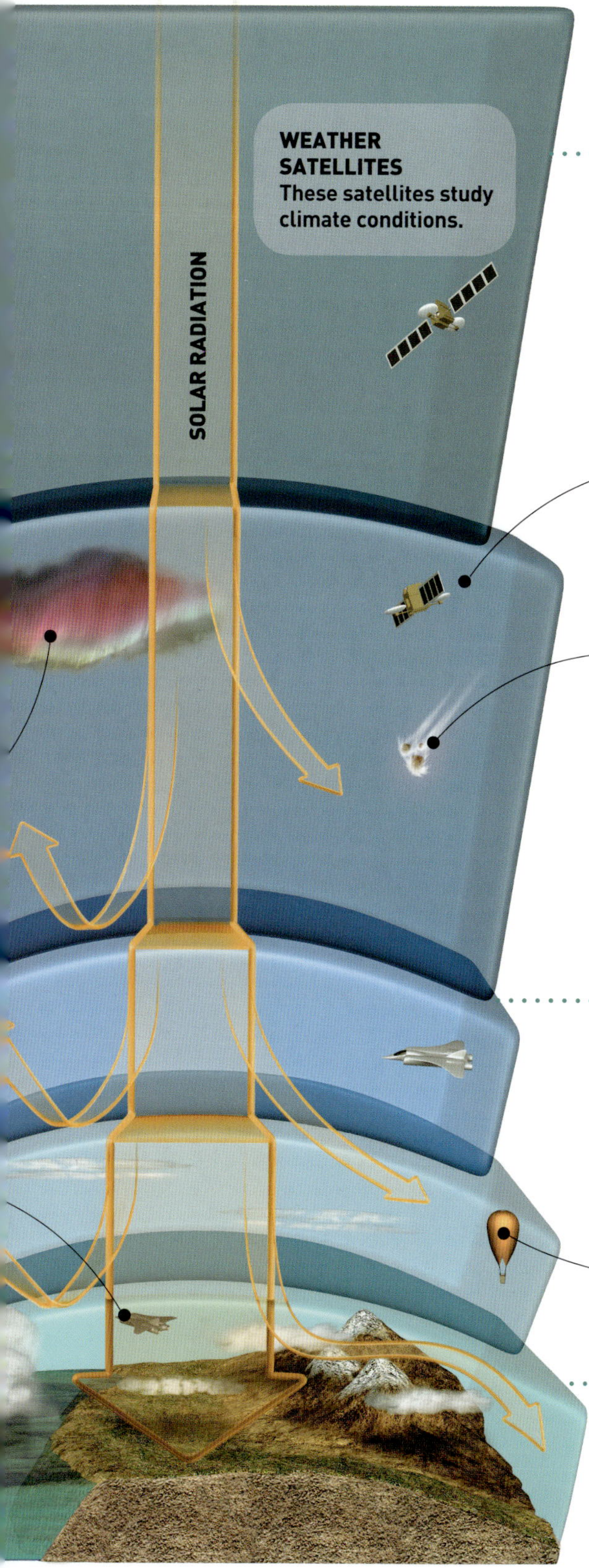

EXOSPHERE

The exosphere is the outermost layer of the atmosphere, which eventually disappears into space. It begins at about 700 km above the ground.

ARTIFICIAL SATELLITES
These orbit in the ionosphere, sending back communications to Earth.

METEORITES
Every day, millions of small rocks called meteorites enter our atmosphere from space. Most of them burn up before they reach the surface.

MESOSPHERE

This layer extends from an altitude of 50 to 80 kilometres. This is where meteorites burn up, creating shooting stars.

WEATHER BALLOONS
Scientists study the stratosphere using weather balloons.

TROPOSPHERE

The troposphere contains the air that we breathe. Most of our weather, such as rain or hurricanes, is caused by events in the troposphere. It is the thinnest layer, just 12 kilometres thick.

The climate

The Earth's climate is a constantly changing system. It is driven by the energy of the Sun. There are five subsystems to our climate: the atmosphere, the biosphere, the hydrosphere, the cryosphere and the lithosphere. The interaction between these subsystems creates different climate zones where the temperature, wind and rain are all similar.

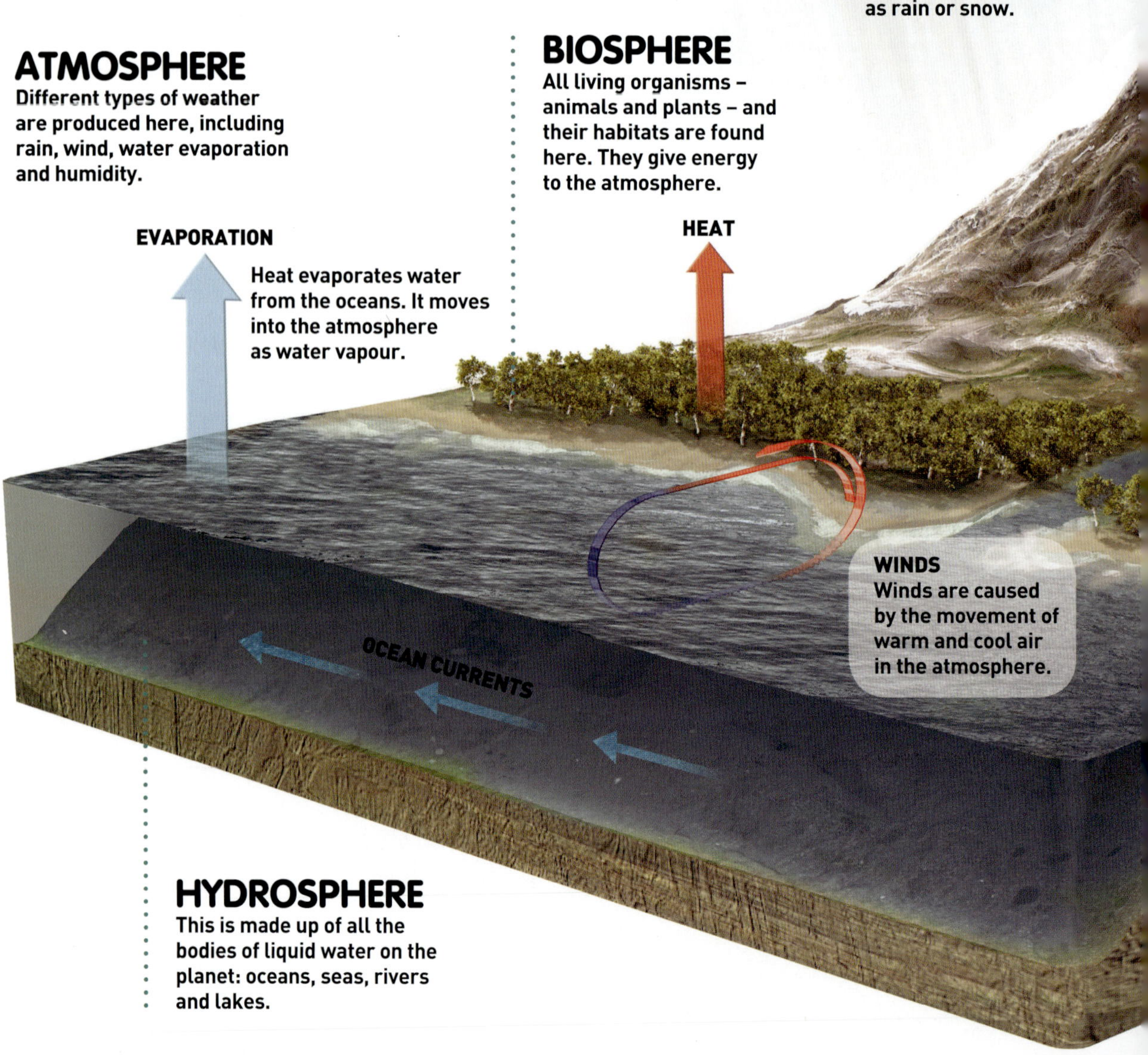

15 °C

The average temperature at the Earth's surface.

THE SUN
The Sun provides energy and drives the changes in each subsystem.

LITHOSPHERE

The lithosphere is the outer layer of the Earth, formed of the continents and the ocean floor. Continuous changes to its surface affect the climate.

CRYOSPHERE

The cryosphere is the parts of the planet that are covered in ice or where the rock or soil is below 0 °C. It reflects almost all of the Sun's rays back into the atmosphere.

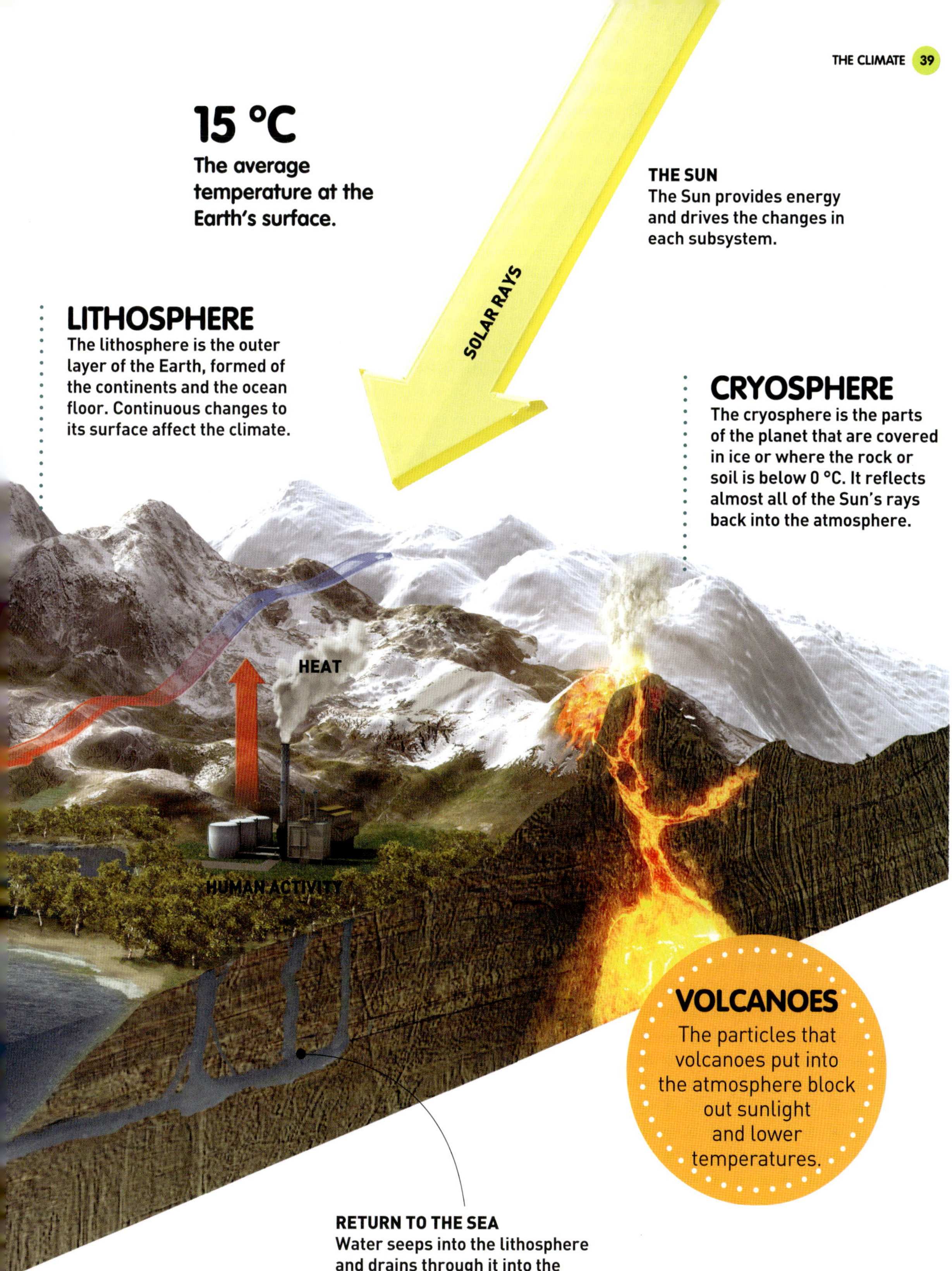

VOLCANOES

The particles that volcanoes put into the atmosphere block out sunlight and lower temperatures.

RETURN TO THE SEA
Water seeps into the lithosphere and drains through it into the oceans, or the hydrosphere.

Climate change

In recent years, the average temperature of the Earth has been slowly rising, causing changes to the climate. This is called global warming. Human activity is the main cause of global warming. Factories and cars, for example, burn a lot of fuel, putting carbon dioxide and other gases into the air. These gases, called greenhouse gases, increase the greenhouse effect. This means that more of the Sun's heat is trapped in the atmosphere and the Earth becomes warmer.

SOLAR ACTIVITY

Almost all of the energy received on Earth comes from the Sun. The amount of energy that reaches the Earth changes over time as the Sun is more or less active.

0.5 °C

The rise in global temperatures over recent decades.

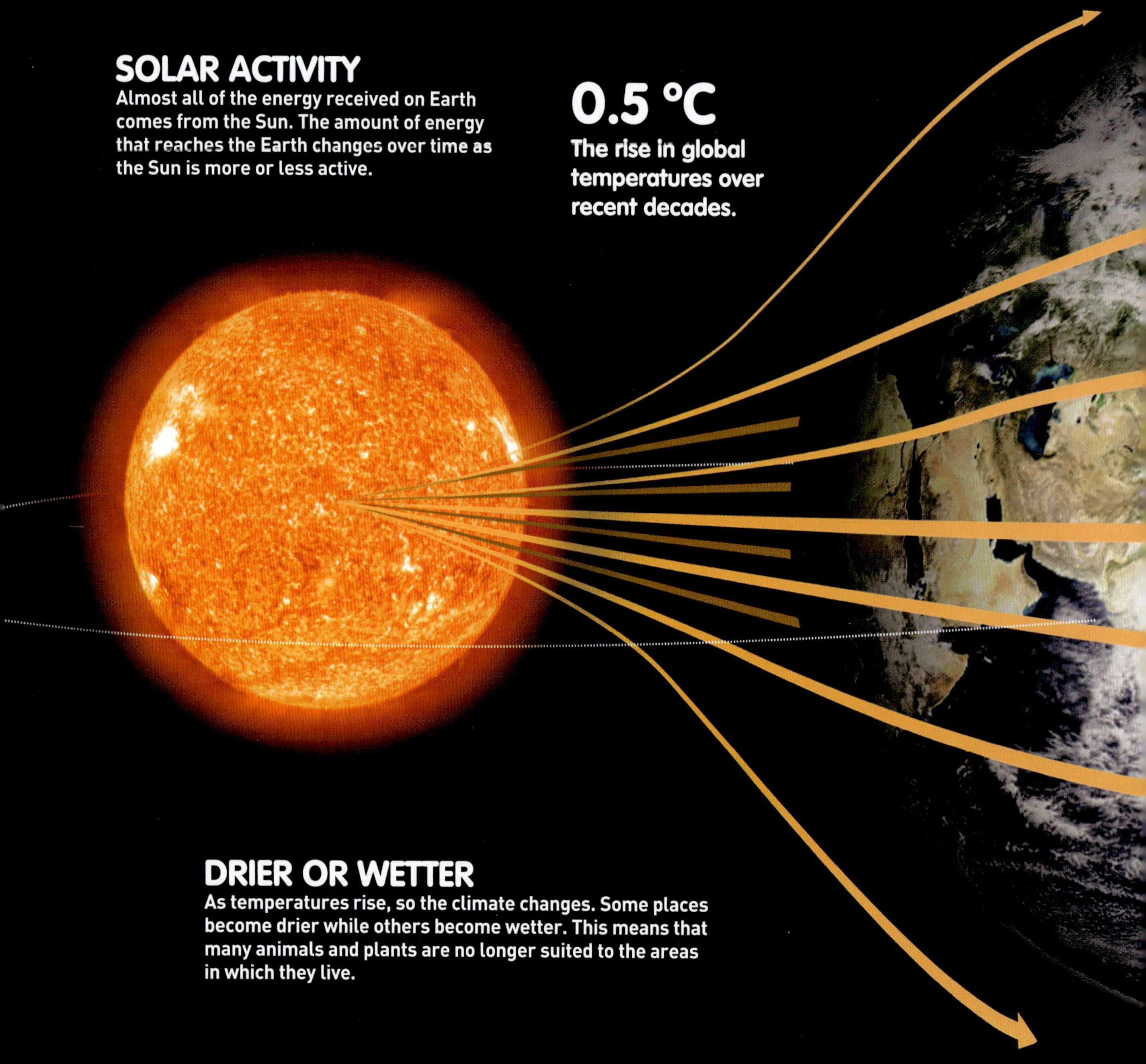

DRIER OR WETTER

As temperatures rise, so the climate changes. Some places become drier while others become wetter. This means that many animals and plants are no longer suited to the areas in which they live.

CARBON DIOXIDE

The most important greenhouse gas is carbon dioxide. When coal, oil and gas are burned, they give off carbon dioxide, adding to the greenhouse effect. Plants take in carbon dioxide and give off oxygen, but many trees are being cut down to make way for human activity. As industry increases and forests shrink, the amount of carbon dioxide in the air is increasing.

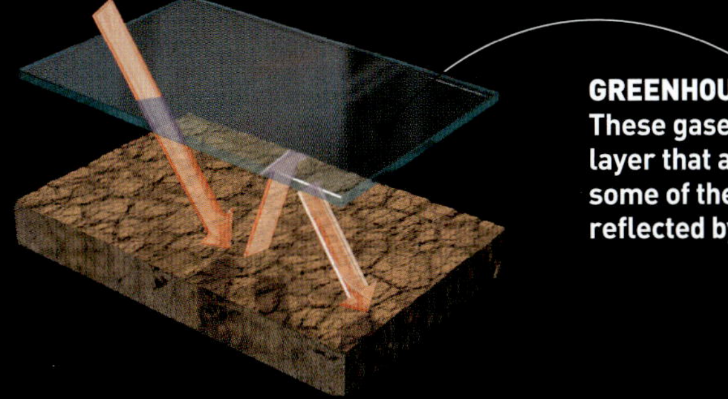

GREENHOUSE GASES
These gases form a layer that absorbs some of the heat reflected by the Earth.

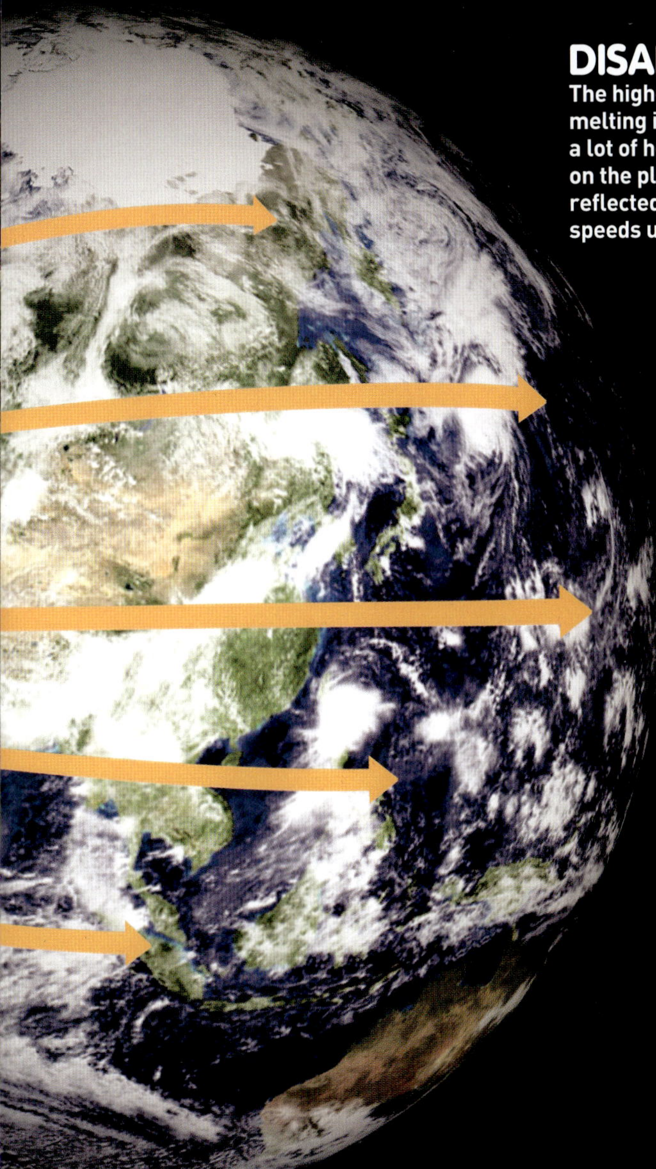

DISAPPEARING ICE

The higher temperatures are melting ice at the poles. Ice reflects a lot of heat, so the less ice there is on the planet, the less heat is reflected back into space. This speeds up global warming.

ICE MIRROR
Ice reflects most of the heat that hits it.

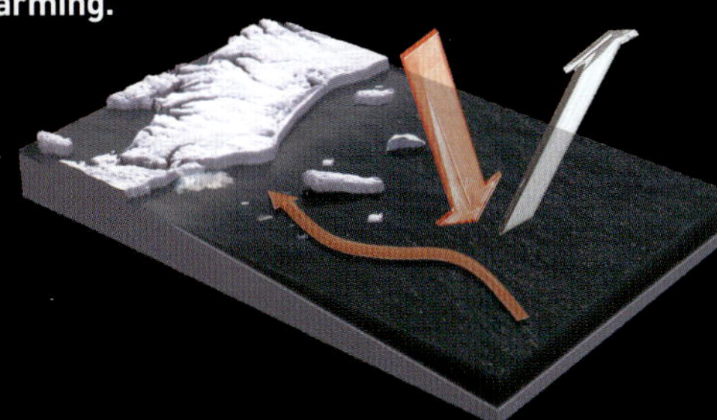

THE OZONE LAYER

The ozone layer protects us from the Sun's harmful ultraviolet rays. Pollution created by people has caused the ozone layer to thin, creating a hole.

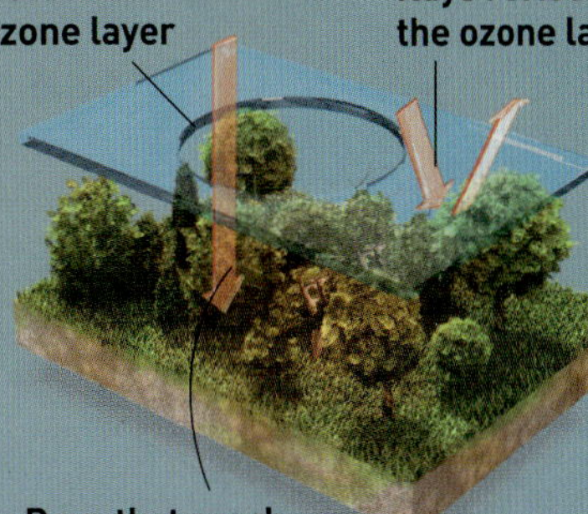

THE NATURAL WORLD

Living organisms come in lots of different shapes and sizes. They range from tiny bacteria that are too small to see, to giant trees that are more than 100 metres tall. Millions of different types, or species, have developed over billions of years in a process called evolution.

INSECT HUNTER
Chameleons have long sticky tongues, which they use to catch insects. They are a type of animal called a reptile (see page 54–55).

The origins of life

When the Earth first formed, about 4,600 million years ago, it was as hot as the Sun. Just over 1,100 million years later, the Earth's surface had cooled, and life had begun. The first living organisms were bacteria, which developed into other forms of life. This process, called evolution, is the key to different types of life on Earth.

LIFE STARTS

EARTH
The oldest rocks date from about 4,400 million years ago (mya). Before then, the planet did not have a solid surface.

OXYGEN
Life on Earth would not be possible without oxygen.

FOSSILS
This fossil contains algae that lived 3,500 mya.

MAWSONITE
This is the fossil of an animal that lived in Australia 650 mya.

4,600 mya
Earth is formed mostly of iron and silicon.

4,000 mya
The first land masses form.

VALVES
The lifeforms of the Cambrian Period had bodies protected by valves or shells.

CRINOID
Fossils of sea lilies have been found from the Silurian Period.

CAMBRIAN
Around 530 mya, the first animals with solid bodies appeared.

AMPHIBIANS
The first amphibians had four legs and a tail. They had webbed feet.

300 mya
The Earth's land masses come together to form one continent: Pangea.

250 mya
The continents separate.

ARCHEAN | PROTEROZOIC

PRECAMBRIAN 4,600–542 mya

CAMBRIAN | ORDOVICIAN | SILURIAN | DEVONIAN | CARBONIFEROUS | PERMIAN

PALAEOZOIC ERA 542-251 mya

EXTINCTION

The fossil record shows us that life on Earth is fragile. Huge numbers of species have become extinct. Dinosaurs became extinct after a dramatic change in the climate 65 mya. This change in climate may have been caused by a large meteorite hitting the Earth.

PREDATOR
Giganotosaurus carolinii was the largest carnivorous dinosaur.

SHARP TOOTH
This is a tooth from a Tyrannosaurus rex, a large, carnivorous dinosaur.

LONG NECK
Barosaurus had one of the longest necks of any dinosaur.

63 mya
Africa, India and America break apart.

TITANIS
This giant flightless bird lived 4 mya.

SABRE-TOOTHED CAT
Thylacosmilus looked like modern cats. It dominated after dinosaurs became extinct.

OUR RELATIONS
Remains of our closest relation, Homo neanderthalensis (right), were found in 1856.

AUSTRALOPITHECUS AFARENSIS
lived 3.7–2.9 mya (above). It was much smaller than a modern human.

60 mya
The continents take the form they are in today.

TRIASSIC	JURASSIC	CRETACEOUS	TERTIARY	QUATERNARY

MESOZOIC ERA 251–65 mya

CENOZOIC ERA 65 mya to present

The plant kingdom

There are about 350,000 different plant species. Plants make their own food using sunlight and a special green substance called chlorophyll. This process is called photosynthesis. Most plants are attached to the ground.

1 GREEN ALGAE

Some algae live on land, in moist conditions on trees, among plants or even in piles of rubbish. They use photosynthesis to make their own food, but they do not have leaves and roots. Today, only green algae (left) are included in the plant kingdom. Other types of algae have their own separate kingdom.

9,550

The age in years of the oldest Norwegian spruce (a kind of pine tree), found in Sweden.

2 BRYOPHYTES

Bryophytes do not have tissues to transport water and nutrients around the plant. These plants include mosses (below).

3 SEEDLESS

Seedless plants reproduce using tiny spores. The spores do not have a store of food. Ferns (left) are the best-known plants in this group.

CLASSIFICATION

Almost all plants are flowering plants. They are called angiosperms. Many plants are vascular. This means that they have special tissues inside them to transport nutrients around the plant.

Plant kingdom

- Green algae
- Non-vascular plants
  - **Bryophytes**
- Vascular plants
  - **Seedless plants**
  - **Seed plants**
    - **Angiosperms (flowering plants)**
    - **Gymnosperms**

SENSITIVE

Saffron flowers open or close depending on the temperature.

4 ANGIOSPERMS

These plants make seeds, flowers and fruit. Angiosperms are found on every continent except Antarctica. They reproduce using flowers, which develop into fruits with seeds inside them. They come in many shapes and sizes and include roses, orchids (above), wheat, coffee plants and oak trees.

5 GYMNOSPERMS

These are plants that make seeds but not flowers. Conifers are examples of gymnosperms. They include pine trees (below) and trees such as cypress, larch and monkey puzzle.

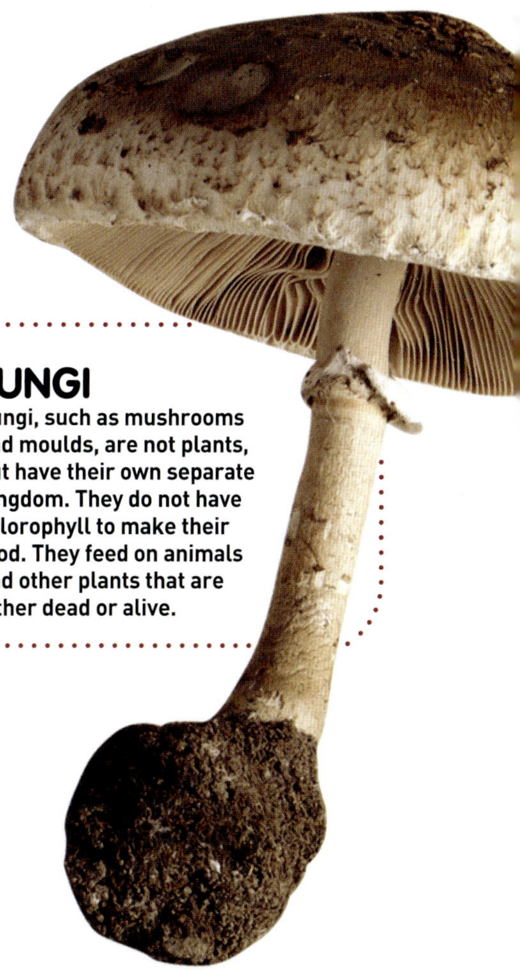

FUNGI

Fungi, such as mushrooms and moulds, are not plants, but have their own separate kingdom. They do not have chlorophyll to make their food. They feed on animals and other plants that are either dead or alive.

Land plants

The earliest plants lived in water. Over millions of years, some of these plants gradually changed and were able to invade the land, living in damp places. Changes to their structure stopped them from losing water, and they could use the Sun's energy more effectively than water plants. Land plants first appeared on Earth almost 450 million years ago.

TALLEST

Giant redwood trees are the tallest plants in the world. They can grow to more than 110 metres high.

EPIPHYTES
These plants grow on other plants, without fixing themselves to the ground.

TREES
The woody trunks of trees give them strength and allow them to grow more than 100 metres tall.

FLOWERS
Flowering plants use their colourful displays to attract birds and insects.

CONQUERING THE LAND

Roots allow plants to grow on the land. They fix the plant to the ground and take in water and minerals from the soil.

The plant cuticle is a waterproof covering that protects land plants from damage by the wind or the Sun. Tiny holes called stomata open and close to control water loss.

MOSSES
These are some of the simplest of all land plants.

60

The number of centimetres a day some species of bamboo can grow. They are the fastest-growing plants.

Photosynthesis

Plants are able to live on substances that are not plant or animal matter. The process that allows them to do this is photosynthesis. Plants photosynthesize by using a green substance called chlorophyll. Photosynthesis is vital to life on Earth because almost all living beings depend on plants as a source of energy.

LEAVES

These parts of a plant are adapted for photosynthesis. Leaves need a constant supply of water, which reaches them via the plant's roots and stems.

PLANT TISSUES

Plant cells take in carbon dioxide from the air. During photosynthesis, they use the carbon dioxide to make sugars and give off oxygen.

GREENERY

Chlorophyll gives plants their green colour. Plants use the Sun's energy to turn inorganic matter (such as minerals) into organic matter, which feeds the plants and allows them to grow.

170,000

The amount of carbon (in million tonnes) that is changed into energy by the world's plants every year.

CHLOROPLAST

This is where photosynthesis takes place. A chloroplast contains a stroma in which there are bags called thylakoids. Chlorophyll is found in the thylakoids.

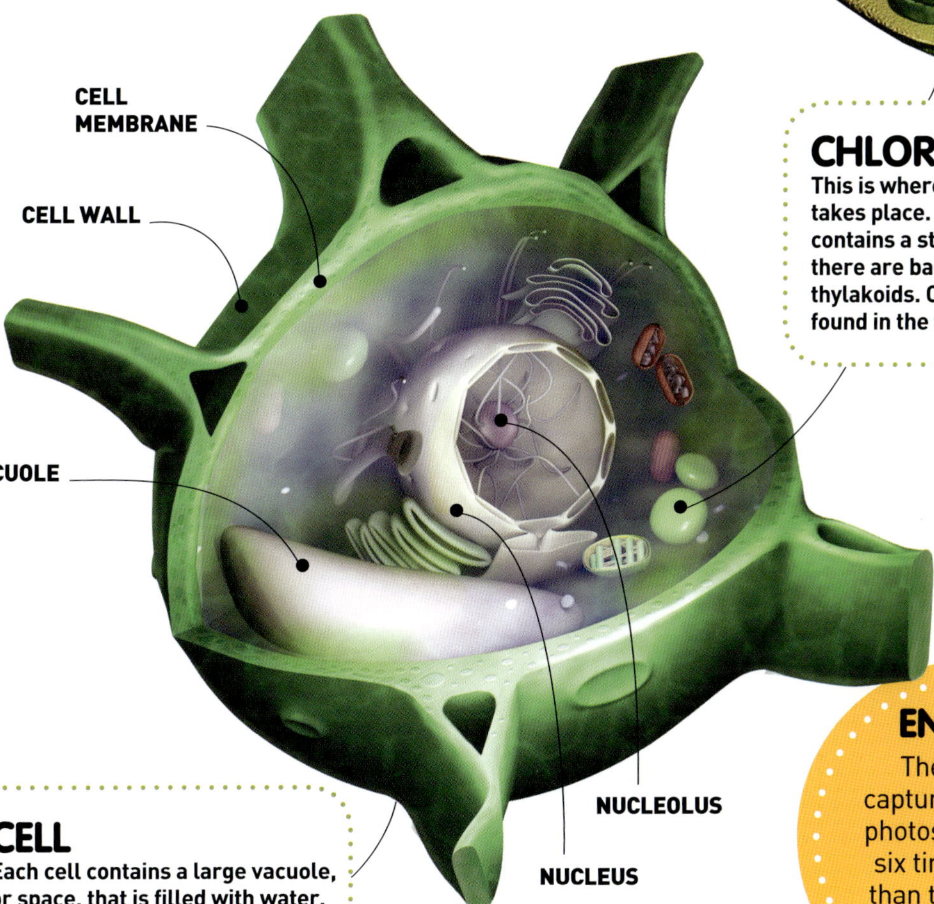

CELL

Each cell contains a large vacuole, or space, that is filled with water, a cell wall made partly of cellulose, and chloroplasts.

ENERGY

The energy captured through photosynthesis is six times larger than the amount of energy used by humans.

Invertebrates

Animals without a backbone are called invertebrates. They are the largest group in the animal kingdom – 98 out of every 100 animal species are invertebrates. More than 1.5 million species have been identified. They can be very different in size and shape, from zooplankton that measure fractions of a millimetre to giant squid, which are more than 10 metres long.

SIMPLE INVERTEBRATES

Simple invertebrates include medusas, anemones, sponges and polyps. Many of these organisms have bodies that are arranged around a central point.

ANEMONES
These animals fix themselves to rocks. They have stinging tentacles that they use to catch their prey.

ECHINODERMS
Echinoderms are also arranged around a central point and base their design on a pattern of five. This group includes starfish (below) and sea urchins.

ANCIENT

Invertebrates were the first organisms from the animal kingdom to live on land.

BIVALVES
These are molluscs with two hinged shells. This group includes mussels, clams and oysters.

CEPHALOPODS
These molluscs have no outer shell. They include octopuses, squid and cuttlefish (right).

MOLLUSCS

Molluscs are animals with soft bodies and no joints. Many molluscs have a hard outer shell. They often live in water and the group includes snails, mussels and octopuses.

18 METRES

The length to which a giant squid can grow.

ARTHROPODS

Most of the world's invertebrates are arthropods. They have jointed limbs and an outer skeleton. This group includes insects, crustaceans, myriapods and spiders.

MYRIAPODS
These arthropods have many legs, such as centipedes and millipedes.

CRUSTACEANS
With two pairs of antennae and legs attached to the abdomen, crustaceans include crabs and lobsters.

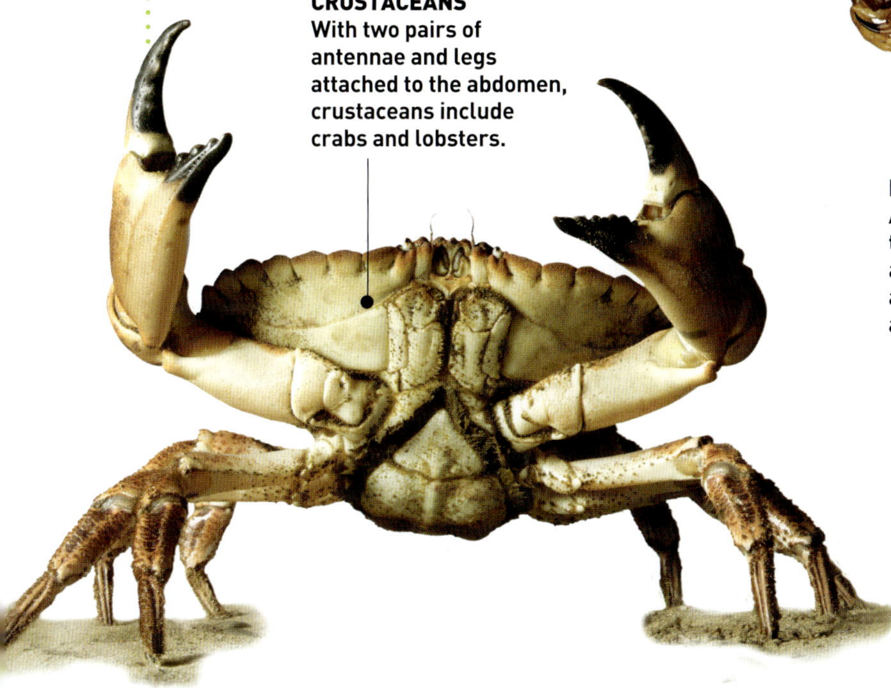

INSECTS
All insects have three pairs of legs and one pair of antennae. Some also have wings.

Reptiles

Reptiles are vertebrates with scaly bodies and waterproof skin. Their young hatch from eggs. They are cold-blooded, which means they need the Sun's energy to keep their blood warm. They live in almost every habitat on the planet, except in Antarctica, and are found both in water and on land.

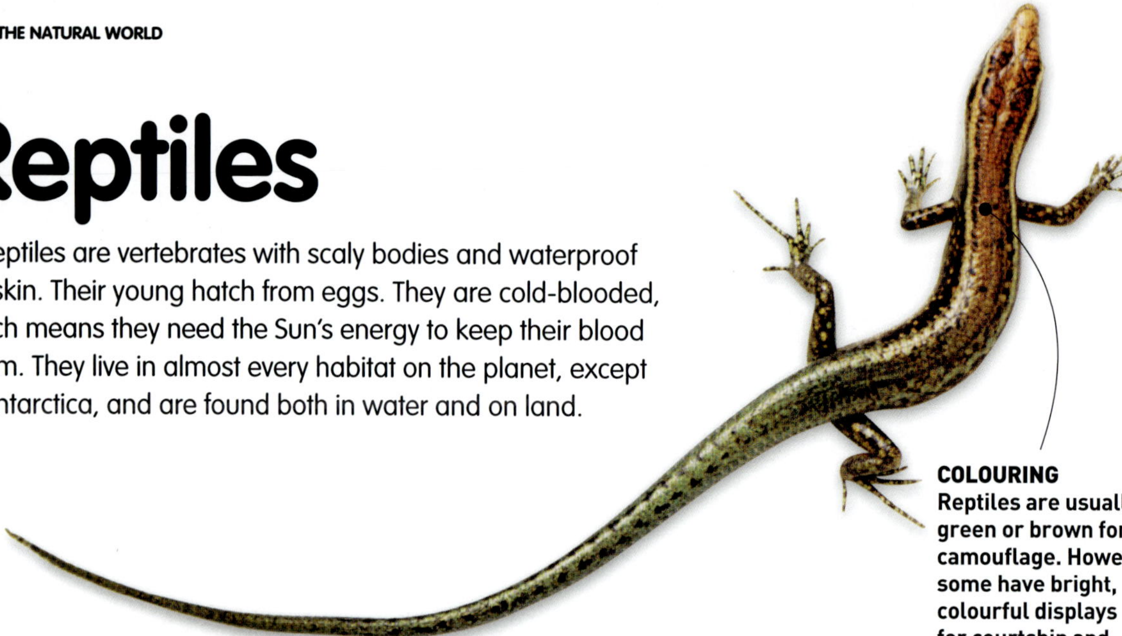

COLOURING
Reptiles are usually green or brown for camouflage. However some have bright, colourful displays for courtship and defence.

ORIGIN

Reptiles first appeared more than 300 million years ago. They developed from early amphibians.

CROCODILES AND CAIMANS

These ancient reptiles have four legs and can grow to enormous sizes. They spend most of their time in water. Most species live in rivers or lakes, but some crocodiles also live in salt water.

BREATHING
Reptiles breathe air using lungs. Some can stay underwater without breathing for a long time.

SCALES
Reptiles' scales are made from keratin, the same substance that your fingernails are made from.

TEMPERATURE
To warm up, reptiles need to find heat sources such as sunlight or stones, tree trunks and other surfaces that have been warmed by the Sun.

TUATARA
These reptiles are known as 'living fossils' because they have hardly changed in millions of years. There are only two species, which are both found in New Zealand.

SNAKES AND LIZARDS

About 95 per cent of all reptiles are snakes or lizards. Snakes are the only reptiles with no legs.

7,000

The number of reptile species alive today.

TORTOISES AND TURTLES

These reptiles can be large or small, with a body protected by a shell. Tortoises live on land, while turtles live in water.

TOOTHLESS
Tortoises and turtles are reptiles with a beak.

Crocodilians

Crocodiles, caimans and gharials are all crocodilians. They are all excellent swimmers and their eyes and noses are located at the top of their heads so that they can breathe in the water. They live in tropical regions in Asia, Africa, the Americas and Australia. Crocodilians are found mostly in rivers, but some crocodiles live in the sea. They are all fearsome hunters.

TEETH
They use their teeth to catch and hold onto their prey.

TAIL
Powerful tails help them to swim and jump.

GHARIALS

These reptiles are adapted to hunt fish. They have a long, narrow snout with small, sharp teeth. They live in swamps and rivers in Asia.

REPLACING TEETH

Crocodiles grow new teeth to replace any that they lose when they are hunting.

HOW THEY MOVE

Crocodiles are very good swimmers, but they can also walk and jump. When they feel threatened, they can run, reaching speeds of up to 15 km/h.

IN WATER
To swim, they use their tails to push themselves forwards.

ON LAND
To run, they lift their bodies and support themselves on slightly bent legs.

CAIMANS

Caimans are closely related to alligators and are very similar to crocodiles, but they are smaller and have a shorter, wider snout. They mostly live in rivers and swamps in Central and South America. They lay their eggs in nests made from grass, mud and leaves.

LEGS
They use their legs to walk on land, dragging their bellies along the ground.

CROCODILES

Crocodiles are large and ferocious. Some species can grow to more than six metres long. When hunting, they surprise their prey. They then hold their victims in their powerful jaws, and pull them underwater to drown them, before spinning them round to rip them to pieces.

NASAL PITS
These close when the animal is underwater.

EYES
They are able to work out how far away prey is. When they dive, they cover their eyes with a transparent film of skin.

1 HOUR

The length of time a Nile crocodile can stay underwater.

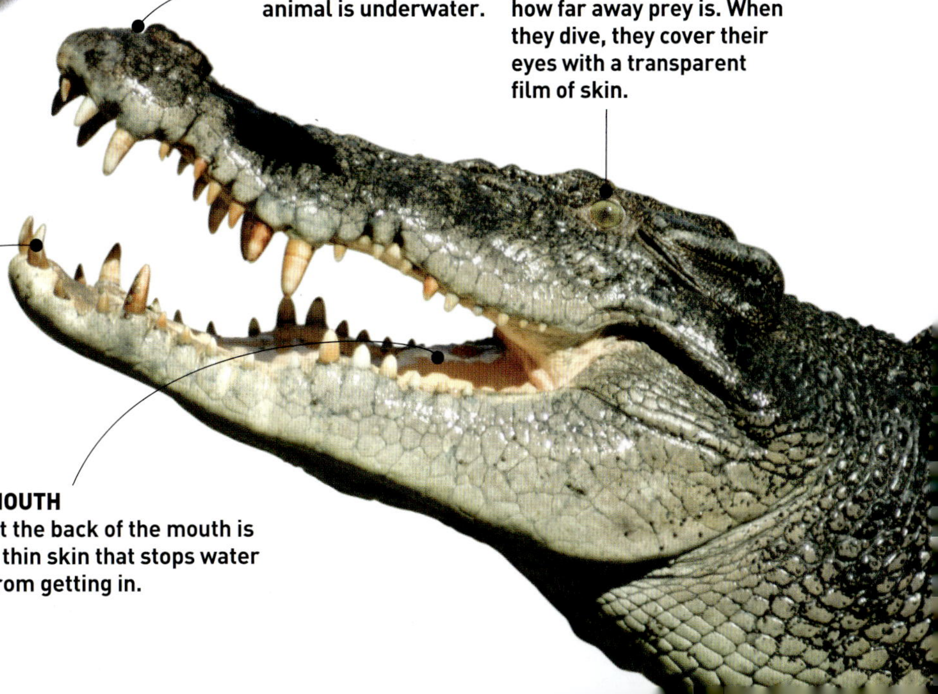

TEETH
Crocodiles have 64–68 teeth. The fourth tooth of their lower jaw sticks out when their mouth is closed.

MOUTH
At the back of the mouth is a thin skin that stops water from getting in.

Ocean life

The oceans are the largest habitat on the Earth. Many different species live in the oceans. The sizes and shapes of the species change depending on the conditions and the food that is found in each ocean zone.

UP TO 500 METRES
In this zone, there is enough light for animals to see during the day.

UP TO 4,000 METRES
There is no longer enough light for plant life and there is not a lot of food.

MORE THAN 6,000 METRES
At this depth, it is extremely cold.

TEMPERATURE

Water temperature is very important in deciding which species are found in each zone. There are five major climate zones in the planet's oceans (right).

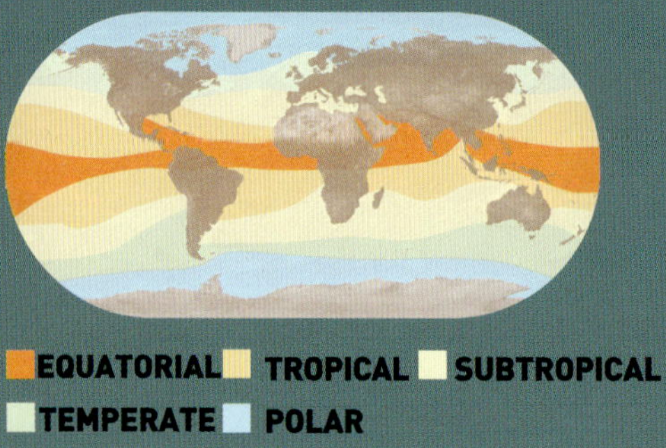

ENDEMIC SPECIES

These are species that only live in one specific place. For example, the globefish on the left is found only in the tropical waters of the Atlantic Ocean.

MAKING YOUR OWN LIGHT

Some animals give off a greenish light. They use the light to attract prey or to surprise possible enemies.

OCEANIC ZONES

Life in the oceans can be grouped into different layers according to how deep the water is. The deeper you go, the harder it becomes for creatures to live. There is less light and it becomes colder.

80

The number of marine species that are in danger of extinction.

Strange fish

All fish have a similar basic body on the inside. However, they do not all look the same on the outside. Some of them look very strange. This is because each species has adapted to survive in its own environment.

DARTFISH
Small and very colourful, the dartfish gets its name from the shape of its dorsal fin.

FEATHERY FILEFISH
This fish has feathery extensions all over its body.

VERY UNUSUAL FISH

Some fish are unusual because there are few of them alive, some because they have a strange shape, and others because we know little about them. The megamouth shark fits in all three groups. The shark was first discovered in 1976, and only 40 have ever been seen. It is related to the whale shark, and like the whale shark, it feeds on plankton. It is named for its extremely large mouth.

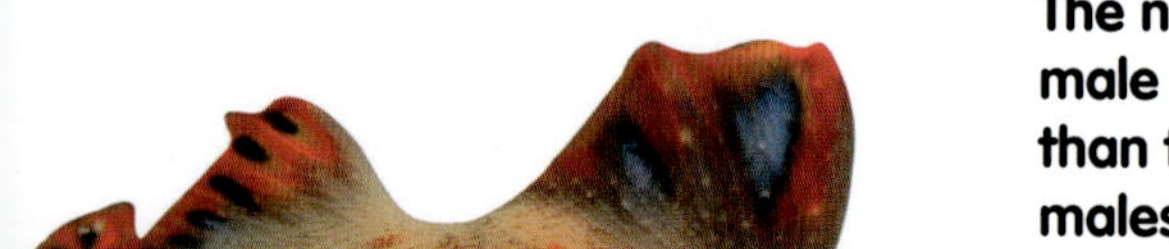

TRUMPETFISH
The trumpetfish is a relative of the seahorse.

10

The number of times the male anglerfish is smaller than the female. The tiny males live attached to the side of a female.

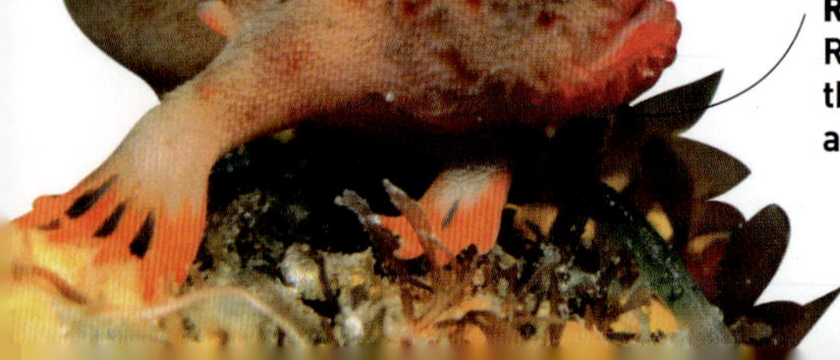

RED HANDFISH
Rather than swimming, this fish drags itself along the seabed.

SCORPIONFISH
This fish is camouflaged to blend in with the seabed.

KNIFEFISH
This fish lives in rivers in Asia. It takes its name from its very long anal fin.

CLOWN CORIS
The young of this species have dots in the shape of eyes on their bodies to confuse predators.

FRESHWATER ANGELFISH
The angelfish's strange shape allows it to move unnoticed through plants in the water.

EARS

Fish have internal organs for hearing, but no ears. Some fish have horn - or ear-shaped additions.

Amphibians

There are about 6,000 species of amphibian: frogs, toads, salamanders, newts and caecilians are all amphibians. They are vertebrates, which means they have a backbone. When they are young, amphibians live in water but when they become adults, they usually live on land.

SOUNDS

Male frogs and toads can make a much louder sound than the females. To make their sounds louder, they inflate sacs next to the larynx (voice box).

ANATOMY

As larvae (tadpoles, in the case of frogs and toads), amphibians live in water and breathe through external gills. As adults, they develop simple lungs, but they do most of their breathing through their skin, which can take in the oxygen dissolved in water.

OLDEST

The Japanese giant salamander is the longest-living amphibian (and the second-largest). It can live for 55 years.

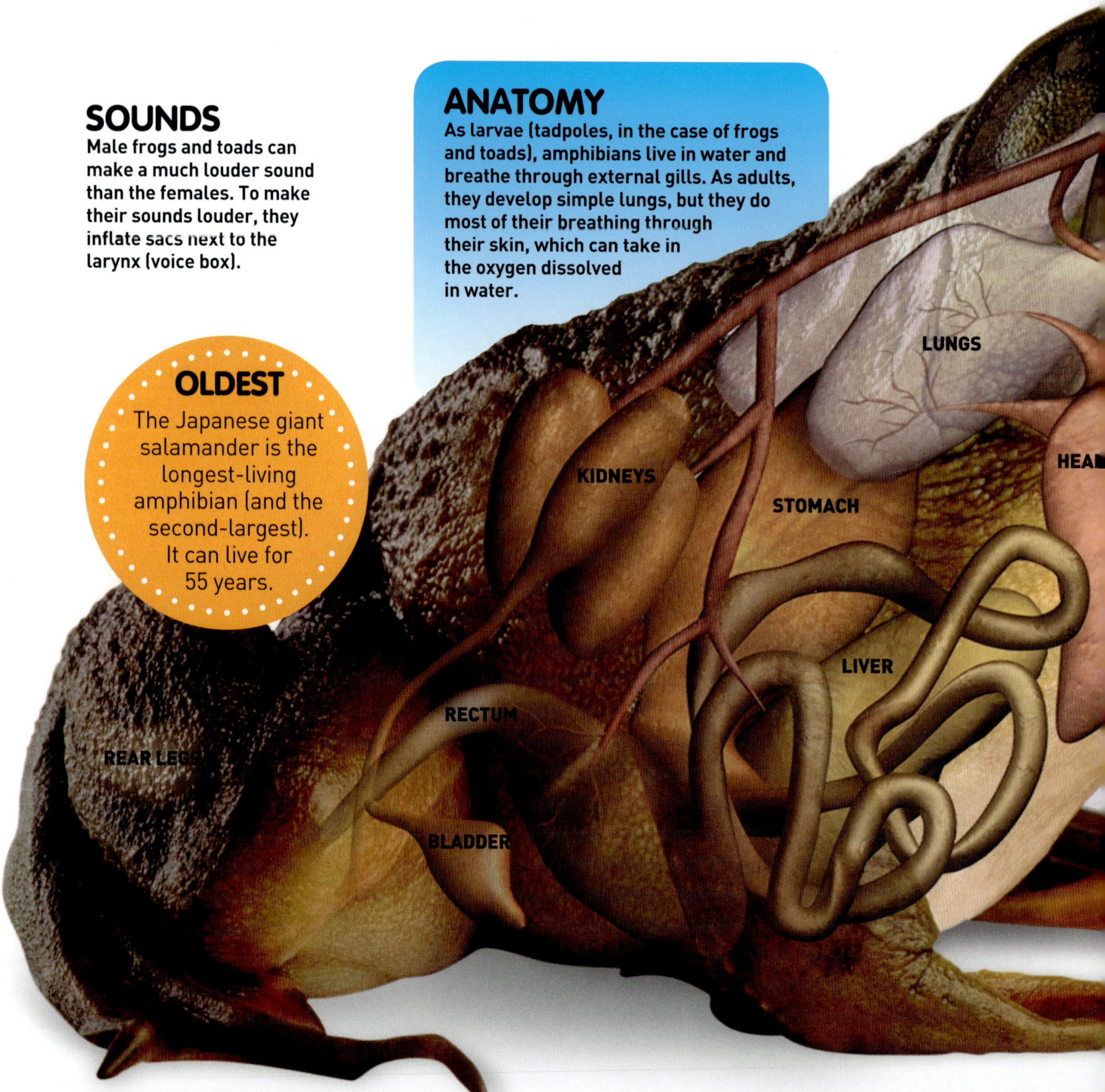

DIET

As adults, amphibians feed mostly on small animals such as spiders, caterpillars, flies and beetles. Their tongues are long and sticky to help them catch their prey.

180 CENTIMETRES

The length of the Chinese giant salamander, the largest amphibian in the world. It is now a highly endangered species.

CLASSIFICATION

Amphibians are divided into three orders:

1. Anura
   Do not have tails when adults. Includes frogs and toads.
2. Urodela
   Includes salamanders and newts, which have tails their whole lives.
3. Apoda
   Have neither legs nor tails, and look like worms.

1 EUROPEAN TREE FROG
This frog is often found living near humans.

2 TIGER SALAMANDER
One of the most colourful amphibians.

3 RINGED CAECILIAN
Looks like a large, thick worm.

Birds

Birds have bodies that are covered in feathers, and beaks with no teeth. Their wings are arms that have adapted for flight, although some birds can no longer fly. Birds are warm-blooded animals. They reproduce by laying eggs.

READY TO FLY

The shape of a bird's body and its feathers, allow it to stay in the air and to fly. Birds have strong muscles and light bones that are hollow and filled with air.

VARIETY

Birds are found in many different habitats, including water, air and land. Some birds are very small, such as the hummingbird, while others are very large, such as the ostrich, which is the largest bird of all.

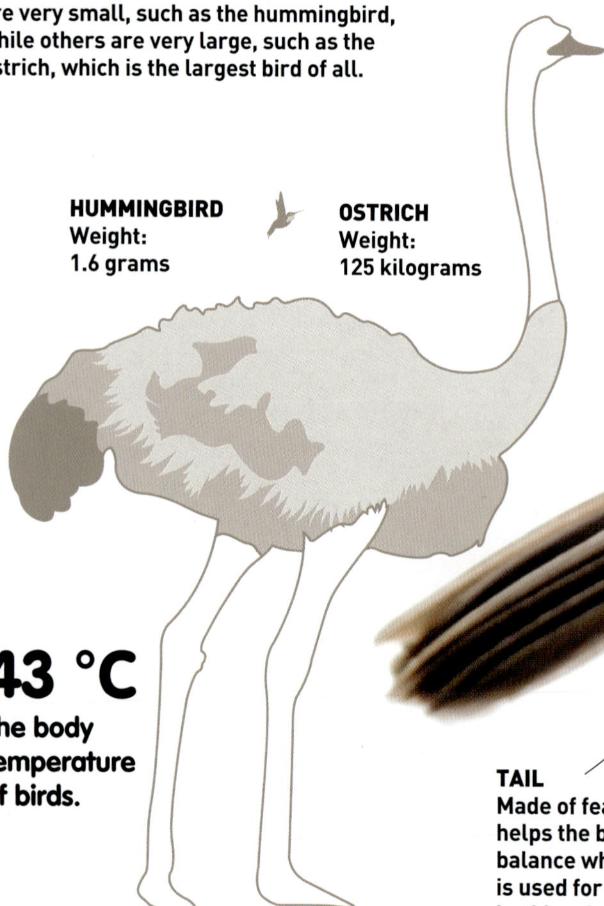

HUMMINGBIRD
Weight:
1.6 grams

OSTRICH
Weight:
125 kilograms

PENGUIN
Can survive at temperatures of -60 °C in Antarctica.

WINGS
When they fly, birds use their wings to stay in the air, move forwards and change direction. The wings have special feathers to make this possible.

TAIL
Made of feathers, the tail helps the bird to keep its balance when it lands, and is used for steering and braking during flight.

BALANCE

Birds keep their balance when flying by using both their wings and their legs.

43 °C

The body temperature of birds.

VISION AND HEARING
Birds have very good vision and well-developed hearing.

BEAK
Like their claws and feathers, birds' beaks grow all through their lives.

CHEST

FEET
Birds usually have three toes pointing forwards and one pointing backwards.

9,600

The number of bird species.

IDENTIFYING BIRDS

Birds can be told apart by looking at differences in their feathers and their skin, and also the shape of the beak. These are some of the features used to tell them apart:

How birds fly

Most birds fly just by beating their wings, but some change between beating their wings and gliding. Beating wings uses a lot of energy, so birds have adapted the way they fly to suit their size and their needs. Larger birds have more powerful, but slower, wingbeats.

FLIGHT

For most birds, flying is not only a way to get around, but also of escaping predators, catching prey and showing off to a mate.

GLIDING

When it glides, a bird saves energy because it uses the wind to fly without beating its wings. The bird climbs with the help of air currents, gains height, then glides downwards until it reaches another current that will carry it back up again.

TAKE-OFF
The bird is already flying after a couple of beats of its wings.

GAINING HEIGHT
The angle of the wings and the wind allow the bird to climb.

GLIDING
It slowly goes lower in a glide.

FLYING IN A WAVE

In this way of flying, the bird beats its wings to gain height, then folds its wings and allows itself to fall. It then beats its wings again, using the strength gained by falling to go up again.

GROUP FLYING

Flying together is a way of saving energy. The bird at the front of the group makes a pathway through the air, making it easier for the rest of the birds to fly. Normally, birds fly either in an 'L' shape - such as pelicans - or a 'V' shape – such as geese.

CHANGING PLACES
When the leader of the group tires, another bird takes its place.

BEATING ITS WINGS

A bird flies through the air as if it were rowing with its wings. With each beat, the wings both keep the bird in the air and push it forwards.

LOWERING ITS WINGS
When it lowers its wings, the feathers close up again.

RAISING THE WINGS
From bottom to top, the feathers at the end of the wings separate.

GAINING MOMENTUM
With the wings behind the body, it gains the strength to raise its wings.

50 km/h

The average speed of a pelican in flight when there is no wind.

FASTEST WINGBEAT

Hummingbirds fly only by beating their wings. They do not glide. A hummingbird can hover in the same place by beating its wings very quickly. Some species beat their wings up to 70 times a second. Hummingbirds are the only birds that can fly backwards.

Flightless birds

There are some species of bird that cannot fly. Some species are too heavy to take off. Others have lost their wings, or their wings have become very small. Some still have large wings but they no longer use them to fly. Flightless birds can be divided into those that live on land (terrestrial) and those that can swim (aquatic).

AQUATIC

Penguins are aquatic flightless birds. Their wings are shaped like flippers, which they use to swim quickly and skilfully.

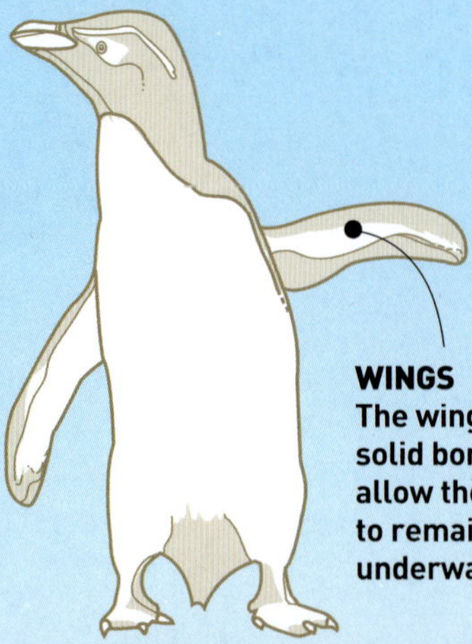

WINGS
The wings have solid bones that allow the birds to remain underwater easily.

72 km/h

The top speed of an ostrich when it runs.

SWIMMERS

The penguin's feet have four webbed toes that point backwards. It uses its toes, wings and tail to swim and change direction.

DIVING
The wings work as flippers. It uses its feet and tail as a rudder.

BREATHING
Between dives, a penguin has to leap out of the water to breathe.

RESTING
When it rests, it swims very slowly using both its wings and legs.

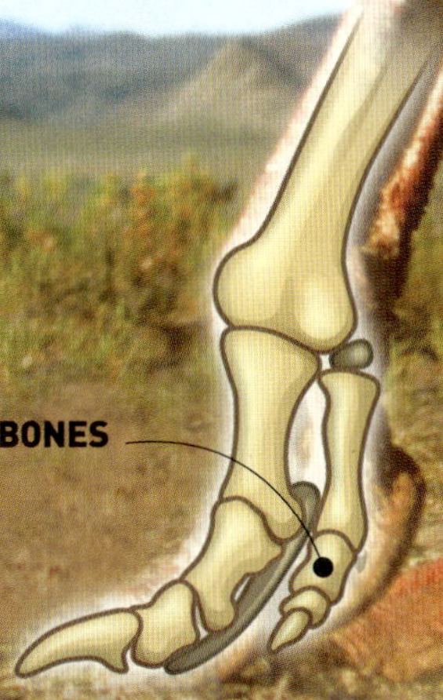

BAD FLIERS

About 260 species of bird, including chickens, can only fly in short bursts. Instead, they use their legs to walk, run and scratch the earth.

1. Runs and jumps.
2. Awkward, fast flap of the wings.
3. Crash landing.

RUNNING

With their strong legs, many land birds can run at high speeds to escape a predator or to hunt prey.

RUNNERS

The ratites are a group of land birds that are powerful runners. Their wings are very small and of no use for flying. Instead, they have developed strong legs, which they use to move around.

OSTRICH
This large bird uses its wings for balance when running.

KIWI
The kiwi has tiny wings, which are hard to see under its feathers.

CASSOWARY
This is a large bird with strong, well developed legs.

RHEA
With long legs and good vision, the rhea is a skilful hunter.

Mammals

Mammals are warm-blooded vertebrate animals. Their bodies are covered with hair, they breathe through lungs, they have a constant body temperature and the females produce milk to feed their young. Mammals are very adaptable – they can live in different environments all over the world.

CONSTANT TEMPERATURE

Mammals are warm-blooded animals. This means they are able to keep their bodies at a constant temperature. The exceptions are species such as bears, which lower their temperatures to hibernate through the winter.

REPRODUCTION

Mammals are divided into three groups according to the way they reproduce:

LIVE BIRTHS

In most mammals, the young develop inside the mother's body.

MARSUPIALS

These mammals give birth to very underdeveloped young. While they develop, the young live and feed in their mother's pouch.

EGG-LAYING MAMMALS

The echidna (right) and the platypus are the only mammals that lay eggs.

LIMBS

Mammals have four limbs. Most use them to walk on land, but sea mammals have limbs adapted to life in the water, and bats have two limbs that they use as wings.

MORE THAN 5,000 different species of mammal exist.

HUMANS

Humans belong to a group of mammals called primates, which also includes gorillas (left) and monkeys.

Life cycle of mammals

All animals go through the same basic stages in their life cycles: they are born, grow, reproduce and die. Among mammals, there are differences in how the animal reproduces, the length of pregnancy, how long the mother feeds its young and how long the animal lives. However, their life cycles all share the same stages.

READY TO REPRODUCE
A rabbit is ready to reproduce at 5–7 months, and a camel at 3–5 years.

LIVE YOUNG

The vital organs of the young develop inside the body of the mother.

90 YEARS

How long some species of whale live.

PRODUCING MILK
The infants of all mammals feed only on their mother's milk until they are old enough to digest solid food.

YOUNG
Rabbits give birth to 3–9 babies in each litter, and can have more than five litters in a year.

NUMBER OF YOUNG

In general, the larger the animal, the fewer young it gives birth to at the same time.

Cow 1

Goat 2–3 kids

Dog 3–8 puppies

Rat 6–12 babies

LENGTH OF PREGNANCY

ANIMAL	MONTHS
Elephant	22
Giraffe	15
Chimpanzee	9
Lion	4
Dog	2

MOVING AROUND
While it is still small, a baby koala clings to its mother's shoulders as she moves from place to place.

IN THE POUCH
When it is born, the infant stays in the pouch, where it feeds on its mother's milk.

PREGNANCY
Pregnancy is the period of time spent in the mother's womb. In rabbits, pregnancy lasts 28–33 days, while in elephants it lasts 22 months.

MARSUPIALS

Marsupials are pregnant for just 9–35 days, depending on the species. After they are born, the babies develop in their mother's pouch, which is a fold of skin at the front of the mother's body.

HUMANS

Humans belong to the group of mammals that give birth to live young.

MONOTREMES

Mammals that lay eggs are called monotremes. An echidna egg takes 12 days to hatch. After it has hatched, the baby echidna spends the next 50 days in its mother's pouch.

Speed and movement

Every mammal is specially suited to live in its particular habitat. The way an animal moves is important to its survival. Some mammals can climb, some can glide or swim, and others, such as the cheetah, can run at high speeds.

LONG JUMP

Some mammals, such as kangaroos and mountain goats, can jump long distances.

TOP SPEEDS

The top speed of mammals changes from species to species.

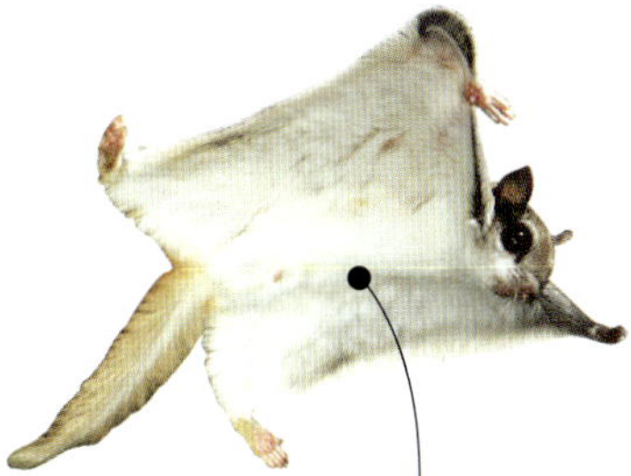

FLYING SQUIRREL
These squirrels throw themselves from one tree to another. They stretch out a thin layer of skin that allows them to glide through the air.

FASTEST

The body of the cheetah is shaped to allow it to catch its prey in a short and fast chase. It has a slender body that stretches as it runs and its legs are longer than those of other cats.

115 KM/H

The cheetah's top speed.

GOOD SWIMMERS
Dolphins and whales are strong swimmers. They move their tails up and down to move forwards. They change direction using their fins.

SLOWEST

The sloth is the slowest-moving mammal.
It spends most of the day hanging from the branches of trees. When it does move, it has a top speed of 2 km/h. Its huge claws allow it to climb through the treetops.

Mammals in danger

Scientists think that within the next 30 years, nearly a quarter of the species of mammals alive today may disappear altogether, becoming extinct.

15

The percentage of European mammal species that are in danger of extinction.

GIANT PANDA
Found in the south of China, the giant panda is in danger of extinction. The animal's natural habitat has been destroyed, and it is also hunted illegally.

LEVELS OF DANGER

Species in danger are labelled as vulnerable, endangered or critically endangered. These are the latest figures for mammals in danger (2012).

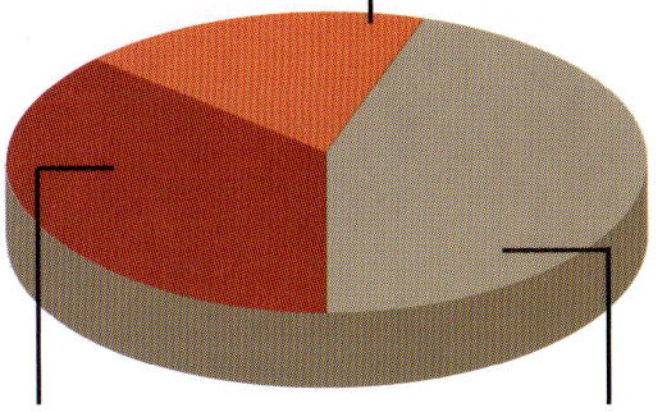

ORANGUTAN
The orangutan is found only on the islands of Borneo and Sumatra. The destruction of tropical rainforest and illegal buying and selling of the orangutans are the main threats to the species.

HUMAN CAUSES

The causes of extinction are habitat destruction and hunting.

IBERIAN LYNX
This wild cat is native to Spain and Portugal on the Iberian Peninsula. It is critically endangered. One reason for this is that there are fewer numbers of its main prey, the rabbit.

RHINOCEROS
Several species of rhinoceros are in danger of extinction because of illegal poaching.

THE HUMAN BODY

Our bodies are among the most complex structures in the Universe. Our brains alone contain more connections than all the computers on Earth put together! The human body is made up of many different organs, which all work together to keep us healthy.

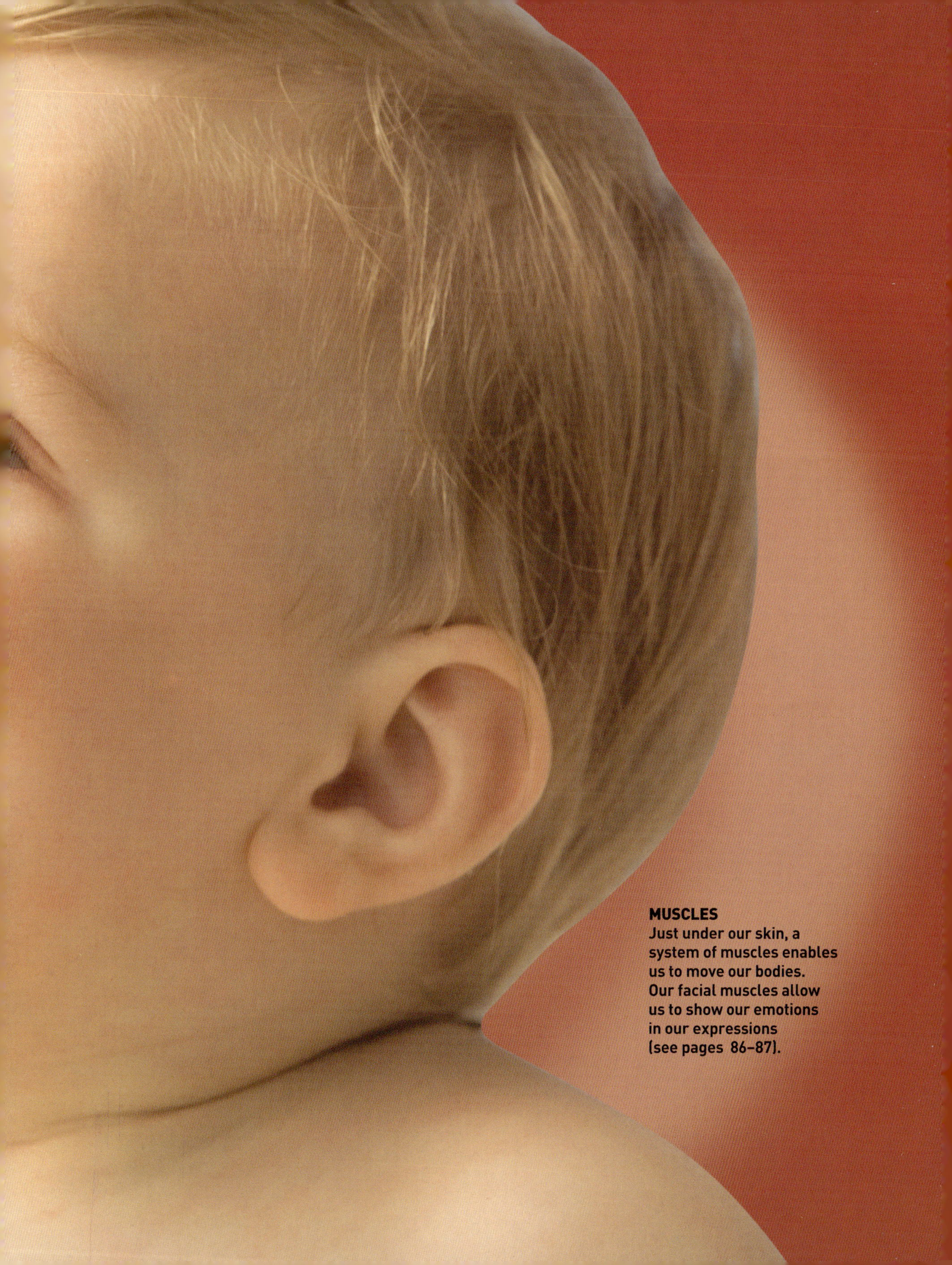

MUSCLES
Just under our skin, a system of muscles enables us to move our bodies. Our facial muscles allow us to show our emotions in our expressions (see pages 86–87).

Body systems

The human body is very complicated. Inside the body there are different organs that need to work together to keep the body healthy. These organs are grouped together into different systems, depending on what they do.

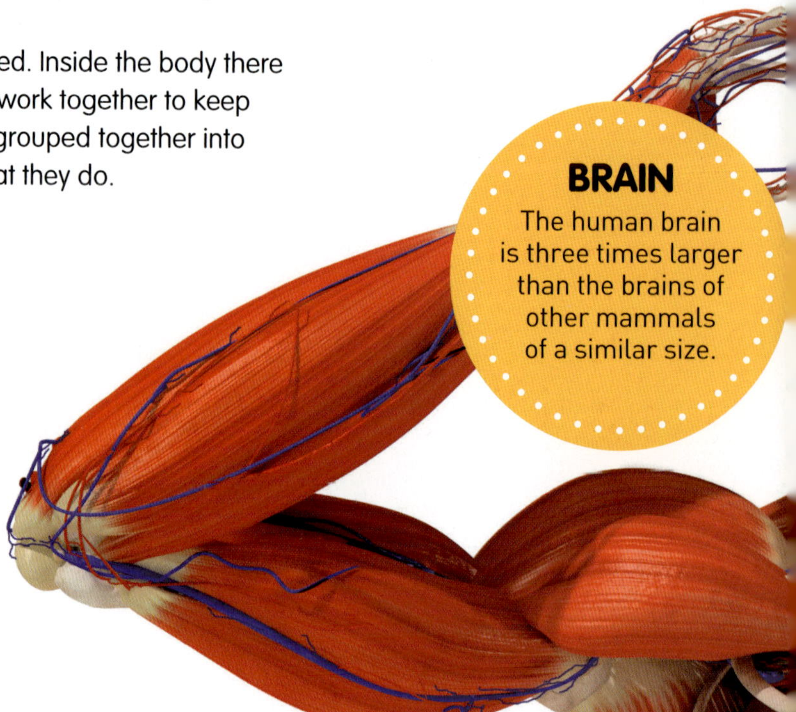

BRAIN

The human brain is three times larger than the brains of other mammals of a similar size.

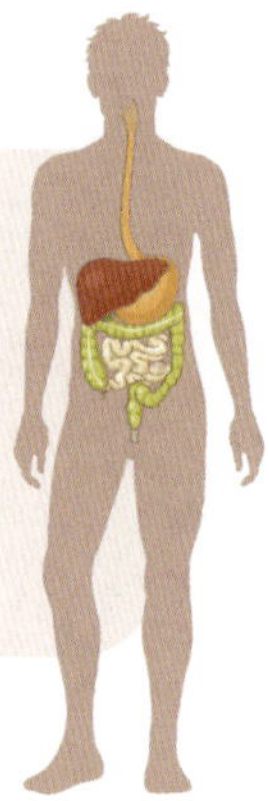

DIGESTIVE SYSTEM
This system helps us to get the energy from our food. It is a tube that starts in the mouth, goes through the stomach and intestines, and ends at the rectum.

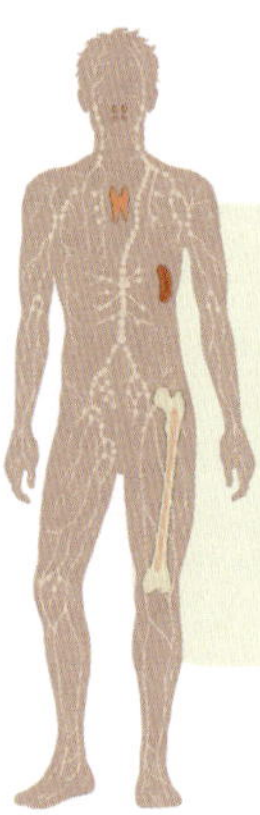

LYMPHATIC SYSTEM
The lymphatic system works with our immune system. This helps the body to fight harmful bacteria and viruses.

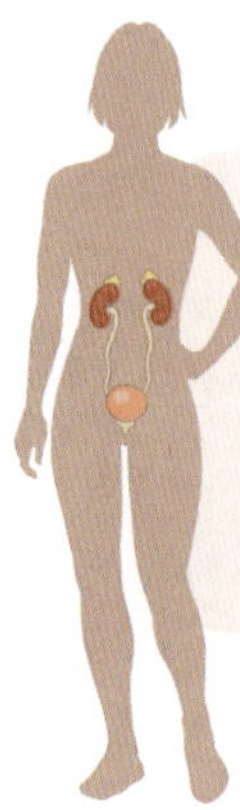

URINARY SYSTEM
The kidneys are the main organs of the urinary system. This system helps the body to get rid of waste by passing urine.

RESPIRATORY SYSTEM
We use the respiratory system to breathe in oxygen. The oxygen passes from the lungs into the blood.

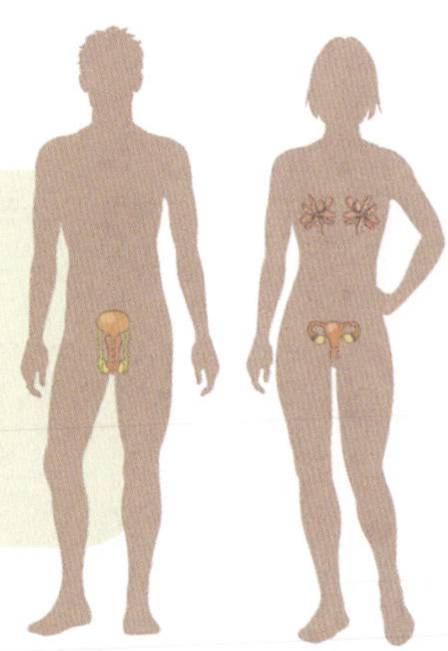

REPRODUCTIVE SYSTEM
This system's function is to make more humans. It is very different in men and women.

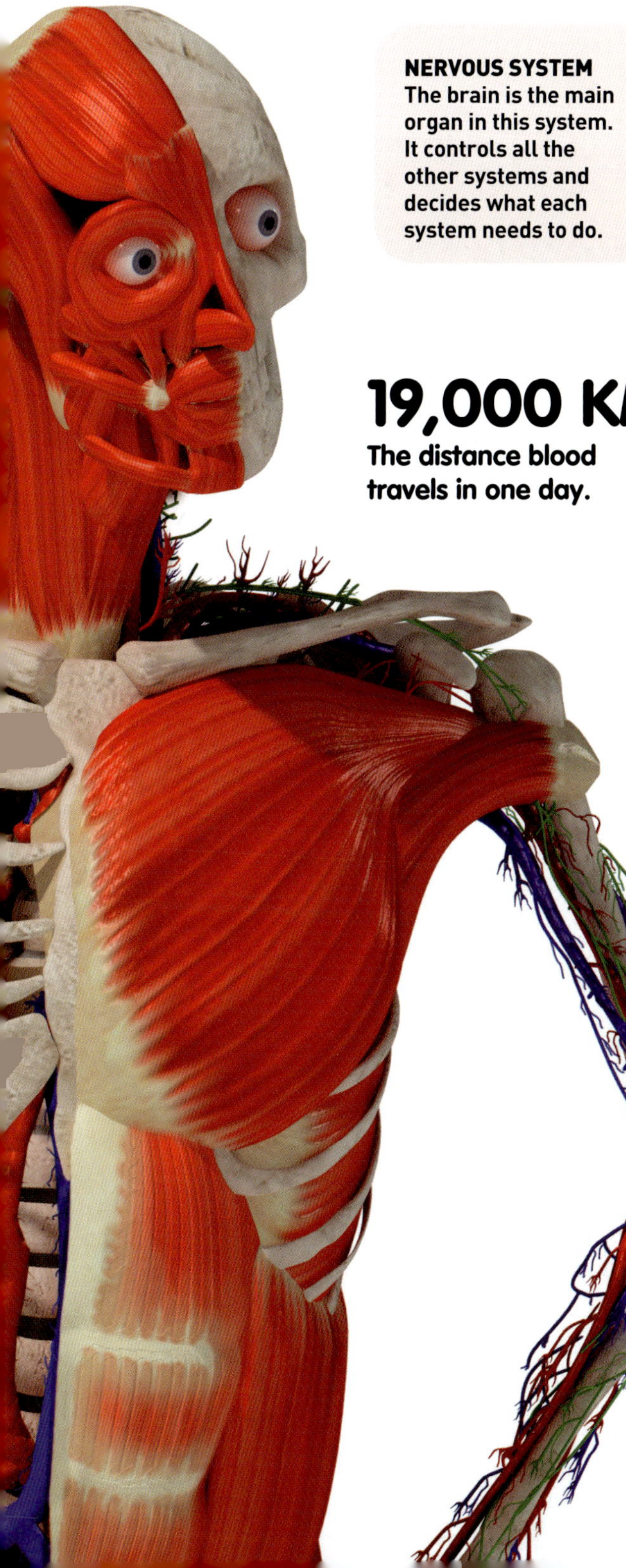

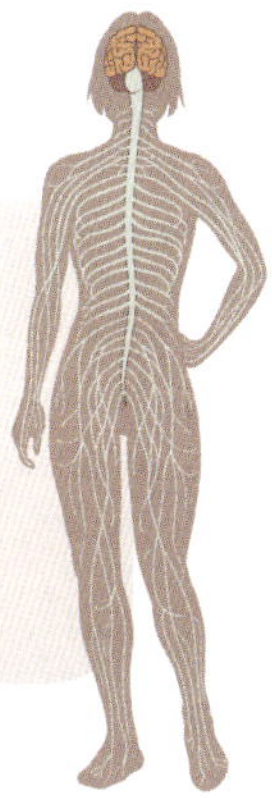

NERVOUS SYSTEM
The brain is the main organ in this system. It controls all the other systems and decides what each system needs to do.

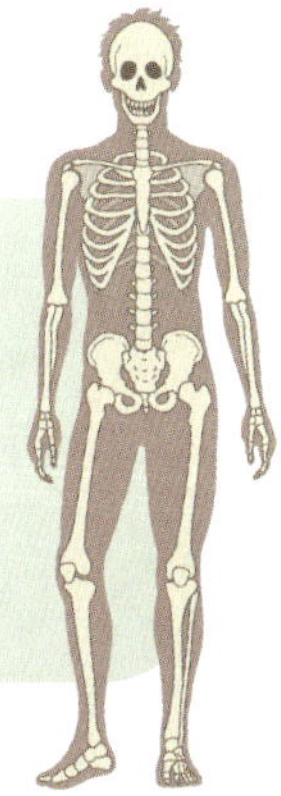

SKELETAL SYSTEM
The skeleton is made up of bones. Bones give shape and support to the body. They also allow the body to move.

19,000 KM

The distance blood travels in one day.

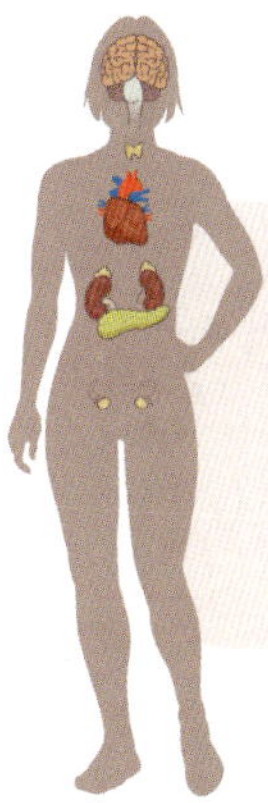

ENDOCRINE SYSTEM
The glands are part of this system. They make chemicals, called hormones, that help the body to work.

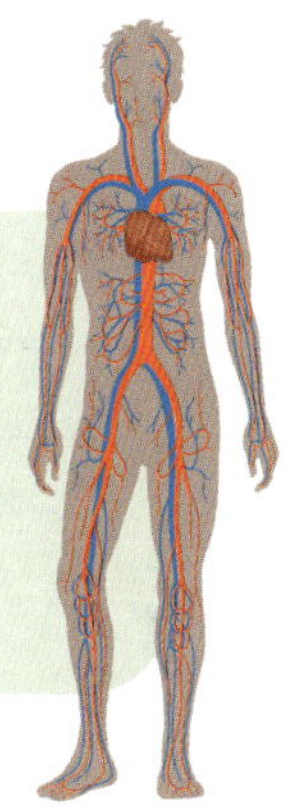

CIRCULATION
Made up of arteries, veins and the heart, this system carries blood around the body.

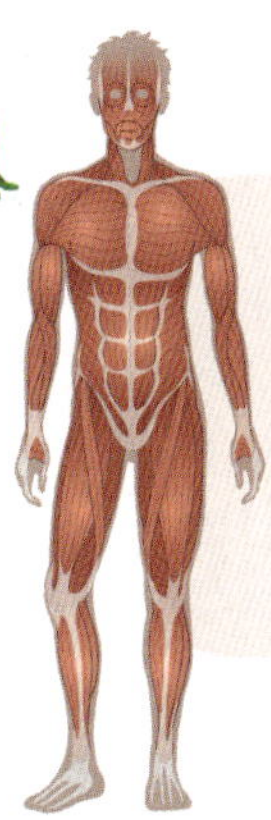

MUSCULAR SYSTEM
The muscles work with the bones to make us move and breathe. They also help digest our food.

The cell

The human body is made up of billions of cells. The cells are so small that they can be seen only through a microscope. Each human cell is made up of the same parts: a nucleus and cytoplasm, surrounded by a membrane.

USEFUL LIFE

Some cells live for only 3–5 days. Others are active throughout a person's life.

CANCER

Sometimes cells go wrong and start growing uncontrollably. This can cause a disease called cancer. To cure cancer, the cells that have gone wrong need to be killed.

CYTOSKELETON
This is made up of strands that keep the cell's shape and allow it to move.

LYSOSOME
Lysosomes break down the cell's waste.

GOLGI APPARATUS
This processes and sends out the proteins made by the rough endoplasmic reticulum.

ROUGH ENDOPLASMIC RETICULUM
Makes and transports proteins.

100 BILLION

The number of cells in an adult human being's body. There are 210 different kinds of human cell.

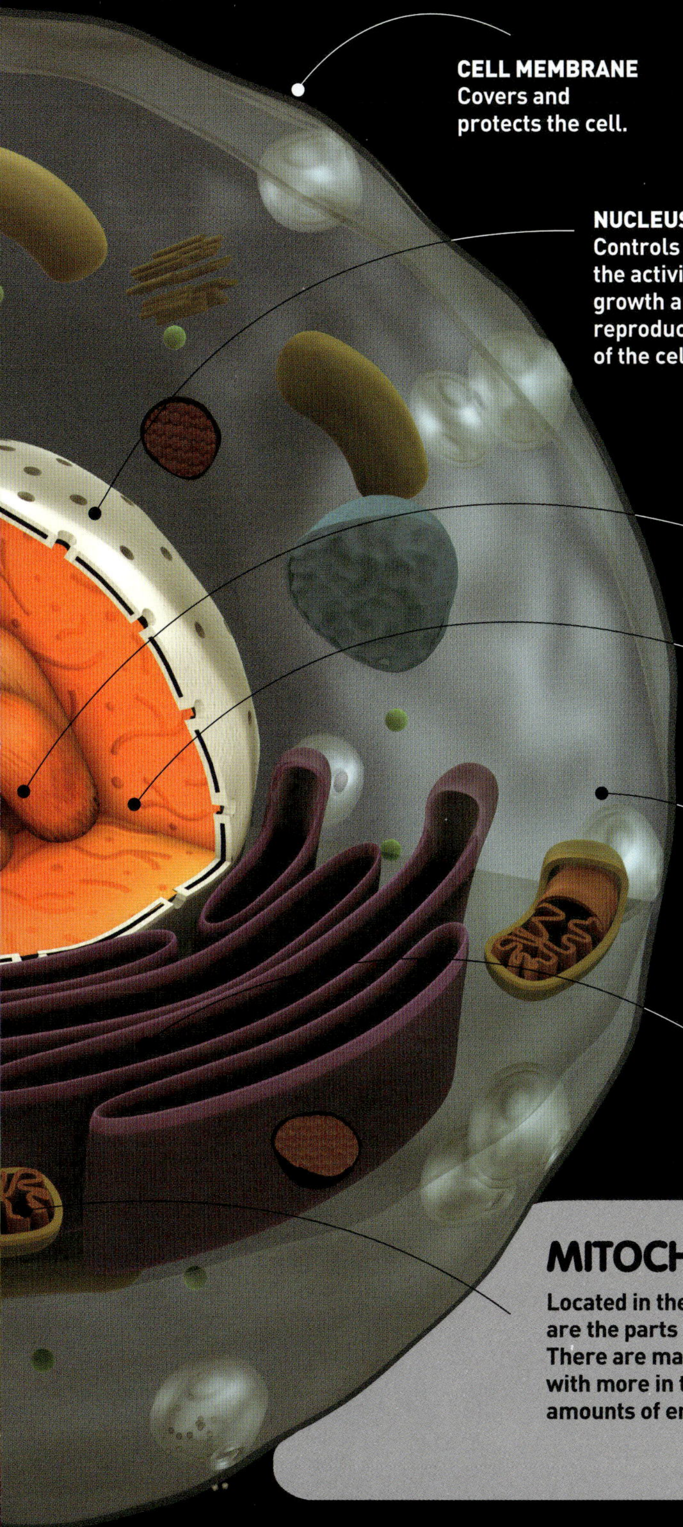

MITOSIS

Two new cells are made from one cell in the process of mitosis. The new cells are exactly the same as the first cell. Mitosis allows an organism to develop, grow and repair itself. Some cells can divide about 50 times.

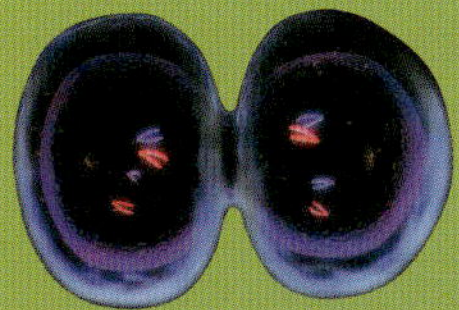

MITOCHONDRIA

Located in the cytoplasm, the mitochondria are the parts of a cell that give it its energy. There are many mitochondria in every cell, with more in those cells that need greater amounts of energy to do their work.

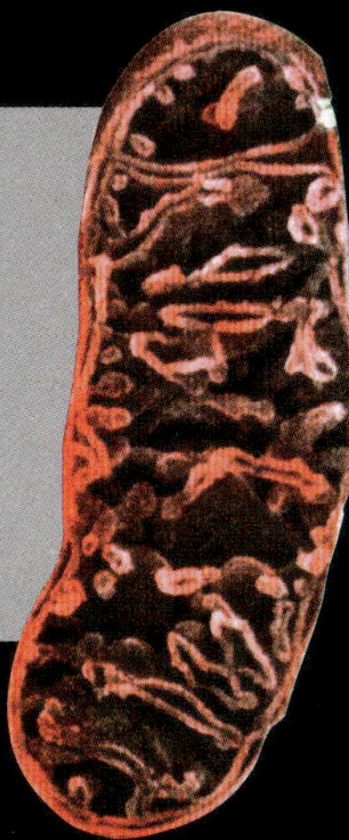

Skeletal system

The skeleton is made of bones. The bones of the skeletal system are made from sponge-like tissue and they contain nerve cells and blood. Bones store minerals that help to keep the body healthy. The skeleton gives the body shape and support and allows it to move. It also covers and protects the organs inside the body.

PARTS OF A BONE

1. **BONE MARROW:** a smooth, fatty substance, which makes blood cells.
2. **BLOOD VESSELS:** carry blood from the bones to the rest of the body and back.
3. **SPONGY BONE:** inner layer of bone.
4. **COMPACT BONE:** outer layer of bone.
5. **PERIOSTEUM:** a film that covers and protects the bone.

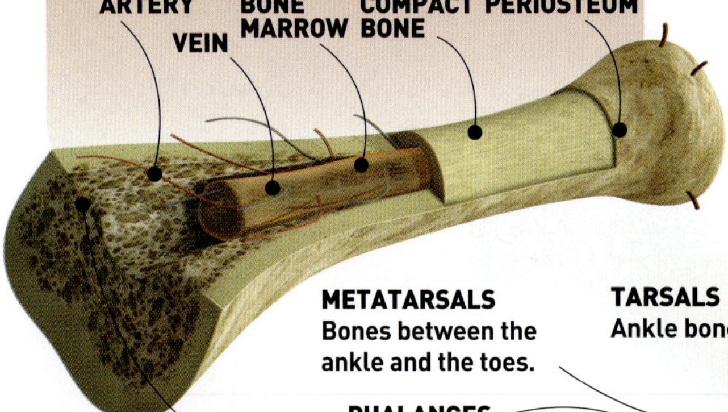

GROWTH

The bones are fully developed by the age of 18–20 years. The calcium in milk strengthens the bones.

206

The number of bones in the human body.

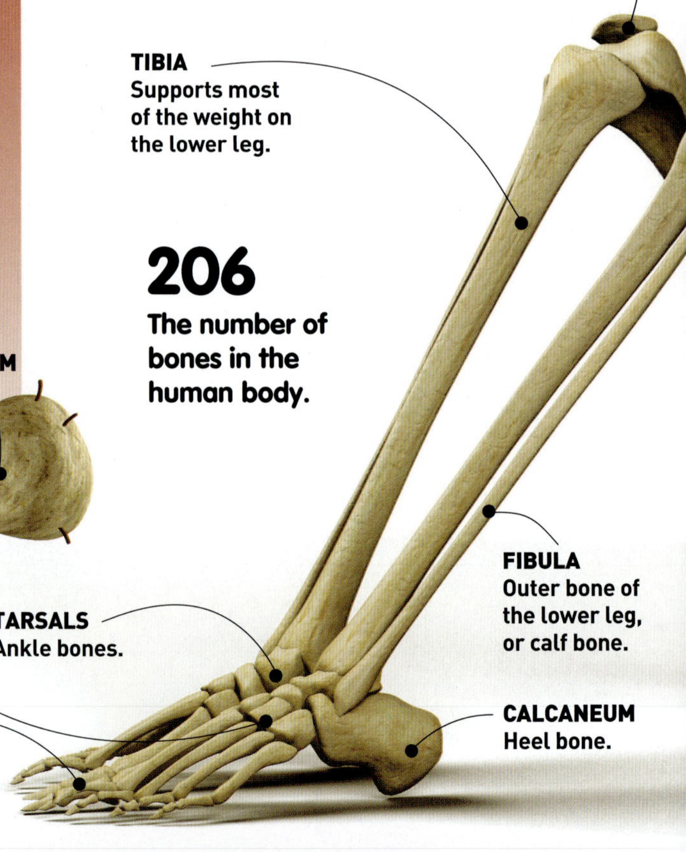

KINDS OF BONE

The bones in the human body can be grouped together, depending on their size and shape:

1. **SHORT BONE:** round or conical in shape, such as the calcaneum.
2. **LONG BONE:** bone, such as the femur, with a central section that stretches between two end points.
3. **FLAT BONE:** sheets of thin bone, such as the bones of the cranium.
4. **SESAMOID BONE:** small and rounded, such as the patella.

JOINTS

The bones are connected to each other by very strong cords called ligaments. In between the bones is a tissue called cartilage, which helps movement.

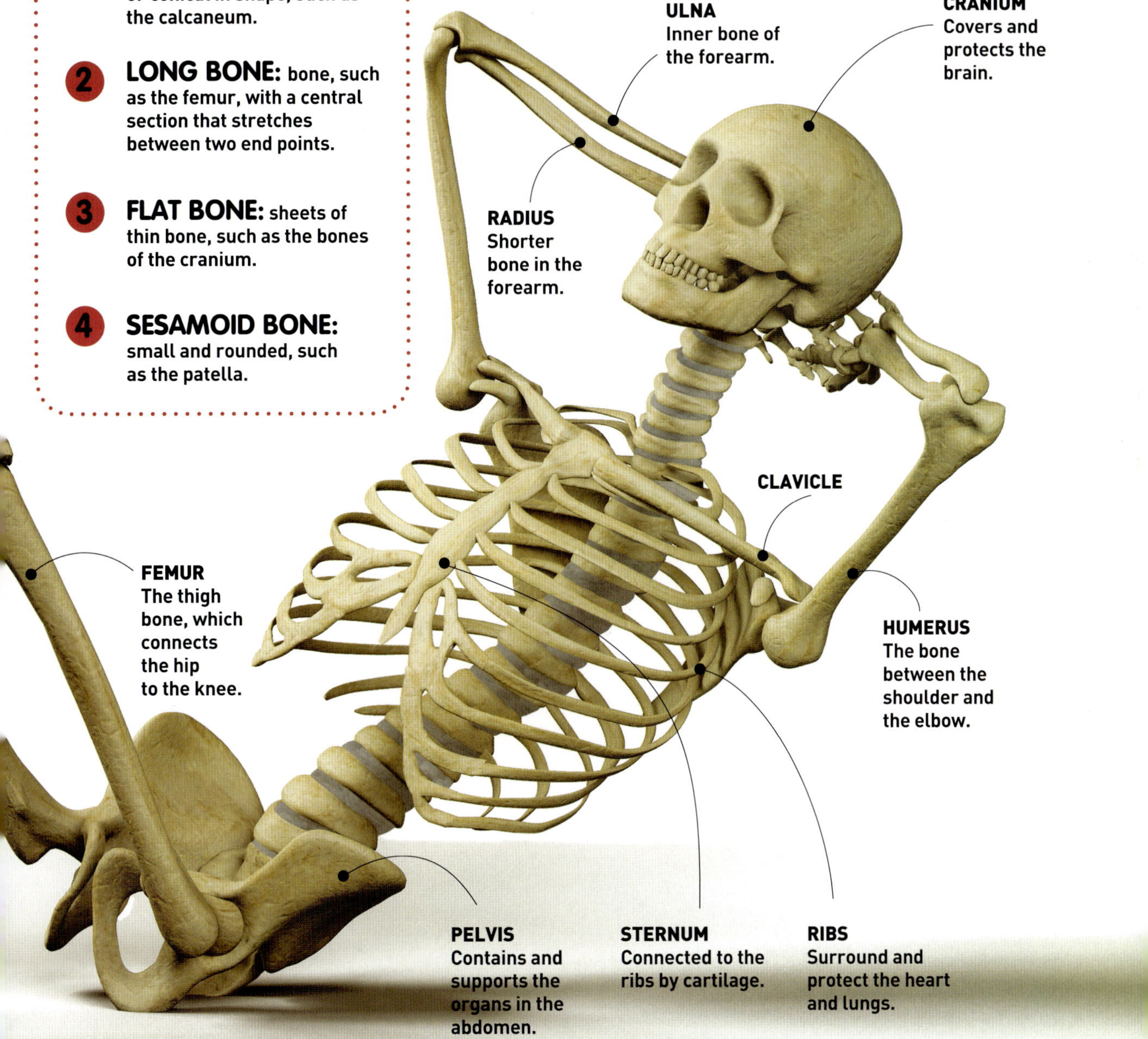

Muscular system

Together with bones, muscles give the body its shape and allow it to move. Muscles work in pairs at each joint on the skeleton, allowing the bones to move in either direction.

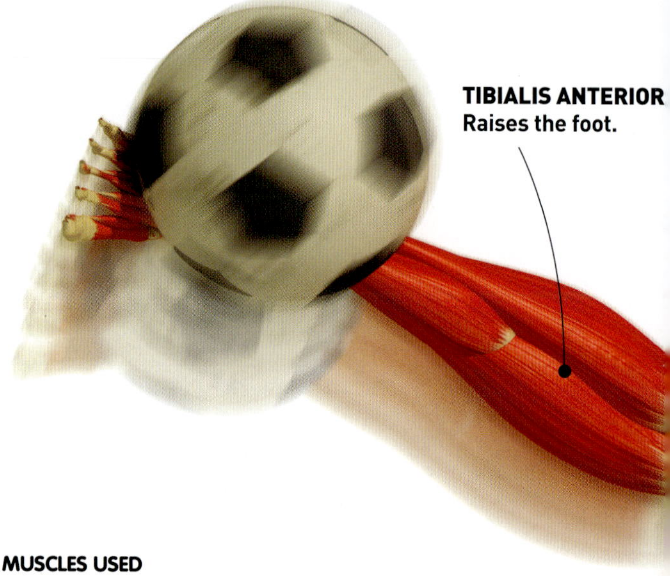

TIBIALIS ANTERIOR
Raises the foot.

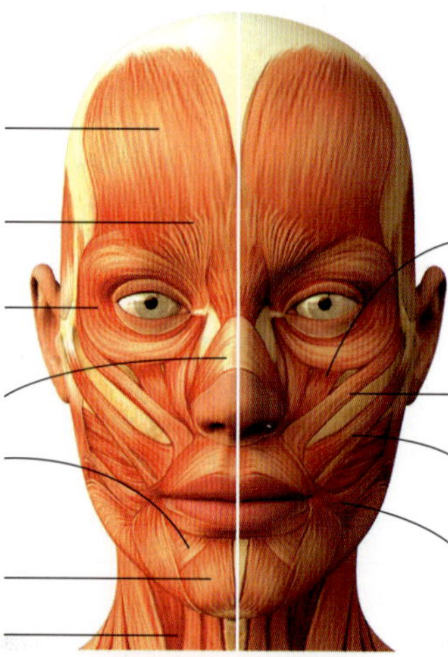

STRONGEST

For its size, the masseter in the lower jaw is the strongest muscle. It works with the rest of the muscles in the mouth to bite.

ACHILLES TENDON
Connects the gastrocnemius to the heel bone.

GASTROCNEMIUS
Bends the foot.

KINDS OF MUSCLE

1 SKELETAL

These muscles are connected to the bones. We have to control these muscles and make them work.

2 SMOOTH

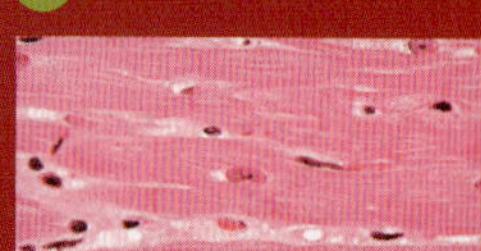

Smooth muscles work without our realizing it. They are found in the walls of the internal organs of the body.

3 CARDIAC

The muscle of the heart also works without our realizing it. It looks like the skeletal muscles.

MASSAGE

A massage relaxes muscles and improves the flow of blood. It can relieve the pain of muscle cramp.

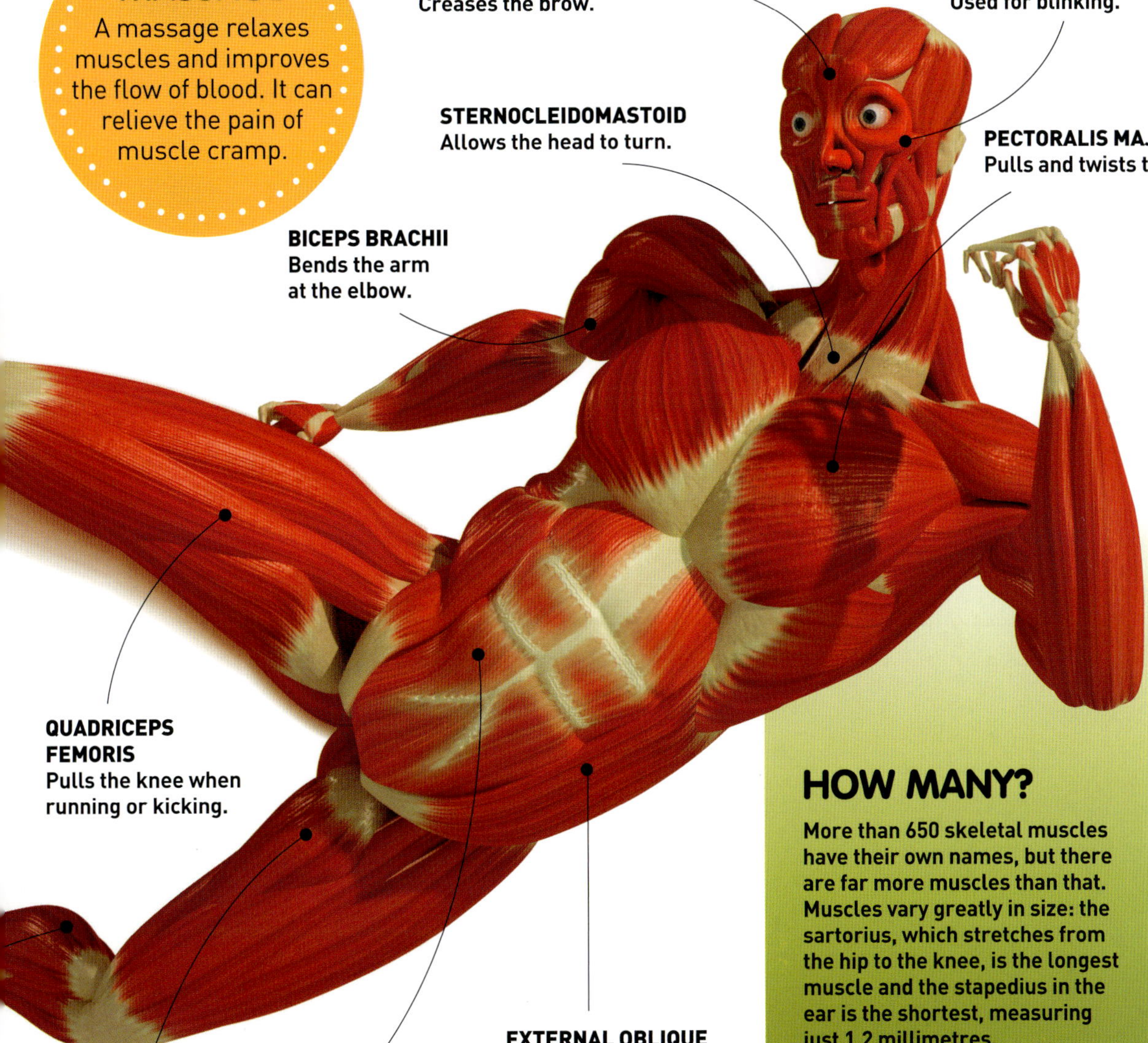

HOW MANY?

More than 650 skeletal muscles have their own names, but there are far more muscles than that. Muscles vary greatly in size: the sartorius, which stretches from the hip to the knee, is the longest muscle and the stapedius in the ear is the shortest, measuring just 1.2 millimetres.

43

The number of muscles in the face that we use to make the expressions to show how we are feeling.

Circulatory system

The cells in our bodies need food and oxygen to live. They also need to have waste taken away from them. The system that does these jobs is called the circulatory system. Substances are carried to or from cells in the blood. Pumped by the heart, the blood reaches all parts of the body along a network of tubes called blood vessels.

BLOOD CIRCUIT

Blood travels around the circulatory system in a figure-of-eight shape, crossing at the heart. The main circuit carries red, oxygenated blood along the arteries from the heart to all parts of the body. The blood reaches individual cells through tiny blood vessels called capillaries. Blue deoxygenated blood returns to the heart along the veins.

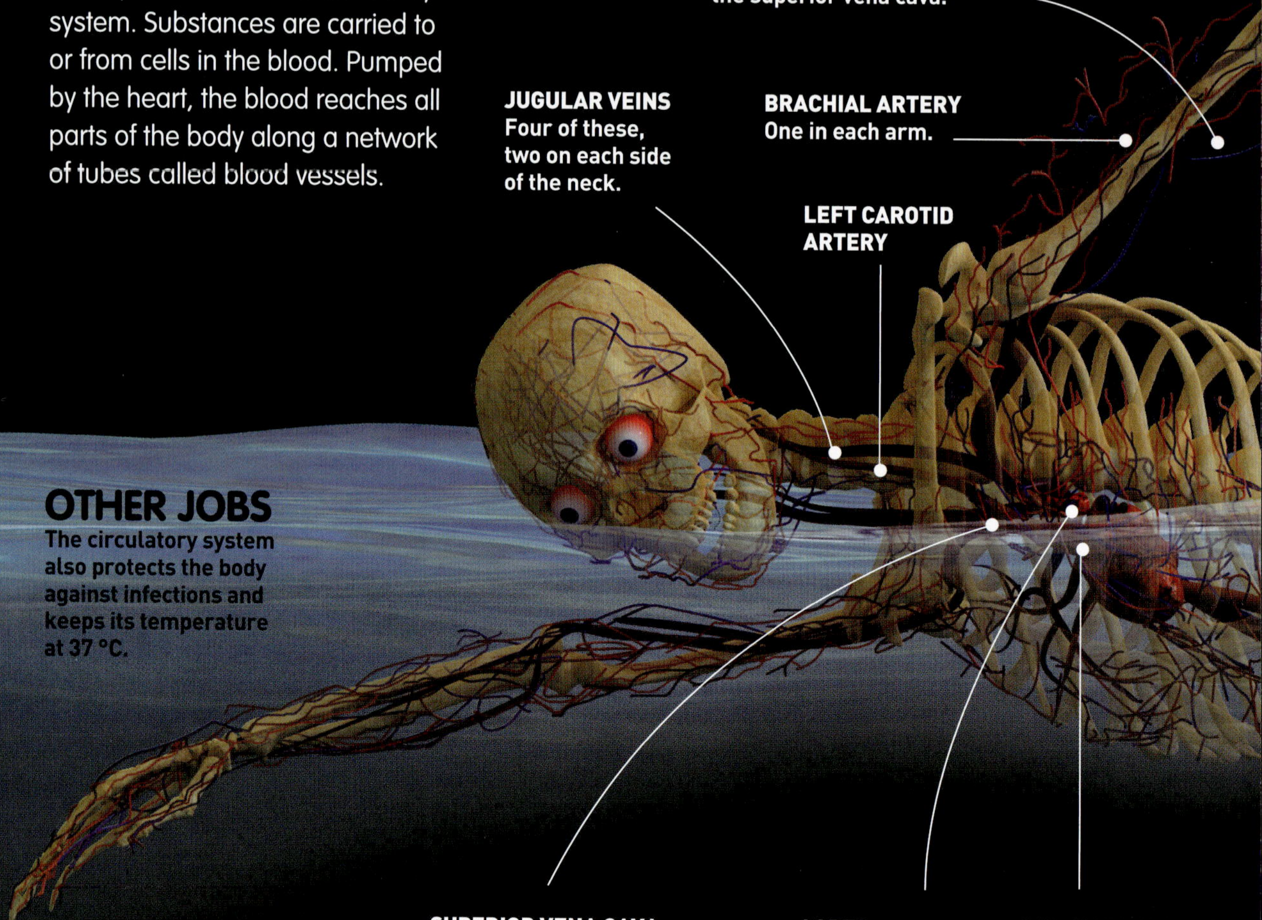

OTHER JOBS

The circulatory system also protects the body against infections and keeps its temperature at 37 °C.

LENGTH

If you were to place all your capillaries end to end, they would be long enough to wrap twice around the world.

ARTERIES

Oxygenated blood is carried from the heart towards the cells by arteries. Arteries have elastic walls that can resist the high pressure of the blood. The capillaries that connect the arteries to the veins, carrying blood to individual cells along the way, are much thinner.

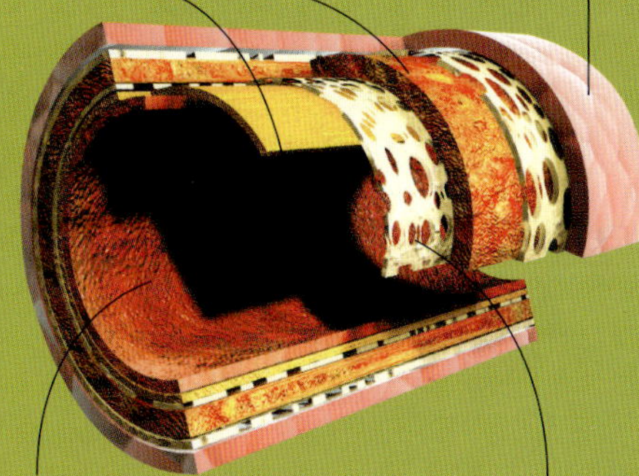

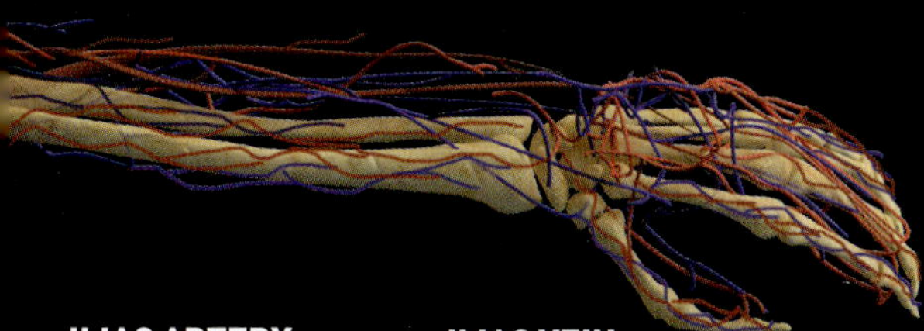

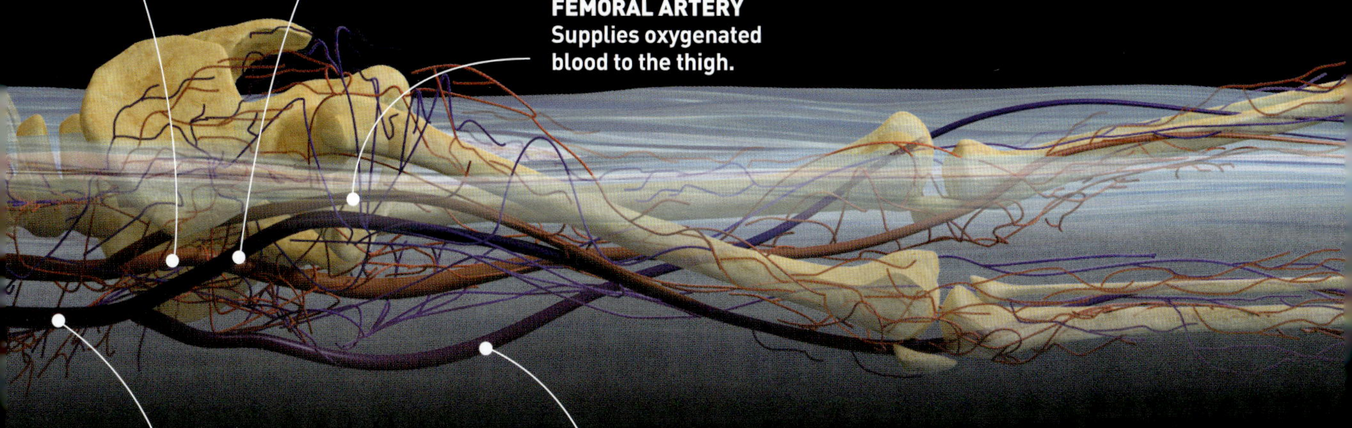

The heart

The heart is a muscle, a little larger than your fist. It is found in the chest between the lungs. It is the main organ in the circulatory system. It pumps oxygenated blood all around the body through the arteries. At the same time, deoxygenated blood arrives at the heart through the veins, to be oxygenated and pumped back around the body.

PUMP
The heart pumps blood to every cell in the body in less than a minute.

70
The average number of heartbeats per minute.

CHAMBERS
The heart is divided into four parts: two atria, in the upper part, and two ventricles in the lower half.

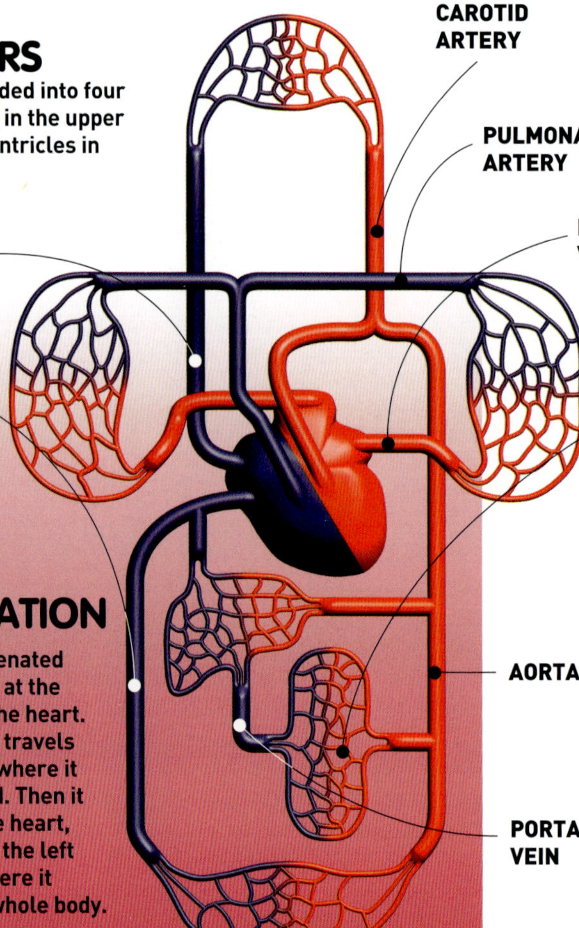

BLOOD CIRCULATION
Blue, deoxygenated blood arrives at the right half of the heart. From there it travels to the lungs, where it is oxygenated. Then it returns to the heart, but is now on the left side. From there it flows to the whole body.

NETWORKS OF VESSELS
All along the circuit, there are networks of blood vessels, located in the lungs, the liver, the digestive system and the upper and lower parts of the body.

HEARTBEATS
There are two phases:
Diastole: the heart fills with blood.
Systole: the heart contracts, forcing blood into the arteries.

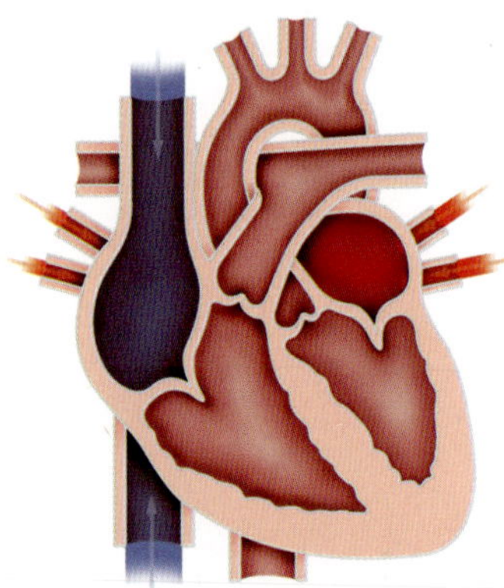

OXYGENATION

The right atrium receives deoxygenated blood from the superior and inferior vena cava. From there, the blood passes to the right ventricle, from which it is pumped to the lungs. This is where it is oxygenated. The left atrium receives oxygenated blood from the lungs and passes it to the left ventricle. From there, the blood is pumped to the whole body, via the aorta.

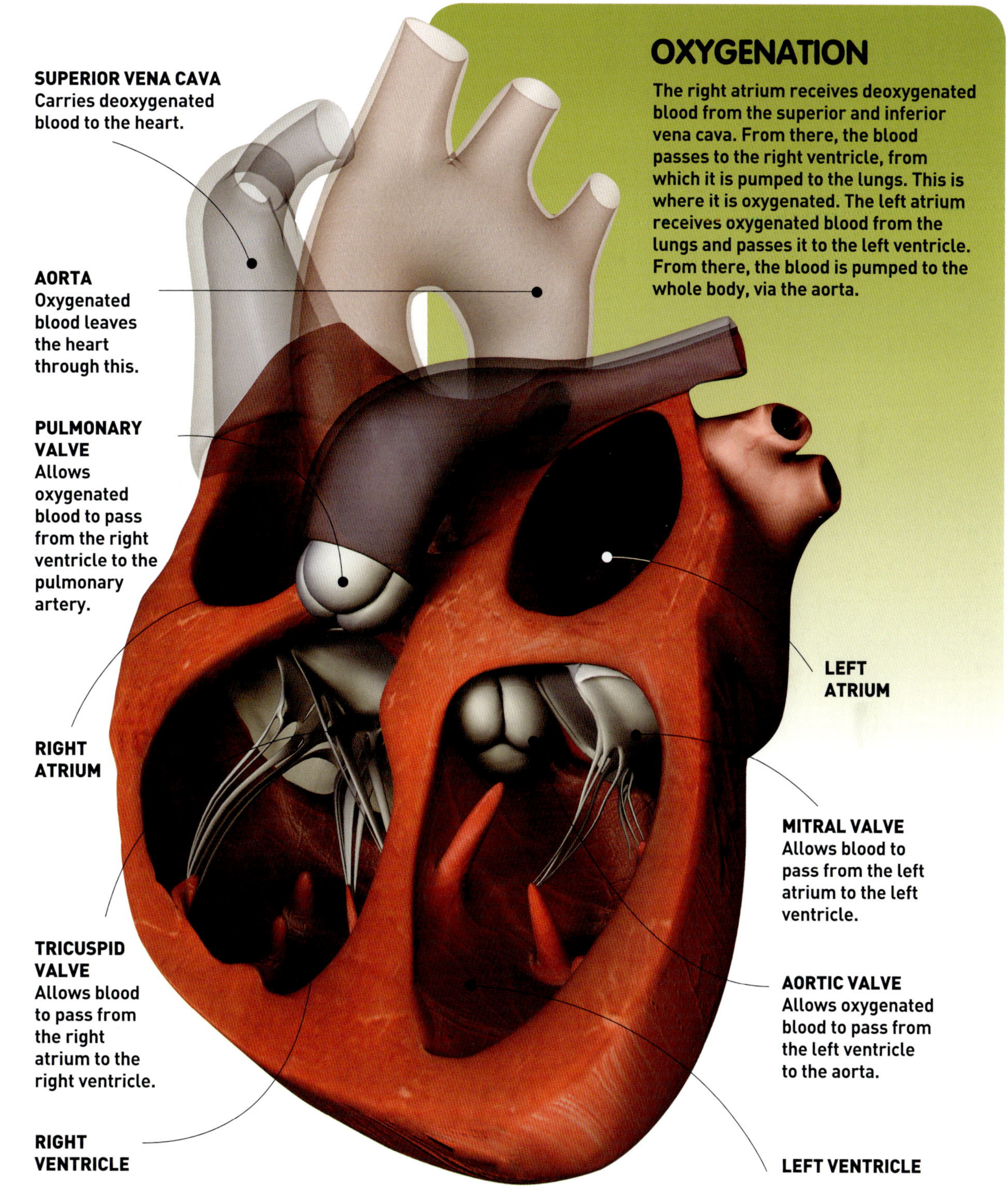

Blood

Blood is a liquid body tissue that moves through the body in blood vessels. It is made of water with substances dissolved in it, and blood cells. It carries food substances taken in through digestion to the whole body. It also carries oxygen from the lungs to body tissues and harmful carbon dioxide from the tissues back to the lungs.

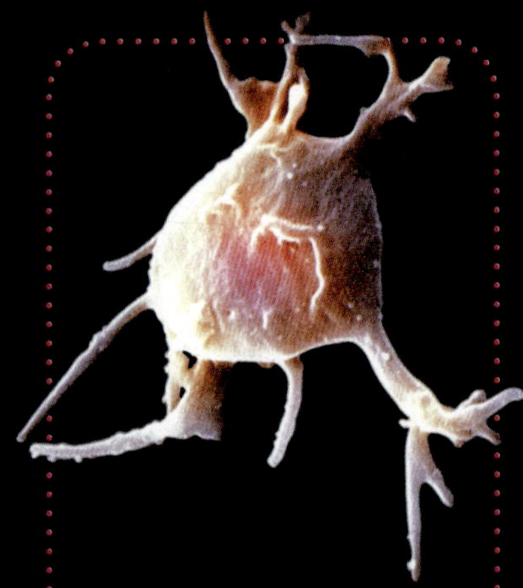

PLATELETS

These repair broken blood vessels. They are found in wounds and help blood to clot.

RED BLOOD CELLS
The main job of red blood cells is to absorb oxygen from the lungs and release it in other parts of the body.

WHITE BLOOD CELLS
These cells protect the body from infections by attacking bacteria, viruses and other harmful organisms.

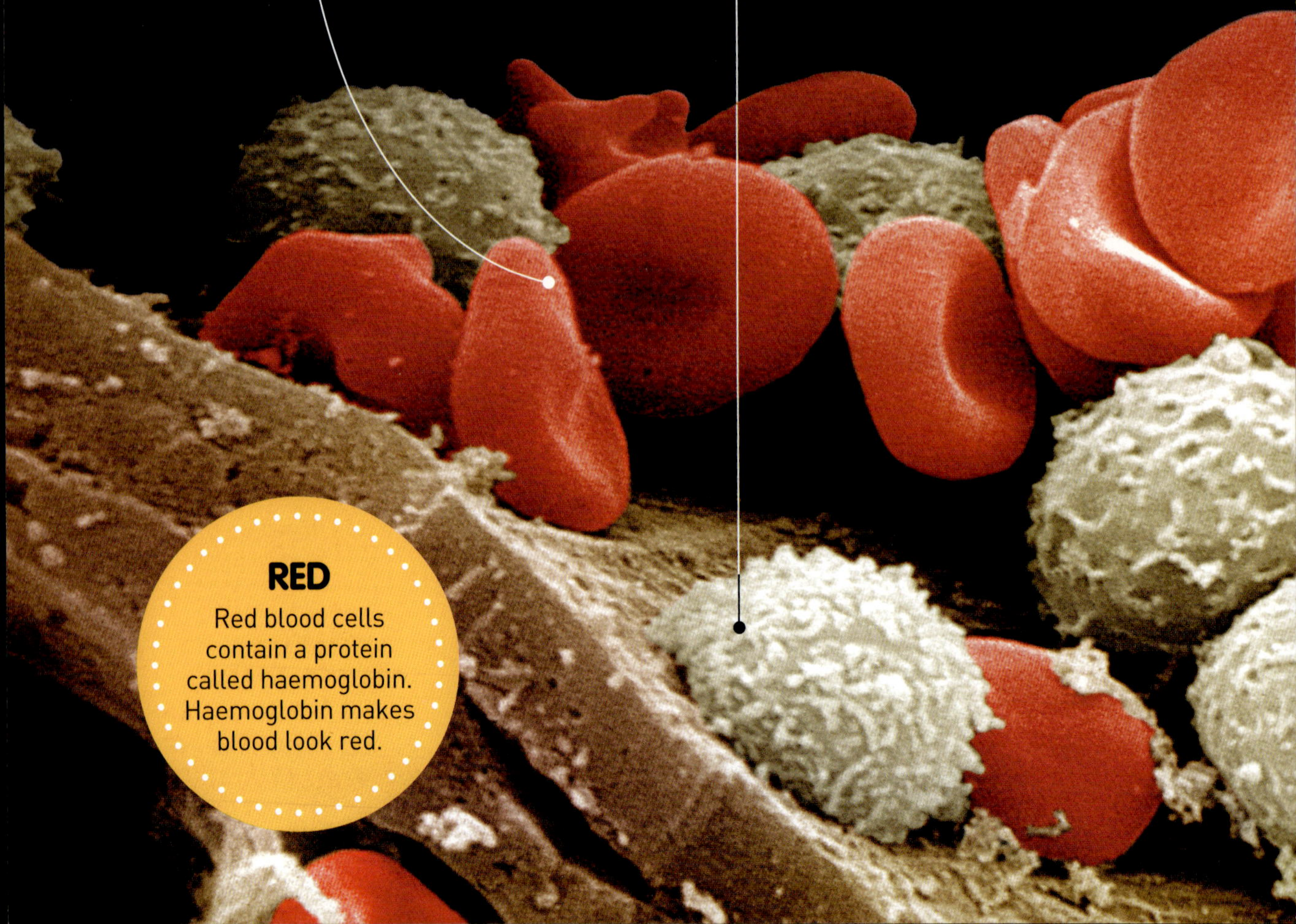

RED

Red blood cells contain a protein called haemoglobin. Haemoglobin makes blood look red.

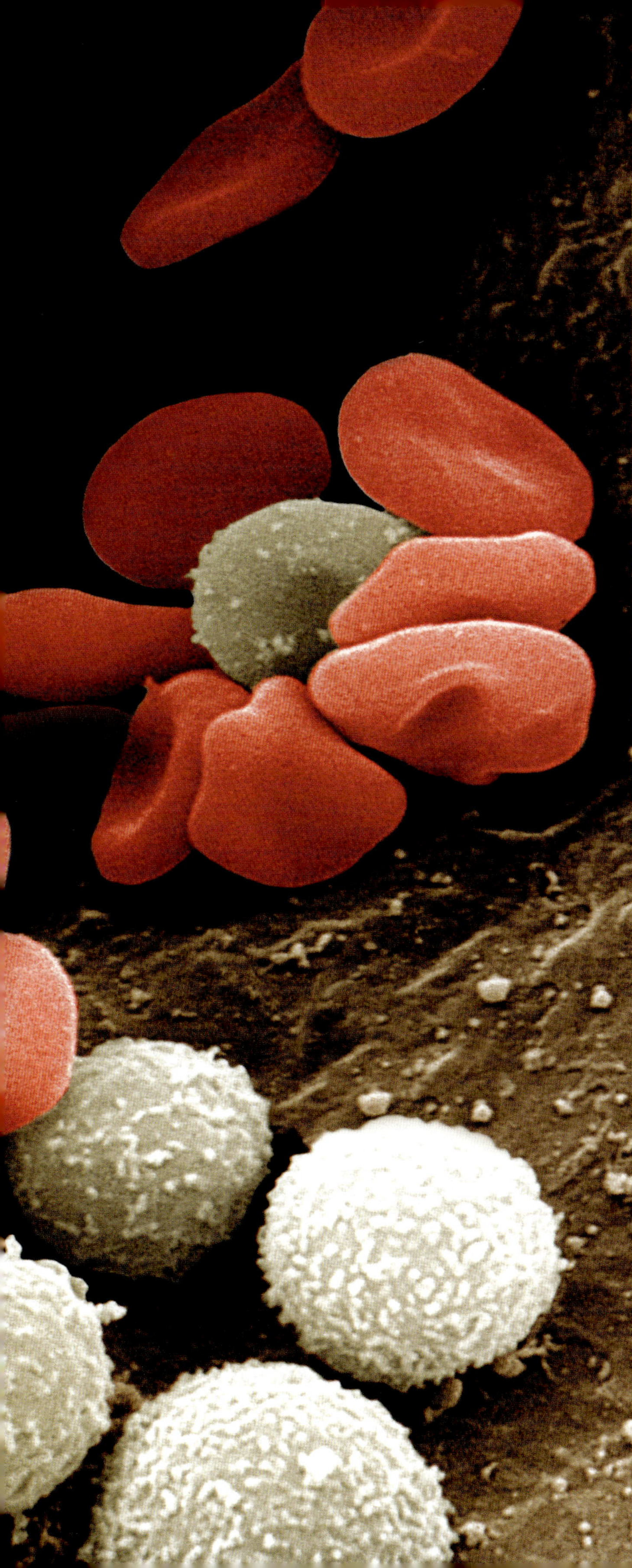

BLOOD CLOTTING

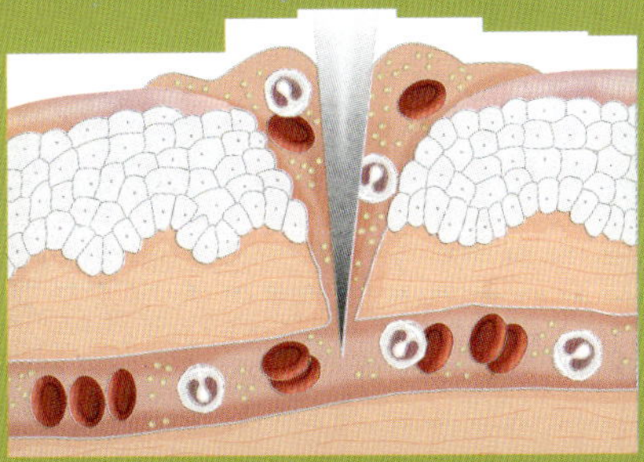

1 When the body is wounded, platelets in the blood around the wound become sticky.

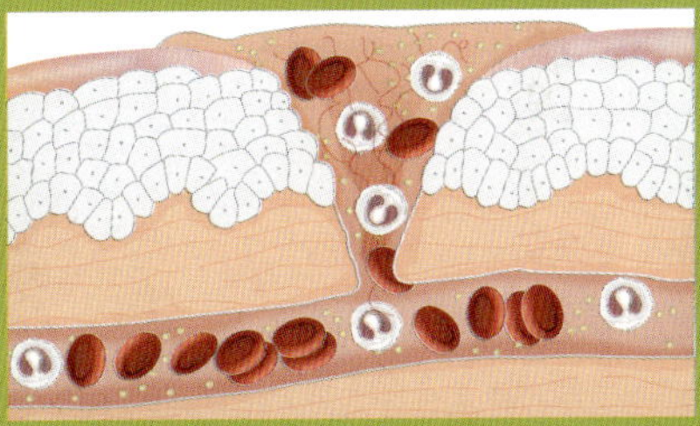

2 The platelets form a cap to stop blood from exiting the wound, and release chemicals that will make the blood clot.

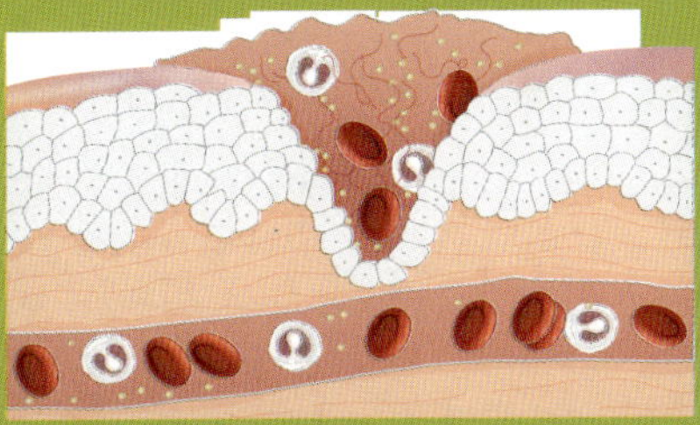

3 Cells divide to cover the damaged area.

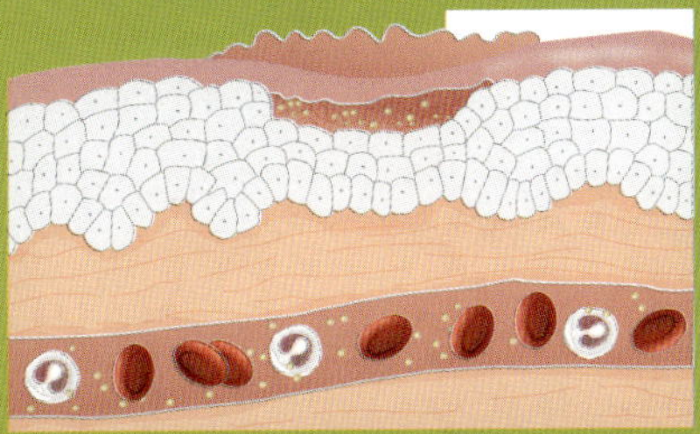

4 At the surface, a crust, or scab, forms. Underneath the crust, the damaged blood vessel repairs itself.

Urinary system

The urinary system is made up of the kidneys, ureters and bladder. It purifies the blood and maintains the levels of water and minerals in the body. The kidneys are the organs responsible for carrying out this task. They filter the blood around the body every five minutes. Unwanted waste, water and salts pass from the kidneys to form urine, which passes out through the bladder.

CELLS
Cells continually release waste products into the blood. These are removed from the body in urine.

RENAL PYRAMID
Urine passes from these triangular-shaped structures into the ureter.

RENAL CORTEX
This part of the kidney filters the blood and helps to remove waste products from the body.

RENAL CAPSULE
The tough layer around the outside of the kidney.

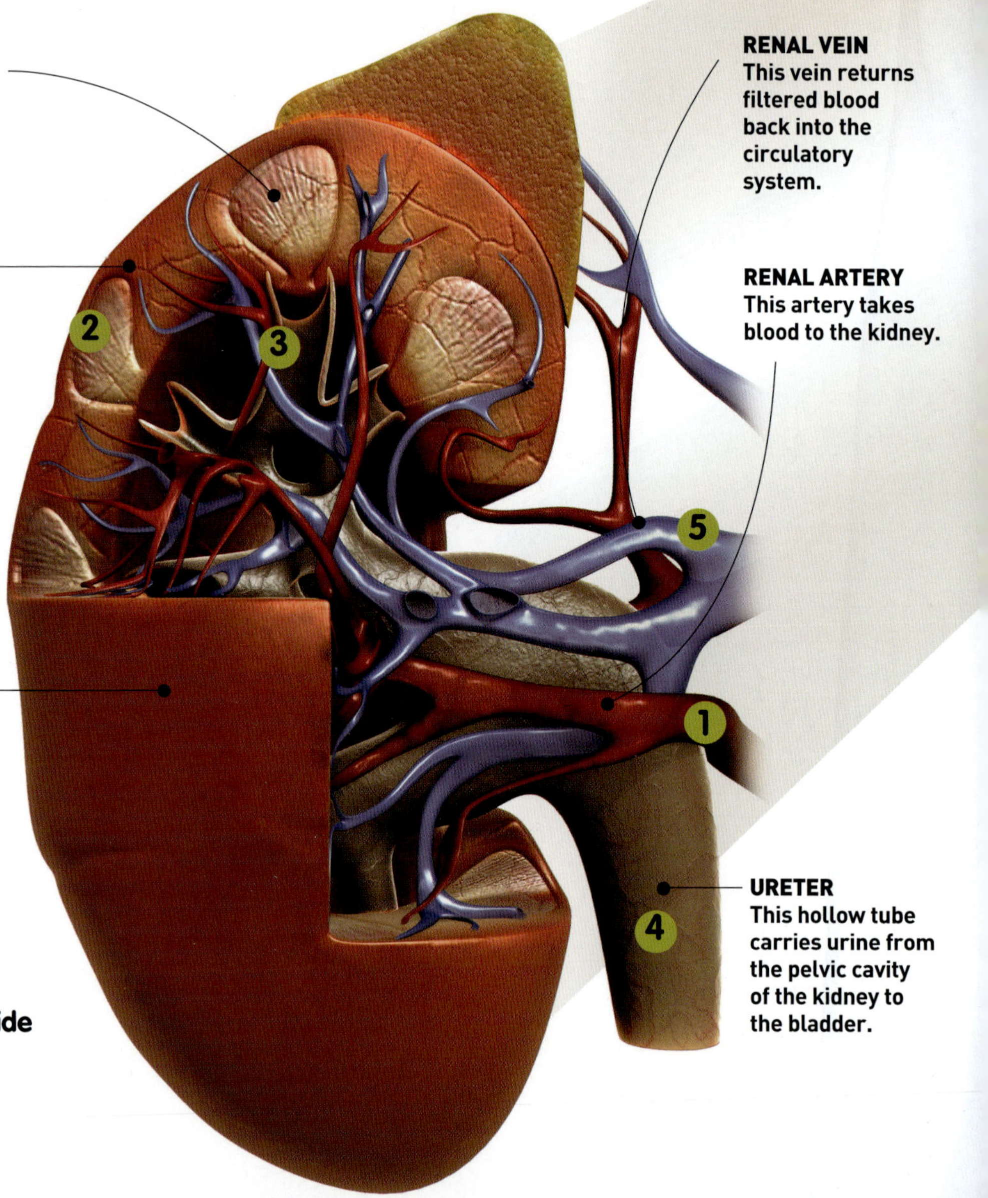

RENAL VEIN
This vein returns filtered blood back into the circulatory system.

RENAL ARTERY
This artery takes blood to the kidney.

URETER
This hollow tube carries urine from the pelvic cavity of the kidney to the bladder.

70,000
the number of kidney transplants performed worldwide each year.

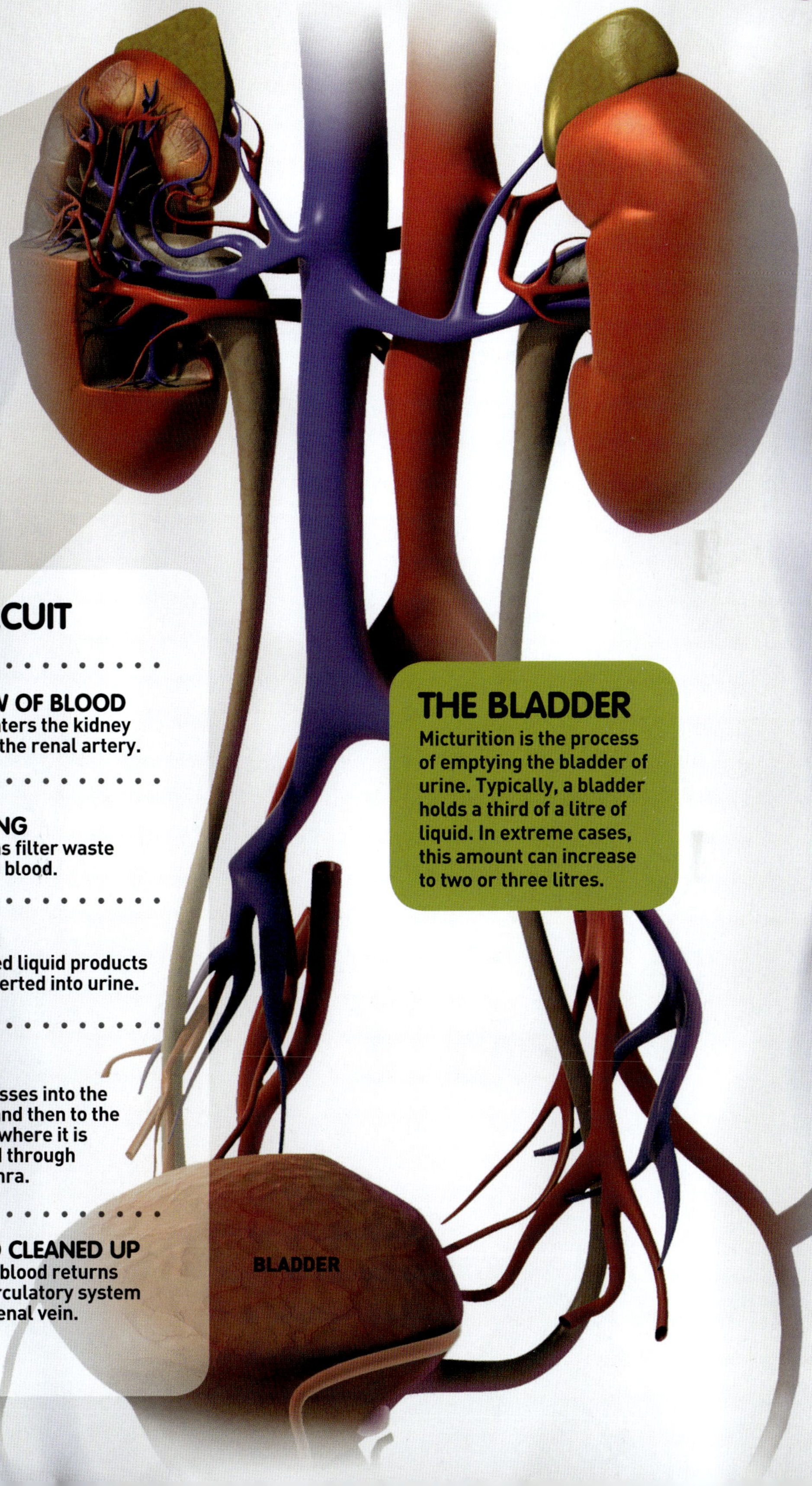

RENAL CIRCUIT

1. **INFLOW OF BLOOD**
Blood enters the kidney through the renal artery.

2. **FILTERING**
Nephrons filter waste from the blood.

3. **WASTE**
Unwanted liquid products are converted into urine.

4. **URINE**
Urine passes into the ureter, and then to the bladder where it is excreted through the urethra.

5. **BLOOD CLEANED UP**
Purified blood returns to the circulatory system via the renal vein.

THE BLADDER

Micturition is the process of emptying the bladder of urine. Typically, a bladder holds a third of a litre of liquid. In extreme cases, this amount can increase to two or three litres.

Respiratory system

Breathing, or respiration, is the process that allows the body to take in air. We breathe in oxygen and breathe out waste gases such as carbon dioxide. The lungs are the main organ of the respiratory system.

15

The average number of breaths per minute taken by an adult.

YAWNING

You cannot control when you yawn – it just happens. When you yawn, you take a deep breath, open your mouth very wide and stretch the muscles in the face. Yawning is a sign of tiredness, relaxation or boredom, and it is contagious – seeing someone else yawn can make you yawn yourself.

CONTINUOUS MOVEMENT

1. **Nose:** Air enters through the nostrils.
2. **Pharynx:** The air passes through the pharynx, where the tonsils detect and destroy dangerous organisms.
3. **Larynx:** The larynx is connected to the trachea. When swallowing, a flap called the epiglottis closes access to the trachea, stopping food or water from getting into the airways, and directing them instead towards the stomach.
4. **Trachea:** The trachea carries air to and from the lungs.
5. **Bronchi:** When it reaches the lungs, the trachea divides into two bronchi, one for each lung.
6. **Blood:** Oxygen passes into the blood, while carbon dioxide is passed from the blood into the air in the lungs. When you breathe out, carbon dioxide is given off.

THE RESPIRATORY PROCESS

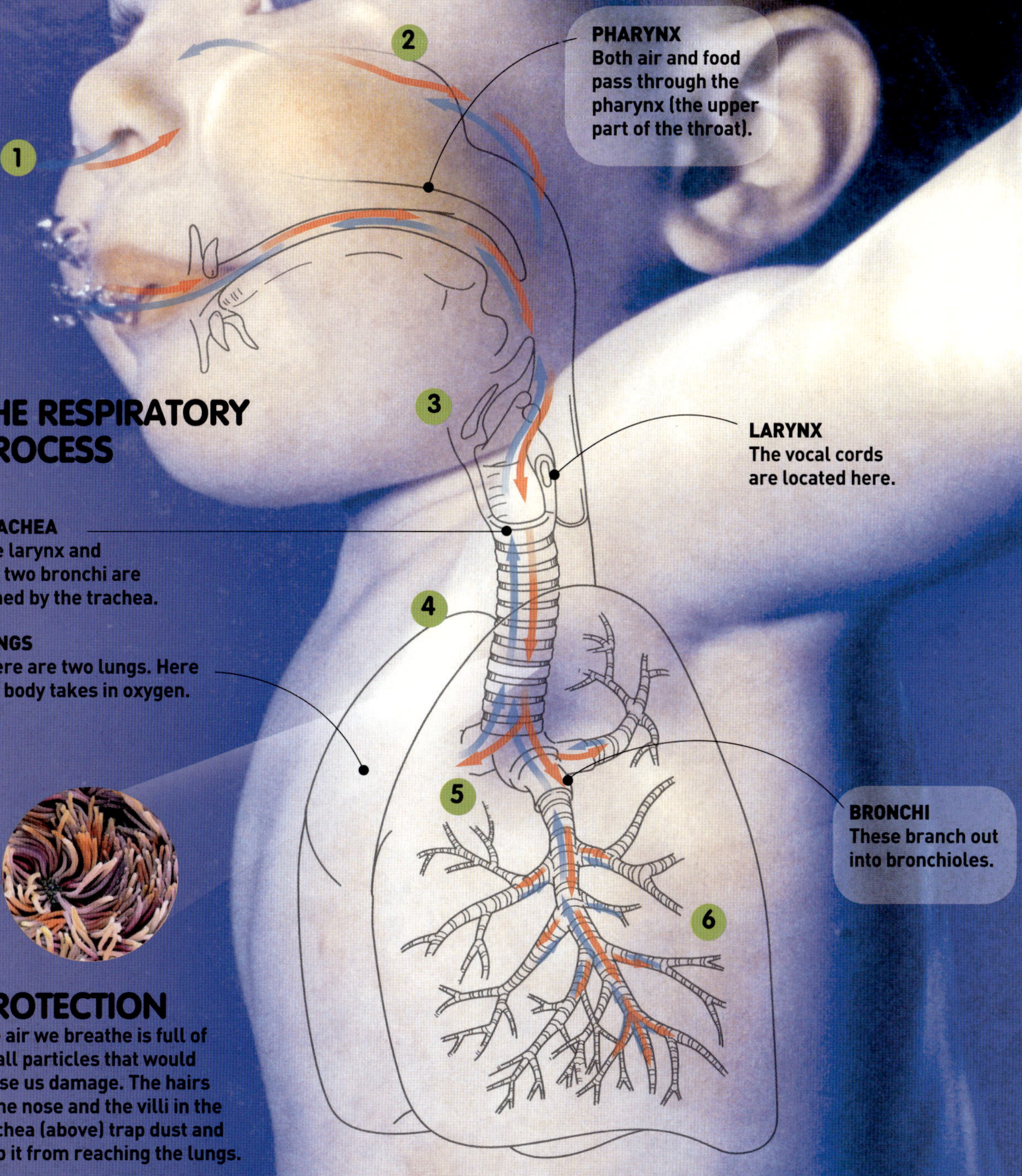

PROTECTION

The air we breathe is full of small particles that would cause us damage. The hairs in the nose and the villi in the trachea (above) trap dust and stop it from reaching the lungs.

Digestive system

The digestive system breaks down the food that you eat into something that the body can use. It also separates material that the body cannot use from food and gets rid of it. In the stomach and the small intestine, food is broken down into simpler substances. Other organs, such as the pancreas and the liver, help in this process, too.

SWALLOW
The muscles in the oesophagus are so powerful that food will reach the stomach even if we are upside down.

3
The number of types of nutrients the body needs: carbohydrates, fats and proteins.

CAVITIES

When we do not clean our teeth and mouths well enough, a layer of plaque can form. This is a mix of food and bacteria. The plaque gives off an acid that harms the teeth and can cause cavities (holes) to form. It is difficult to get rid of plaque because the bacteria in it contain a glue that keeps them stuck to the teeth.

BRUSHING YOUR TEETH
It is important to clean your tongue and your palate as well as your teeth.

TEETH

The food we put in our mouths is broken up by our teeth. Adults have 32 teeth. During chewing, the flexible tongue moves the food around, forming it into a blob called a bolus.

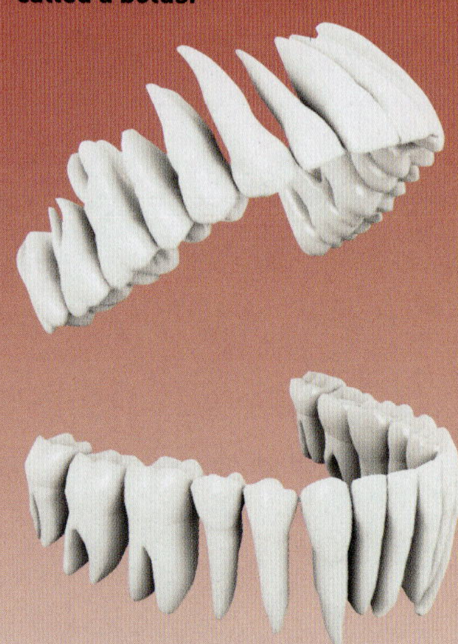

FIRST TEETH
Young children have 20 smaller milk teeth, which fall out at age 6 or 7, to be replaced by adult teeth.

DAY-LONG JOURNEY

1 Mouth
(20 seconds)
Food starts off in the mouth. It is crushed and chewed by the teeth, with the help of the tongue and saliva (spit). The saliva moistens the food and helps to form it into a ball ready for swallowing.

2 Oesophagus
(10 seconds)
The ball passes quickly through the oesophagus. Within 10 seconds, it has reached the stomach.

3 Stomach
(3 hours)
The food stays in the stomach for 3–6 hours. In the stomach, it becomes dough-like.

4 Small intestine
(5 hours)
The digestive process continues in the small intestine for 5-6 hours. The remains, now in a liquid state, pass to the large intestine.

5 Large intestine
(12 hours)
The materials that reach the large intestine stay here for 12–24 hours. Water is taken out of the remains, which form into semi-solid faeces.

6 Rectum
(20 hours)
Waste is expelled from the body through the anus, 20–36 hours after it has been eaten.

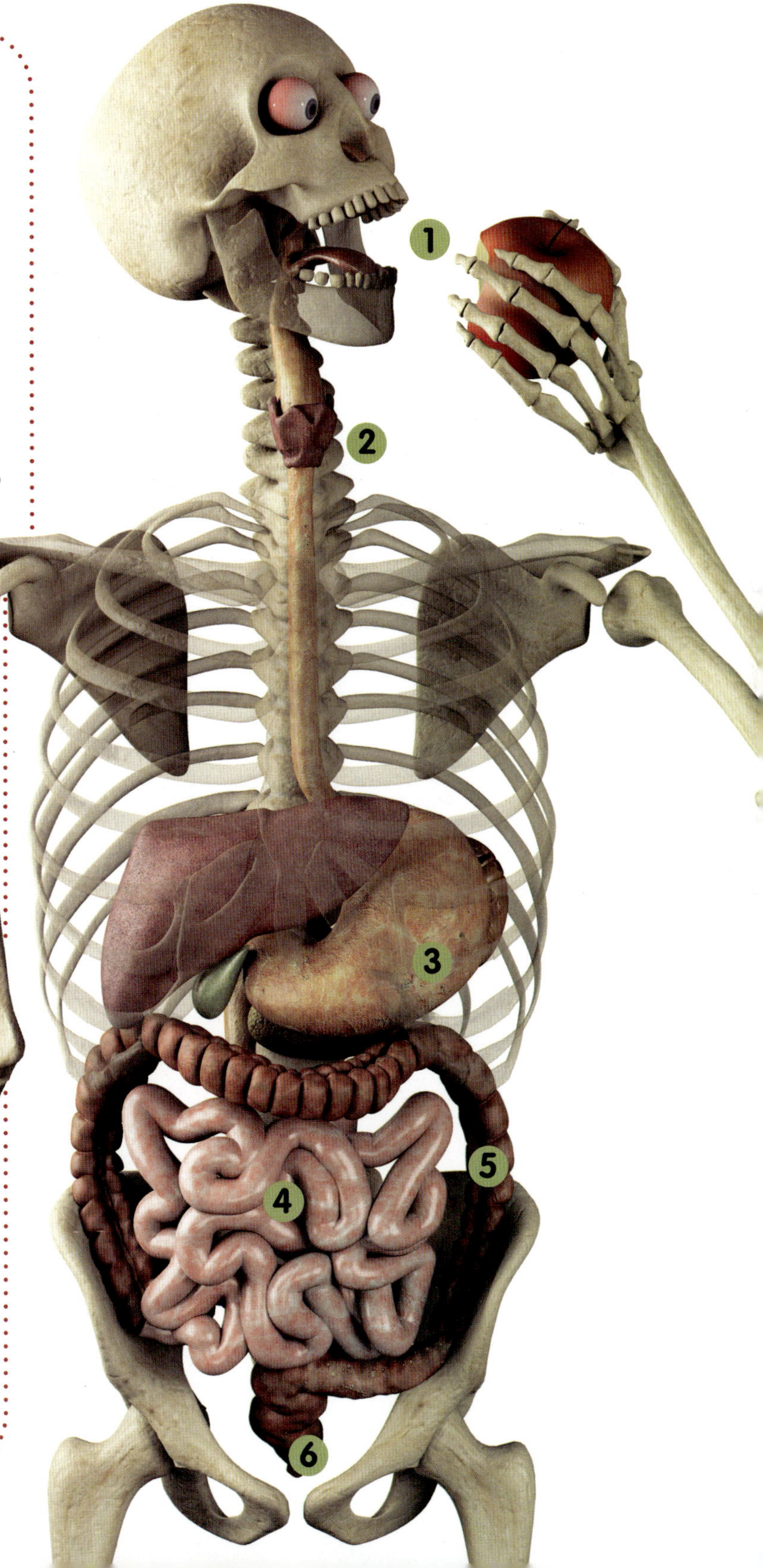

Endocrine system

The endocrine system is a network of glands that makes chemicals called hormones. Hormones keep the body working properly. The whole system is controlled by the pituitary gland at the base of the skull. There are another eight glands, which are in the brain, the neck and the torso.

50

The number of hormones that the body produces.

HORMONES

These chemicals are carried in the blood. They contain information for particular places in the body, telling them how to work. Hormones control processes such as reproduction, growth and how quickly we use energy (metabolism). Before pregnancy, for example, hormones released by the woman's ovaries prepare her body to receive the fertilized egg.

GROWING BODIES

Several hormones are produced that control the rate at which our bodies grow and how they perform. Many of these are produced by the pituitary gland, and these usually control how other endocrine glands perform. The pituitary gland is itself controlled by a part of the brain called the hypothalamus.

GOODBYE

Once they have done their job, hormones are broken down into harmless substances by the liver.

DISEASE

The endocrine glands may produce too much of a hormone or not enough. This can lead to conditions such as diabetes. This disease can be caused by a lack of the hormone insulin.

CONTROLS

The thyroid, in the trachea, is one of the most important glands. It controls the production of energy in our body, and also controls the rate at which tissues grow.

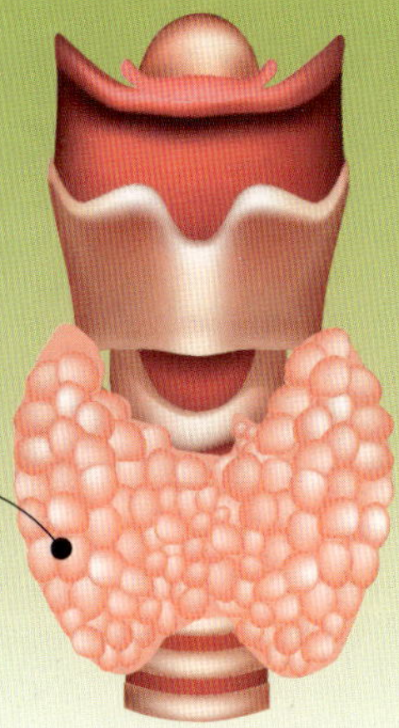

THYROID
The thyroid is a butterfly-shaped gland that is found in the front of the throat.

PANCREAS

The pancreas produces the hormones insulin and glucagon. These are involved in controlling the amount of sugar that is found in the blood.

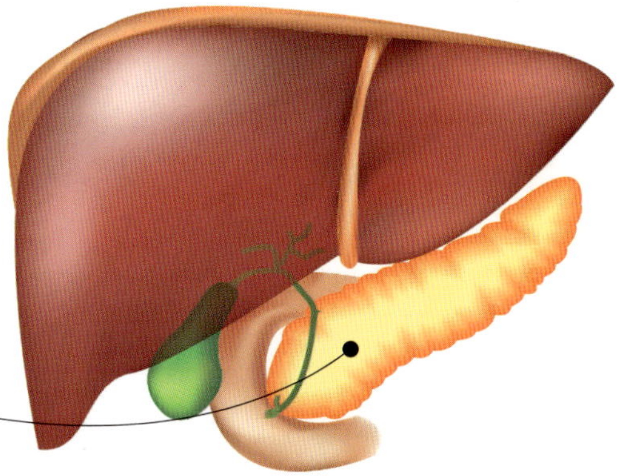

PANCREAS
The pancreas sits just beneath the liver and is connected to the intestines.

ADRENALINE

This is a hormone that is produced when we feel we are in danger. It prepares the body for action by increasing the amount of sugar in the blood, raising blood pressure and the heart rate, increasing breathing and dilating the pupils of the eyes.

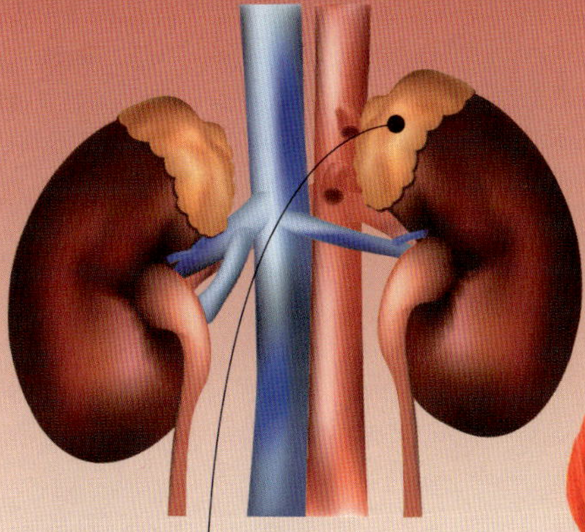

ADRENAL GLANDS
Adrenaline is produced by the adrenal glands, which sit above both of the kidneys.

Nervous system

There are two parts to the nervous system: the central nervous system and the peripheral nervous system. The central nervous system is made up of the brain and the spinal cord. The nerves in the rest of the body make up the peripheral nervous system.

NERVES

Nerves look like tiny ropes made up of a large number of strands. These strands are called nerve fibres. The nerve fibres send signals from one part of the body to another.

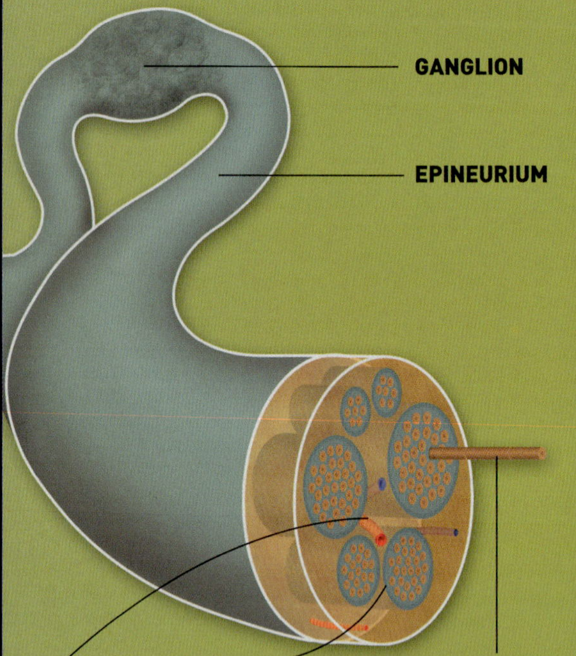

RAPID GROWTH

The brain triples in size during the first year of life.

REFLEXES

Reflexes are responses that you cannot control. Most reflexes are controlled by the spinal cord. The signal from the nerves is 'decoded' in the spinal cord and an instruction to react is sent out without the brain being involved.

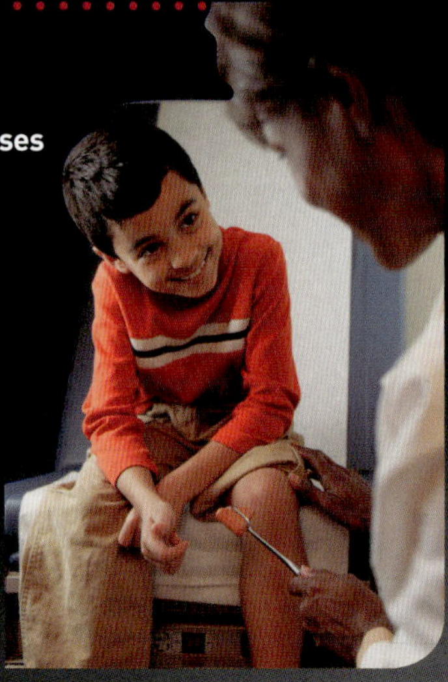

THE VALUE OF SLEEP

We spend a third of our lives sleeping. The brain uses this time to process information that has been gathered during the day.

100

The speed, in metres per second, at which signals can travel along the nervous system.

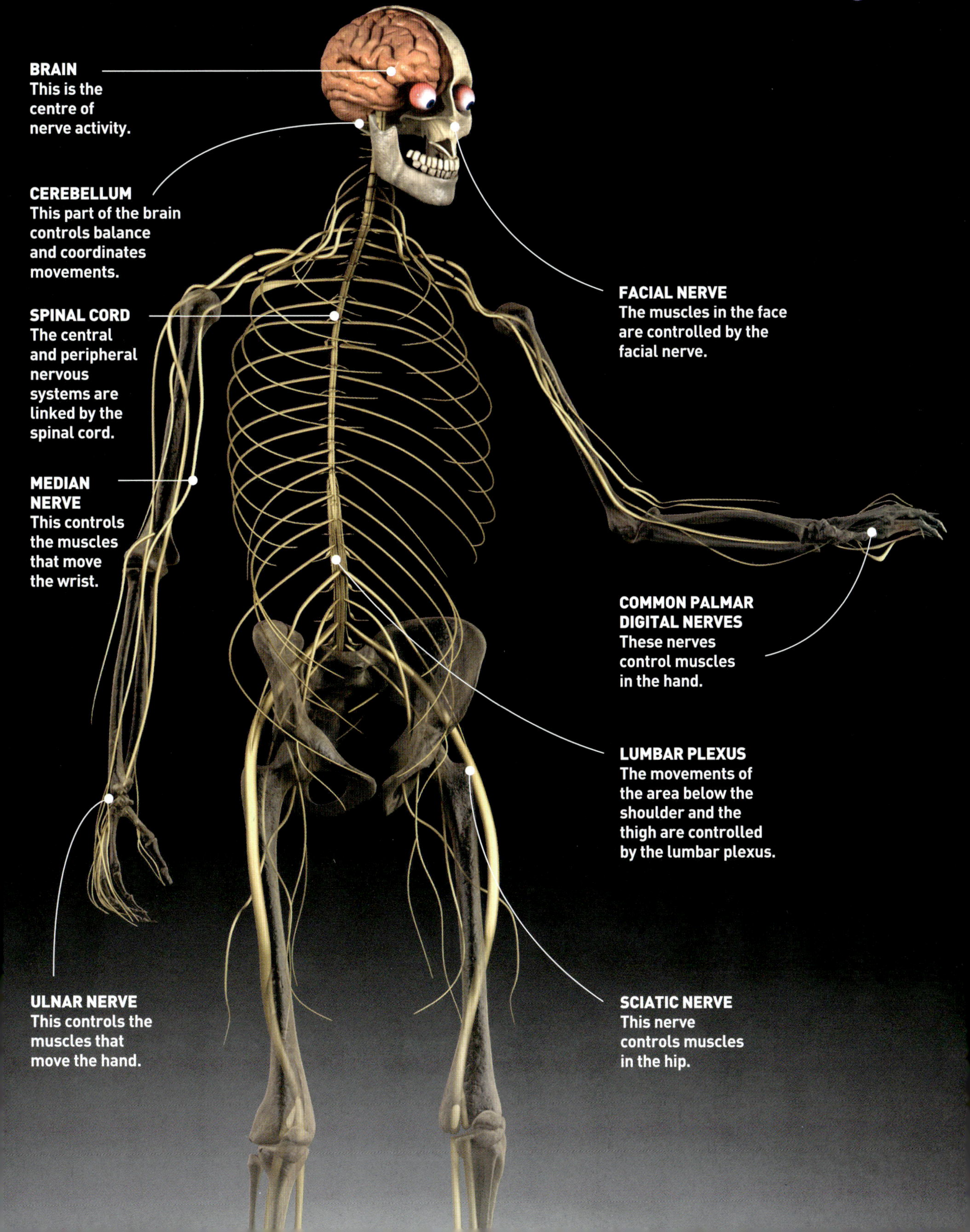
BRAIN
This is the centre of nerve activity.
CEREBELLUM
This part of the brain controls balance and coordinates movements.
SPINAL CORD
The central and peripheral nervous systems are linked by the spinal cord.
MEDIAN NERVE
This controls the muscles that move the wrist.
ULNAR NERVE
This controls the muscles that move the hand.
FACIAL NERVE
The muscles in the face are controlled by the facial nerve.
COMMON PALMAR DIGITAL NERVES
These nerves control muscles in the hand.
LUMBAR PLEXUS
The movements of the area below the shoulder and the thigh are controlled by the lumbar plexus.
SCIATIC NERVE
This nerve controls muscles in the hip.

The brain

The brain is the main organ in the nervous system. It controls every action of our bodies. It is split into two hemispheres, or halves, which are in turn divided into four parts, called lobes.

1.4 KG
The weight of an adult human's brain.

TEAMWORK

There are many different areas within the brain, which must all work together. Each hemisphere is responsible for different abilities and skills. In some people, for example, the language function, usually in the left hemisphere, is swapped to the right.

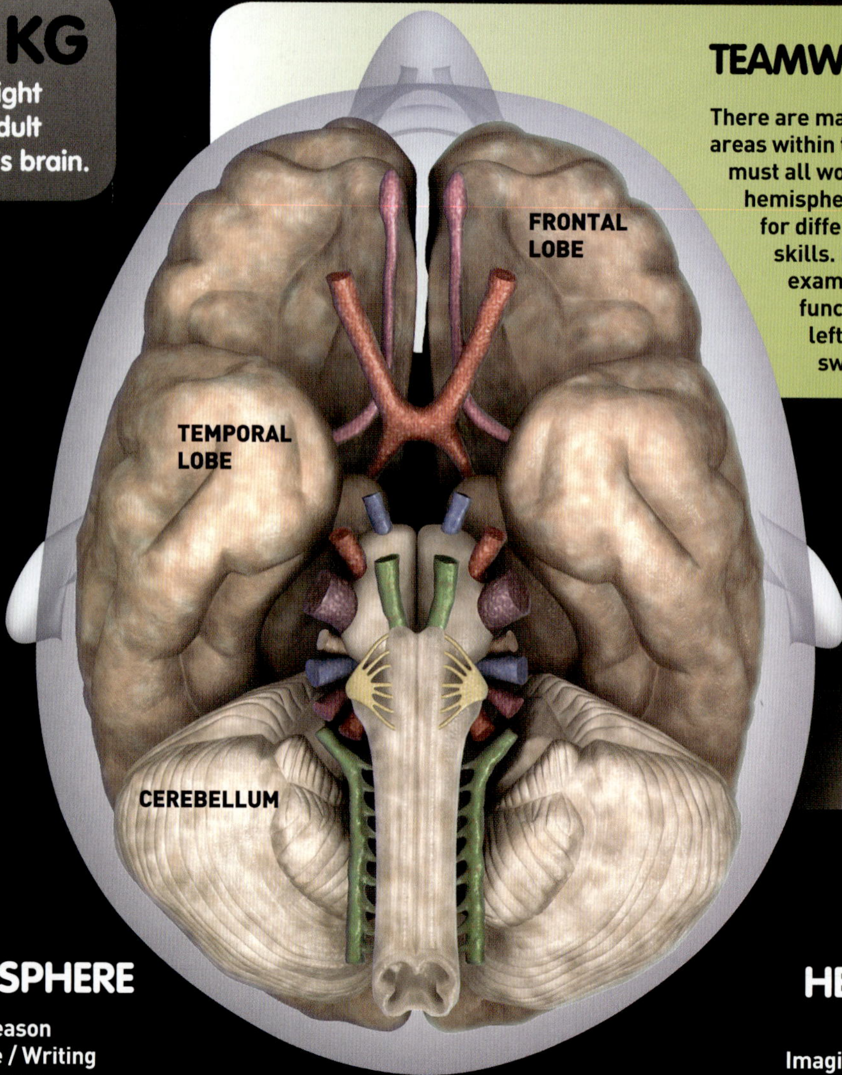

LEFT HEMISPHERE

Logic / Reason
Language / Writing
Body language
Numeracy
Planning

RIGHT HEMISPHERE

Intuition
Imagination and feelings
Thinking in wholes
Creativity
Spatial awareness
Visual imagery

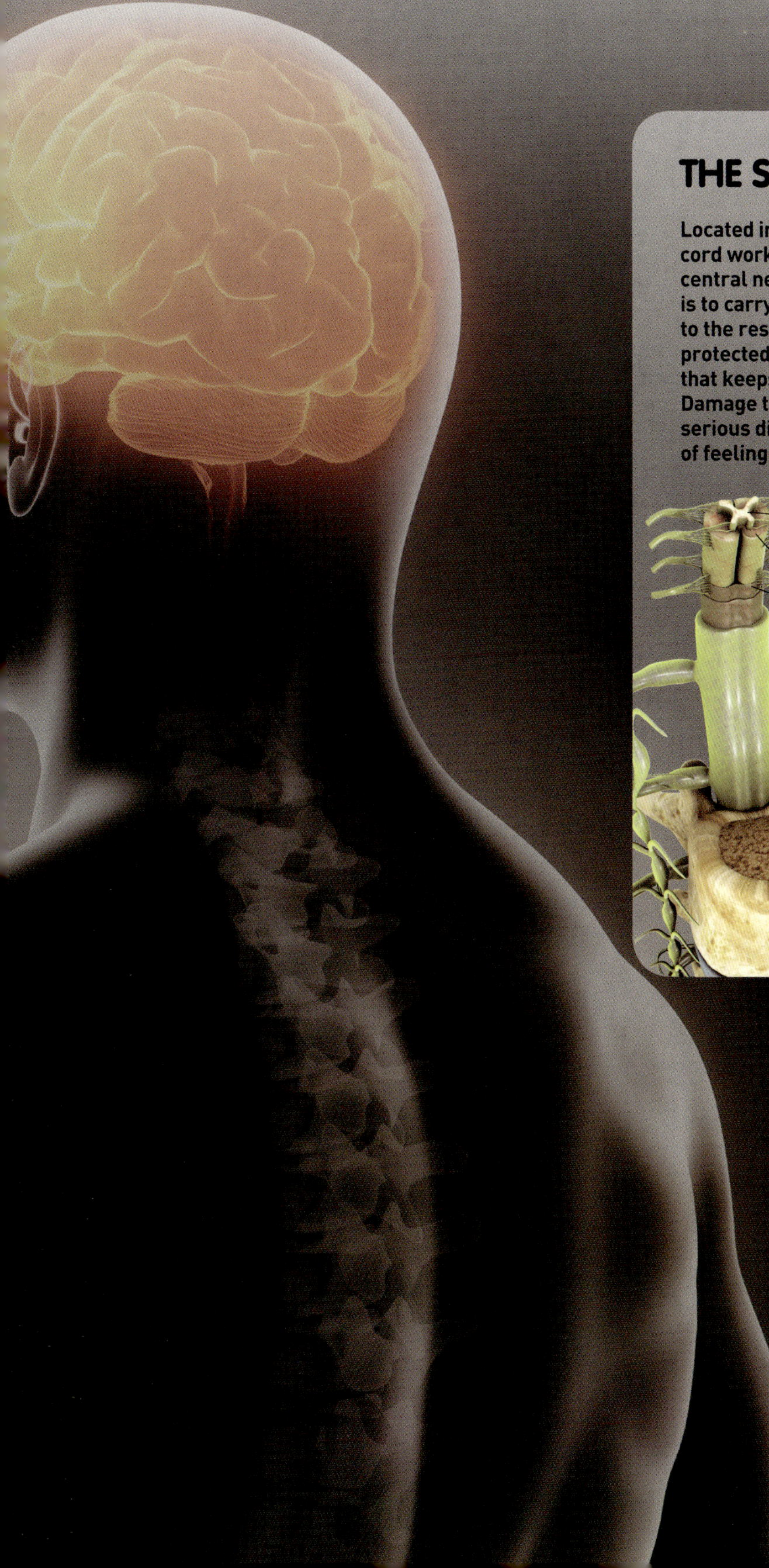

THE SPINAL CORD

Located inside the backbone, the spinal cord works with the brain to form the central nervous system. Its main job is to carry nerve signals from the brain to the rest of the body. The cord is protected by the meninges, a membrane that keeps out harmful substances. Damage to the spinal cord can lead to serious disabilities, including the loss of feeling in the torso and limbs.

OXYGEN

The human brain receives 20 per cent of the oxygen that is taken in by the lungs.

Vision

Our eyes allow us to know the colour, shape and feel of an object before we touch it. We also use our eyes to work out how far away an object is or how fast it is moving. The eye contains large numbers of cells that are sensitive to light.

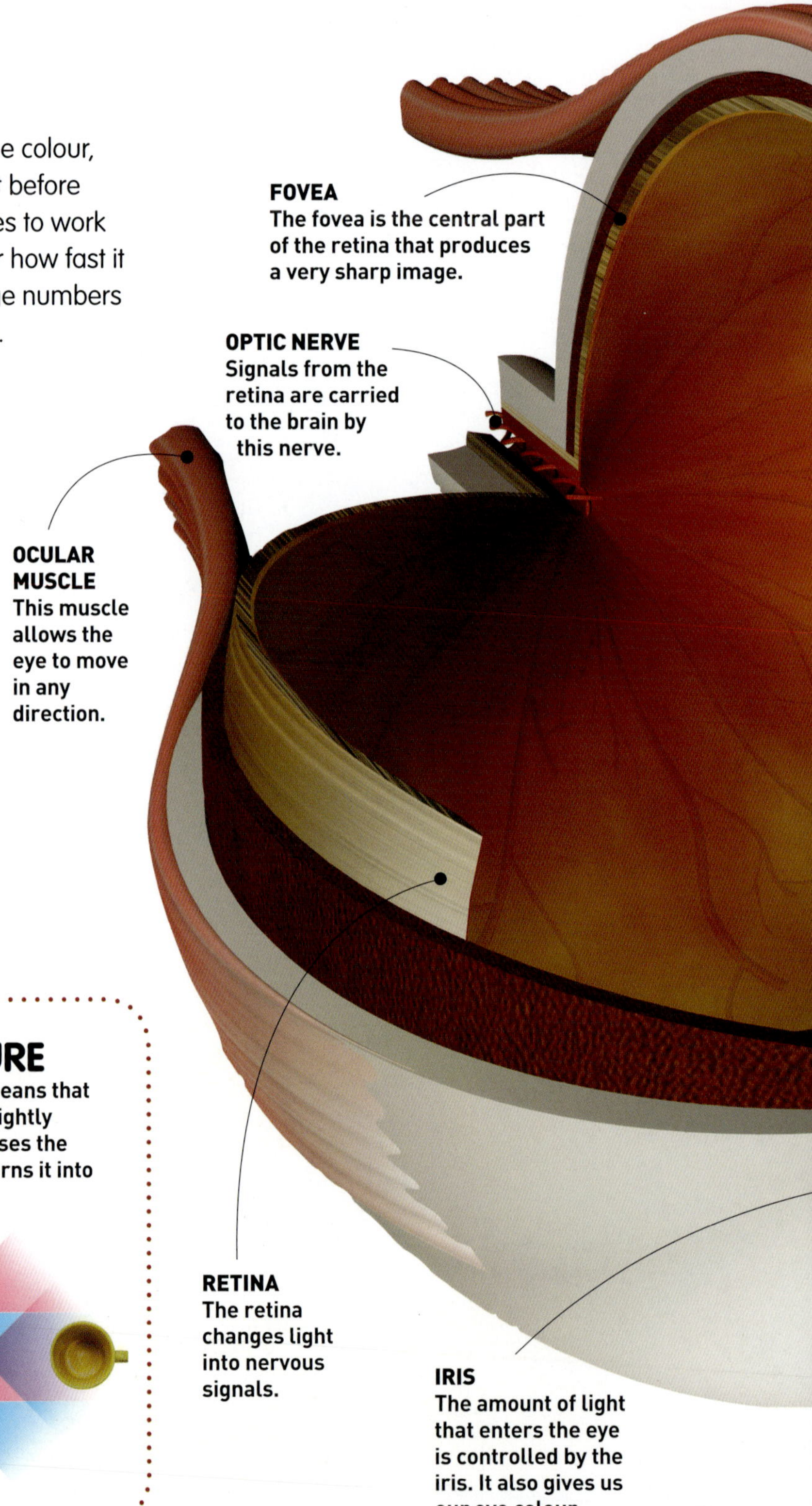

BLINKING

The muscles in our eyelids allow us to blink. We blink about 20,000 times per day.

SEEING ONE PICTURE

The distance between the eyes means that each eye sees an object from a slightly different angle. The brain processes the information from each eye and turns it into one picture.

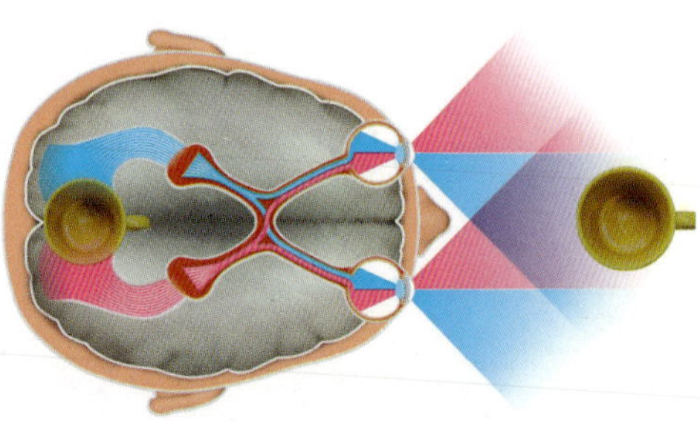

HOW WE SEE

When we look at an object, the light it gives off enters the eye through the cornea and the lens. These both focus the light before it reaches the retina. At the retina, the light produces an upside-down image of the object. The retina sends this information along the optic nerve to the brain. The brain turns the image the right way up.

130 MILLION

The number of cells in the retina.

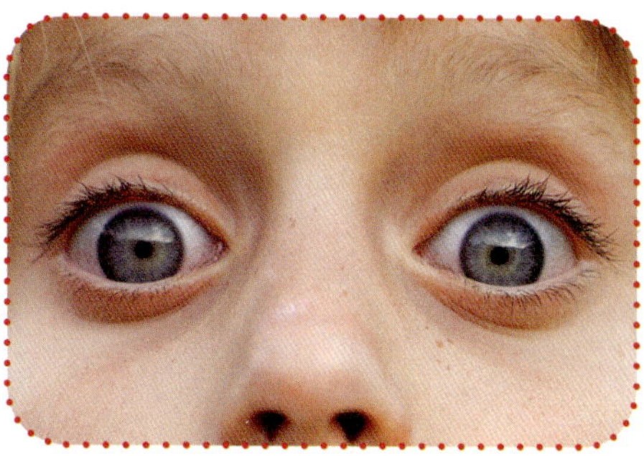

PROTECTION

The eyes are easily damaged, and need to be protected from dust and dirt in the air that might damage them. The first layer of protection is provided by the eyelids. The eyelids also clean the eye and keep it moist by spreading liquid produced by our tear ducts. The eyelashes help to protect the eyes against bright light, while the eyebrows keep sweat away from the eyes.

Hearing

Our ears allow us to hear a great variety of sounds. They can tell the difference between sounds, such as loudness, pitch and timbre, and also the direction from which the sound is coming. Our ears also help us to keep our balance.

2.6 MM

The size of the stapes, a bone inside the ear, which is the smallest bone in our bodies.

STAYING BALANCED

Inside our ears there are fluid-filled canals. When the fluids move, this tells us that the body is moving. The brain takes information from both the ears and the eyes, and uses it to stay balanced. When we are on a boat, the eyes do not sense movement, but the ears do. This confuses the brain and makes us feel seasick.

THE INNER EAR

The ear is divided into three different areas. The outer ear is the part of the ear you can see. It directs sound vibrations towards the rest of the ear; it also protects the ear. The middle ear carries the vibrations to the inner ear. The inner ear translates the vibrations into nerve signals that are sent to the brain. The brain turns this information into sounds.

VOLUME, TIMBRE AND PITCH

Our ears can recognize three different things in the sounds we hear: its volume (how loud or soft it is); its timbre (the quality) and its pitch (how high or low it sounds).

GROWTH

The external ear is made of skin and cartilage. It continues to grow throughout life.

Smell and taste

Our senses of taste and smell work together, and in a similar way. We taste the flavour of food dissolved in our saliva (spit) using our tongues. With our noses, we can sense a wide range of smells that are carried in the air.

THE TONGUE

The tongue is covered in more than 10,000 taste buds. When the taste buds make contact with food, taste receptor cells pass signals to the brain.

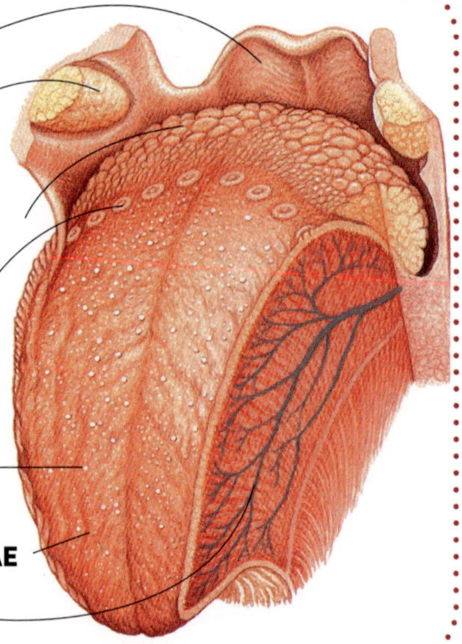

FIVE TASTES

Human beings can recognize five different tastes: sweet, sour, bitter, salty and umami. Umami is the taste found in a substance called glutamate, which is found in meat and cheeses.

HOW WE SMELL

The smell receptors are found in the nose. When we breathe in, smell molecules dissolve in the mucus that covers the receptors. Tiny hairs called cilia pass signals to the brain, which decides what the smell is.

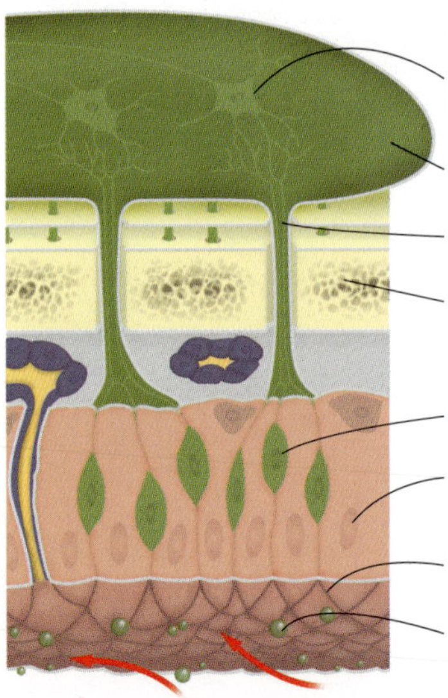

SMELL CELL

A dog's nose contains 200 million or more olfactory nerve cells. Human noses contain only about 5 million.

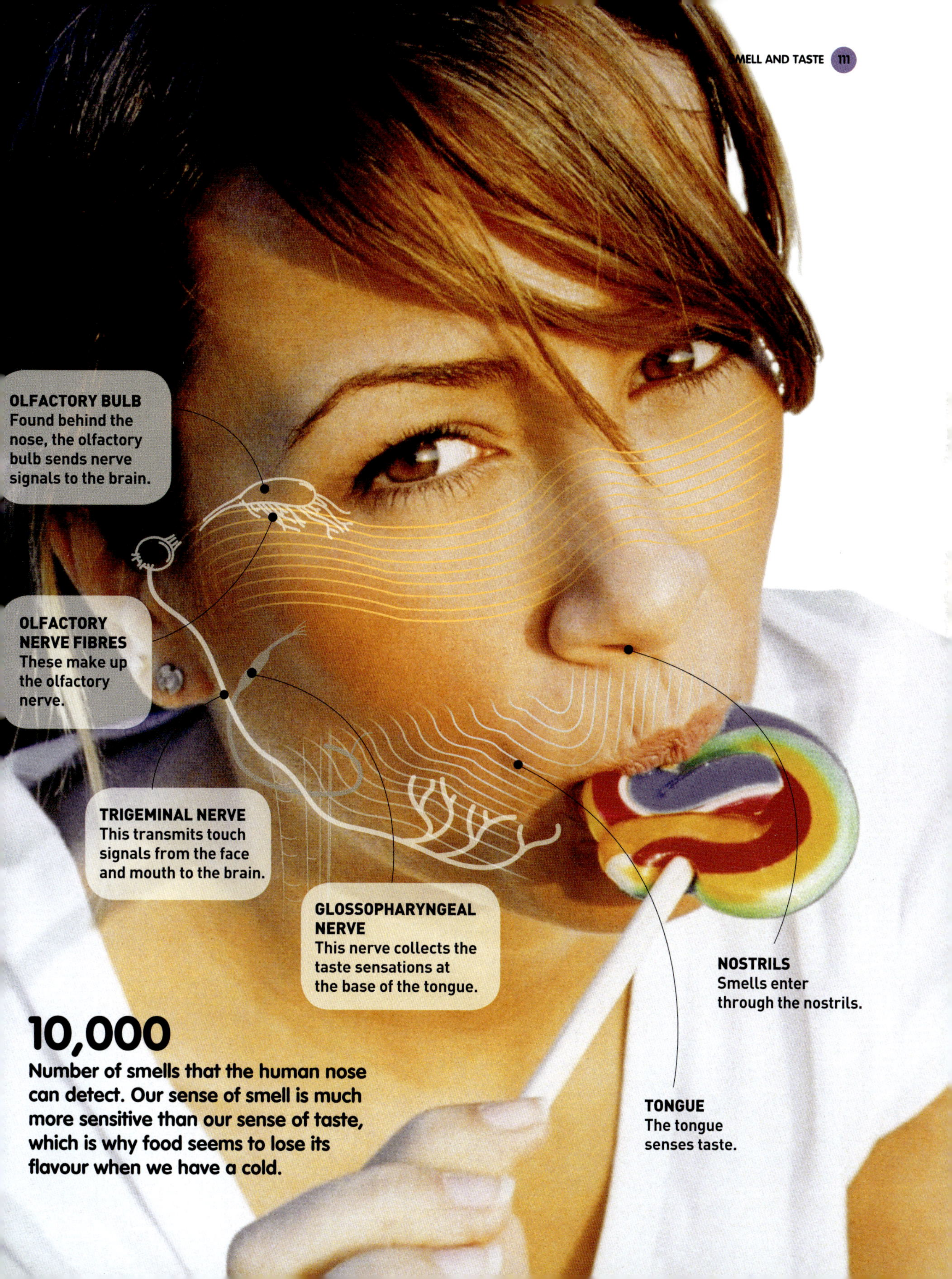

10,000

Number of smells that the human nose can detect. Our sense of smell is much more sensitive than our sense of taste, which is why food seems to lose its flavour when we have a cold.

Lymphatic system

The lymphatic system is the most important part of the immune system, which protects the body from disease and illness. It returns excess body fluid, called lymph, to the bloodstream. The system is made up of a network of lymphatic vessels, which connect the spleen, thymus, lymph glands, tonsils, adenoids and tissues (bone marrow and Peyer's patches).

ALLERGY

An allergic reaction happens when the immune system reacts to substances that the body normally tolerates.

40,000

The number of tiny particles that fly out of our noses and mouths when we sneeze.

LYMPH GLANDS

The lymph glands attack diseases using two different types of white blood cell: lymphocytes and macrophages. These blood cells are made in the bone marrow.

FILTERS

Lymph glands are grouped all around the lymphatic system. They kill harmful bacteria and viruses.

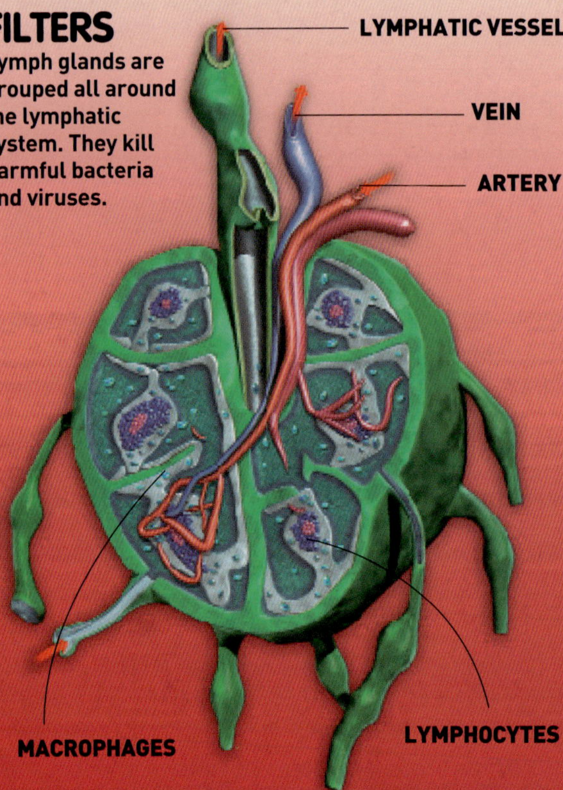

LYMPHOCYTES

Lymphocytes are the smallest kind of white blood cell. They keep the body healthy by killing cells that have become infected with viruses.

OTHER DEFENCES

Other liquids, such as tears, also protect the body and get rid of germs, but they are not part of the lymphatic system.

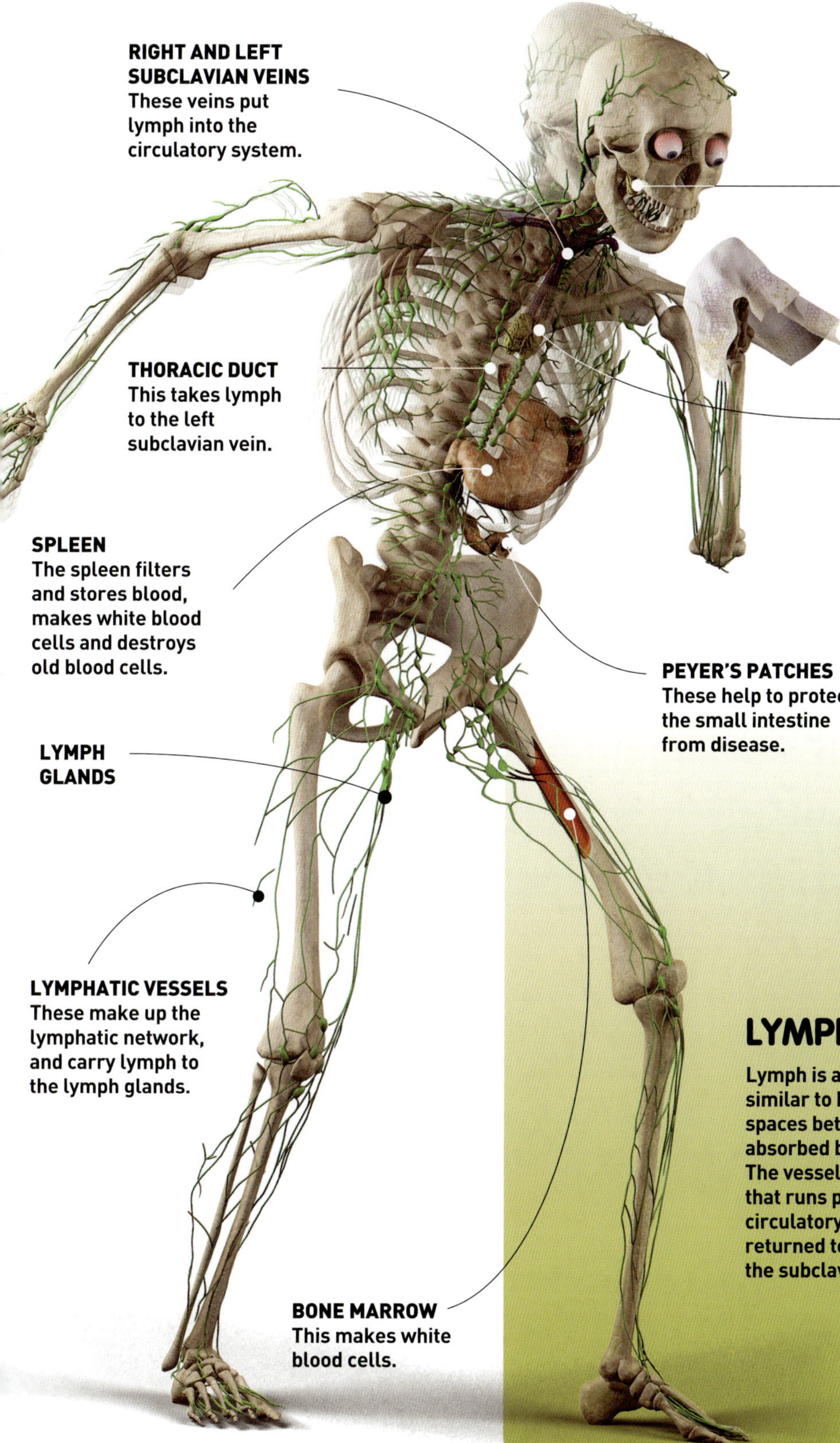

LYMPH

Lymph is a clear liquid that is similar to blood. It forms in the spaces between cells, and is absorbed by lymphatic vessels. The vessels form a network that runs parallel to the circulatory system. Lymph is returned to the blood through the subclavian veins.

HISTORY

About 11,000 years ago, people began to settle in one place and farm the land. Soon afterwards, writing was invented and things could be written down for future generations to read. This marked the beginning of the period of recorded history. The written record tells the story of how we developed from those early days of agriculture to the modern technological world of today.

PERSIAN SOLDIER
This image of a soldier is found in the ruins of Persepolis, Iran, which was the capital city of the ancient Persian Empire (see pages 132–133).

The start of agriculture

People began to farm in the Middle East about 11,000 years ago, and in China about 8,000 years ago. These farmers planted crops and kept animals. They also started to make clay pots for cooking and storing food. These changes were made possible by the easier climate that came with the end of the last Ice Age.

DOGS

The first animal to be kept and tamed by humans was the dog.

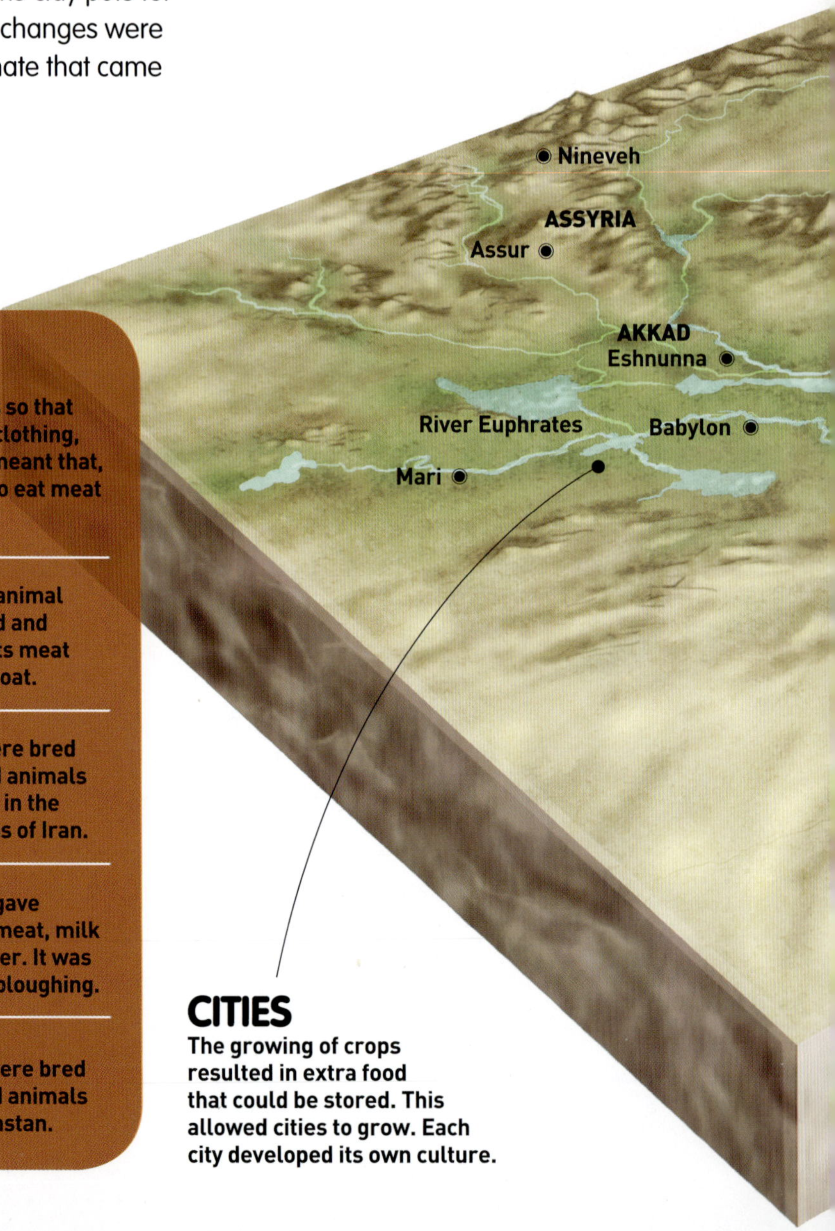

KEEPING ANIMALS

Farmers started to breed animals so that they could use them for food and clothing, and to help with farm work. This meant that, for the first time, it was possible to eat meat without having to hunt.

GOAT The first animal to be bred and kept for its meat was the goat.

SHEEP Sheep were bred from wild animals that lived in the mountains of Iran.

COW The cow gave farmers meat, milk and leather. It was used for ploughing.

HORSE Horses were bred from wild animals in Kazakhstan.

CITIES

The growing of crops resulted in extra food that could be stored. This allowed cities to grow. Each city developed its own culture.

GROWING RICE

About 8,000 years ago, people started to grow rice in flooded fields called paddy fields. They used special axes with holes in the blade to cut the crops.

THE FERTILE CRESCENT

Agriculture first appeared in this area in the south of the Anatolia Peninsula, near the rivers Tigris and Euphrates. For the first time, people no longer hunted, but grew their own food instead. The name Fertile Crescent comes from the shape of the area in which the good farm land was found, which is like the shape of a quarter-moon.

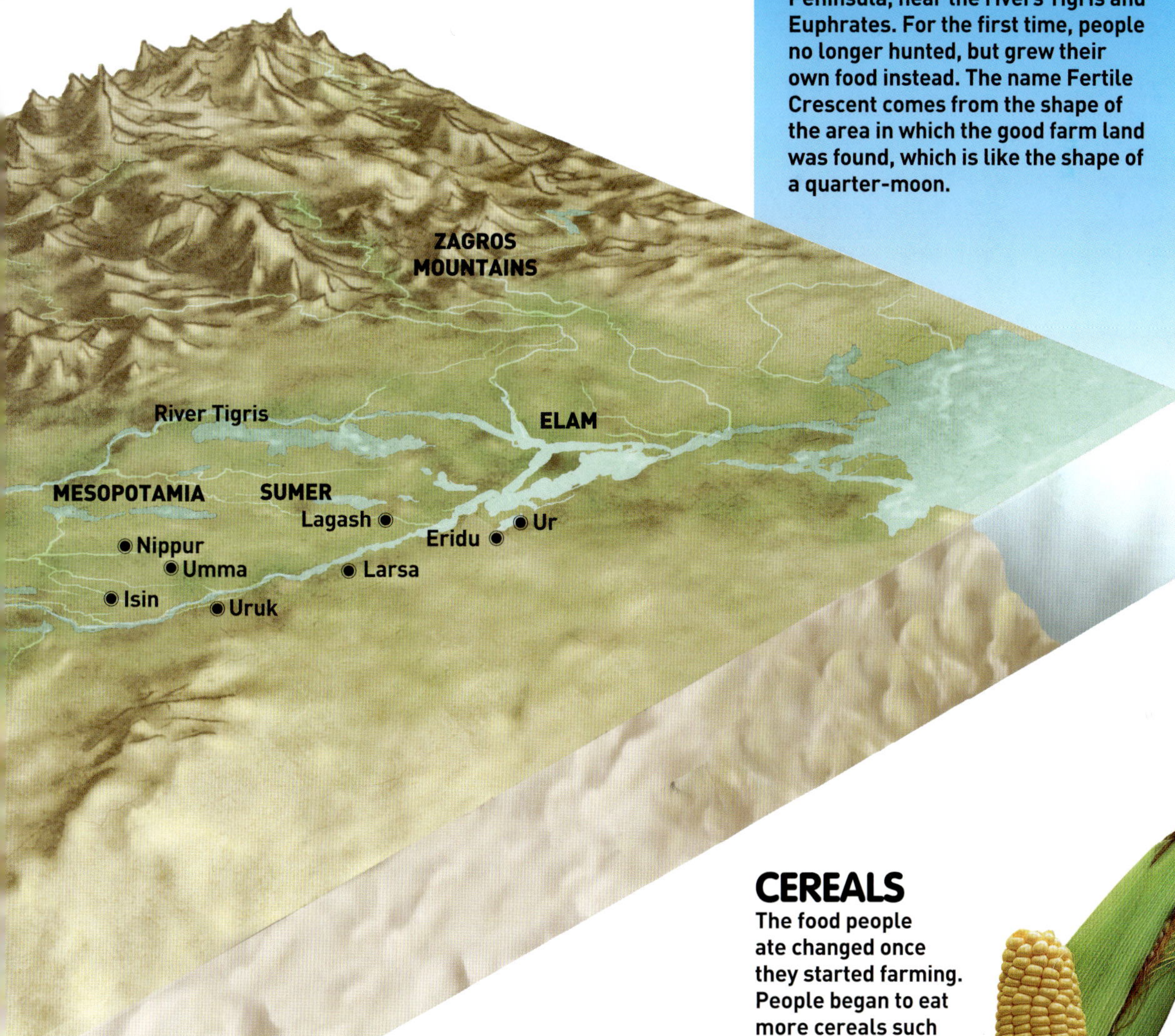

CEREALS

The food people ate changed once they started farming. People began to eat more cereals such as wheat, corn and barley.

11,000

YEARS OLD

The age of sickles (farming tools) that were found in the Nile Valley in Egypt.

The invention of writing

Writing began in Sumer, Mesopotamia, as a means of keeping track of the food stores that farming had made possible. Writing developed as systems of pictograms (symbols that stand for objects). Eventually, the pictograms developed into the phonetic writing that most of us use today. In phonetic writing, the symbols represent the sounds that make up the words. Writing is one of the most important developments in history: it allows us to express ideas and record history.

4000 BC

The first evidence of writing dates from this time.

CUNEIFORM

Sumerian writing is called cuneiform. It is a series of wedge-shaped marks made on clay tablets.

HYMN TO NIDABA

Sumerian scribes wrote down stories about kings and gods. They also recorded the hymns that priests said at religious ceremonies. The Hymn to Nidaba tells how the city of Ur was destroyed by the god Enlil. Nidaba was the Sumerian goddess of writing.

SUMERIAN TABLET

Found in the ruins of Uruk, a city on the banks of the River Euphrates, this tablet contains marks for numbers – the circles – and also simple pictograms. On it, researchers have identified the name of Uruk and that of Dilmun, a small kingdom on the outskirts of the Assyrian Empire.

PHONOGRAMS
Over time, the Sumerians began to use phonograms to represent sounds.

PICTOGRAMS
A pictogram is a picture that stands for an object. For example, the symbol for 'woman' is an upside-down triangle.

WRITING ABOUT MORE
With phonograms, symbols came to represent the sounds that make up the words. This allowed people to write about more things.

WEIGHTS AND MEASURES

To keep trading fair, a system of weights and measures was used. Gold and silver were swapped for goods, as monetary systems appeared in Egypt and Anatolia.

THE EVOLUTION OF WRITING

Over time, the symbols in cuneiform developed from a realistic depiction of the objects they represented into more abstract shapes, similar to the ideograms (symbols) of Chinese writing.

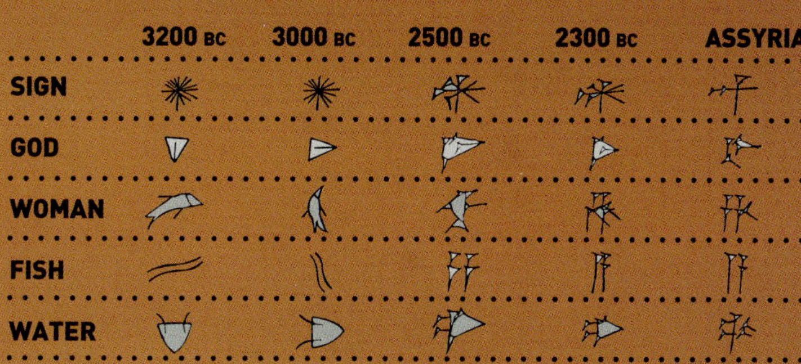

Babylon

Of all the cities in Mesopotamia, Babylon came to be the most powerful. Babylon was founded around 2300 BC. The city is situated in modern-day Iraq. The Babylonians believed that the city belonged to the god Marduk, who appointed the king to rule in his name. The Babylonians were among the first people to use precious metals, such as gold and silver, as a form of money. They also developed new types of medicine.

FOUNDER

Babylon was founded in 2500 BC by Nimrod, a king who was believed to have built the Tower of Babel.

70 METRES

The height of the Babylonian temples, which were known as ziggurats.

THE LION OF BABYLON

This sculpture was in fact made by the Hittites, people who lived in Anatolia between the 18th and 12th centuries BC. The Lion of Babylon is now in the ruins of the palace of Nebuchadnezzar in Iraq. It is thought to have been brought there as treasure won in a war.

GODDESS OF LOVE

Ishtar was the Babylonian goddess of love, war, sex and fertility. In Sumer, she was known as Inanna.

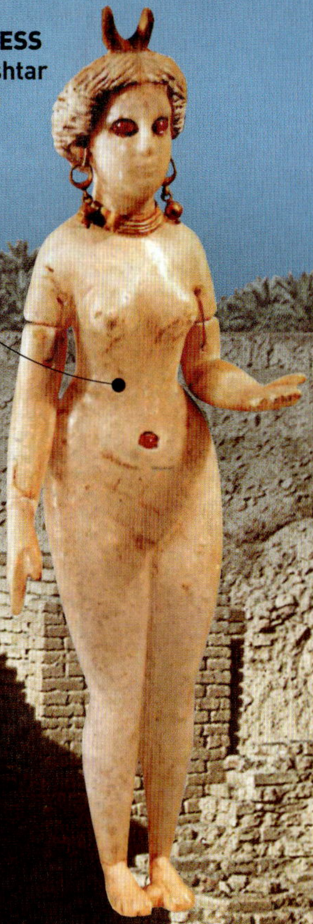

PLANET GODDESS
The goddess Ishtar was thought to represent the planet Venus.

GOD OF WRITING

The Babylonians worshipped Nabu, the god of wisdom and writing. He was shown holding a tablet and writing tools. People believed that he used these to write down the destiny of each person.

The Code of Hammurabi

The Code of Hammurabi was written in around 1775 BC. It is one of the first sets of laws recorded in history, and lists the decisions made by the Babylonian king Hammurabi. Before the Code of Hammurabi, priests had made sure people obeyed the law. The Code provided a list of rules that legal decisions had to follow. In total, the Code contains 282 laws.

STONE STELE

The Code is carved into a basalt column that is 2.25 metres tall.

ONE LAW FOR ALL

Hammurabi carefully spread his Code to the entire kingdom so that every person he ruled was following the same laws.

SYMBOLS

The circle was a symbol used to represent power.

MONOLITH

This monolith gives the details of the people condemned to death by Assyria's King Sargon II. He reigned in the years after Hammurabi, and was the declared enemy of Egypt, Urartu and Elam.

PAY BACK

The idea of paying someone back 'eye for an eye, tooth for a tooth', which appears in the Old Testament, also appears in the Code.

WOMEN IN THE CODE

Babylonian society was ruled by men. Women are hardly ever mentioned in the Code, except to do with adultery or incest. Both of these crimes were thought to be punishable by death.

SCRIPT
On most of the column, the laws are written in a type of cuneiform.

DIVINE LAWS
The king of Babylonia is shown receiving the Code from the god Shamash. Mesopotamians believed that laws were given to them by the gods.

1901

The year the Code was discovered in Iran by Frenchman Jacques de Morgan.

THEMES
The Code gives the punishments for stealing, murder and damage to property. It explains how people should treat their slaves and how they should behave when married.

FOR ALL TO SEE
The Code was displayed in public so that nobody could say they did not know it. However, not many people could read. Those who could, read it out loud to everyone else.

ADVENTURES

The column stood in the temple of the god Shamash in Sippar. When the Elamites invaded Babylonia, they took it to the city of Susa, where it was discovered in 1901. Today, it can be seen in the Louvre Museum in Paris.

Ancient Egypt

For 3,000 years, a civilization flourished on the banks of the River Nile in northern Africa. It was a great kingdom ruled by kings called Pharaohs. The Egyptians made huge monuments, such as the pyramids at Giza, which were tombs built to house the pharaohs' bodies. They invented a form of writing known as hieroglyphs, which was a system of ideograms. Many of the monuments are covered in hieroglyphs.

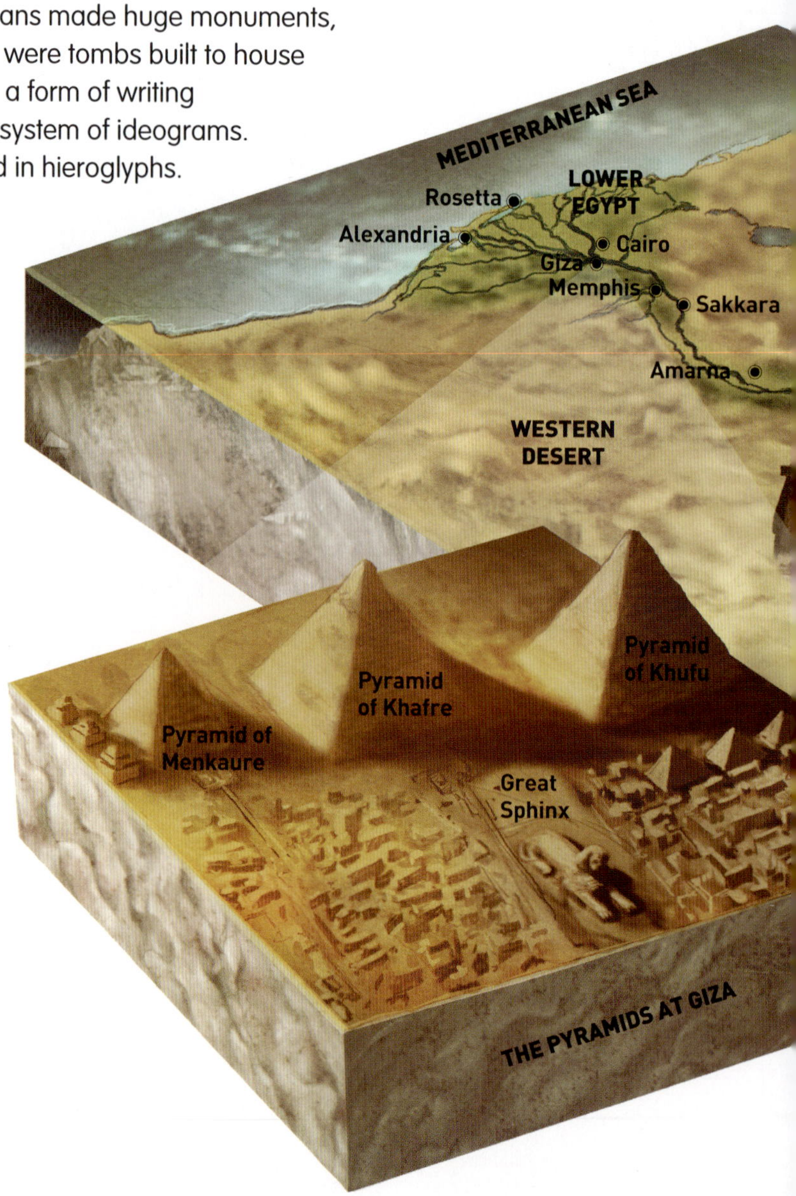

PAPYRUS

This tall plant grows in the Nile Delta. The Egyptians pressed papyrus stems to make a type of paper.

SACRED FLOOD

Every year, the River Nile flooded. When the floodwater went down, it left behind a layer of mud, called silt. The silt was very good for growing crops, and the Egyptians saw the floods as a gift from the gods.

THE GREAT SPHINX
This monument is at Giza. It has the body of a lion. Its head is believed to be that of Khafre, a pharaoh.

4,000
The age in years of the pyramids at Giza.

RED SEA SAILORS

Called the 'sea of rushes' in the Old Testament, the Red Sea was sailed by the Egyptians in small boats with one mast and a rectangular sail.

HISTORICAL PERIODS

Ancient Egyptian civilization can be split into three main periods, ruled over by 30 different dynasties (royal families). The pyramids were built in the Old Kingdom.

3200–2300 BC: Old Kingdom

2100–1788 BC: Middle Kingdom

1580–1090 BC: New Kingdom

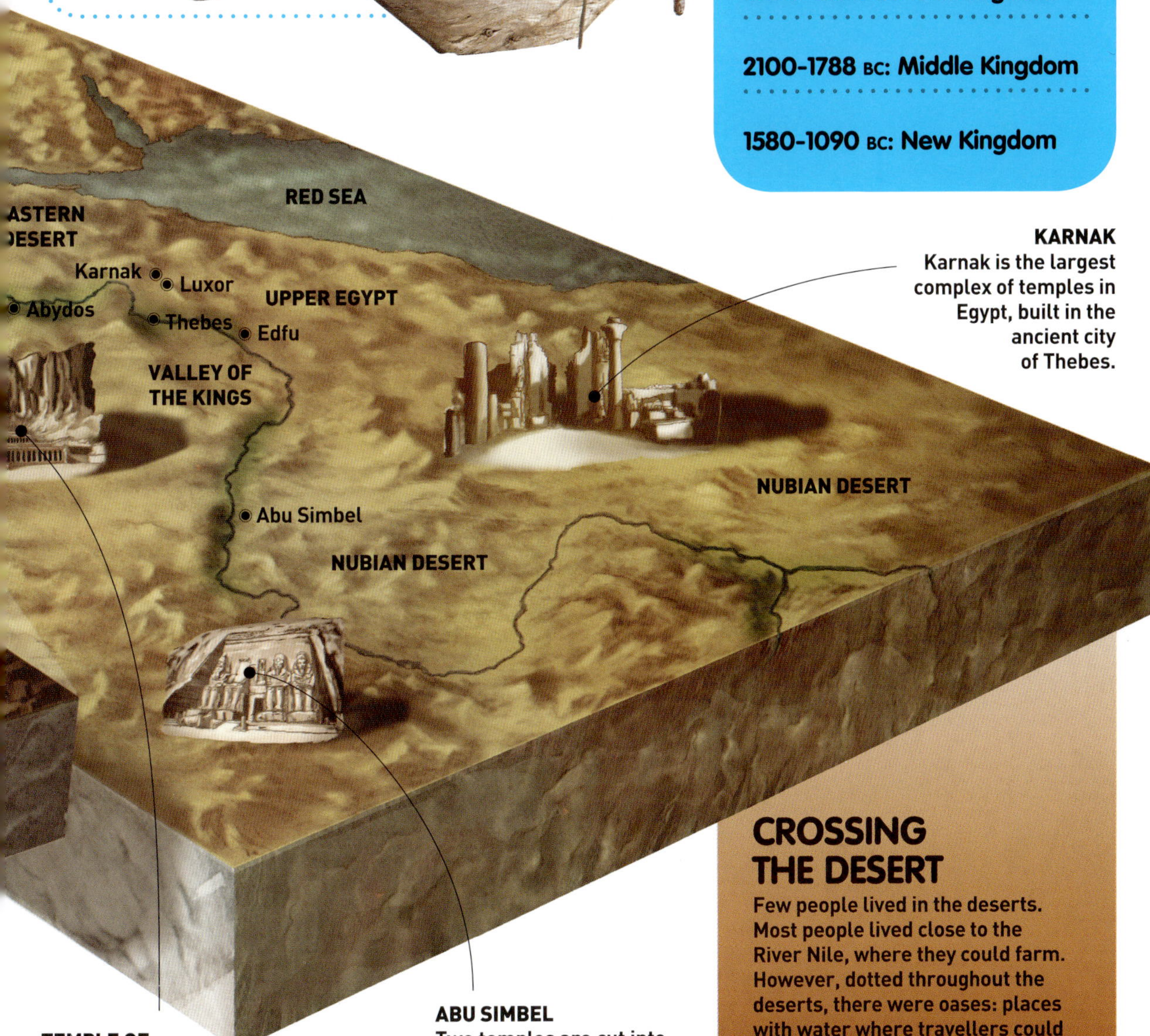

KARNAK
Karnak is the largest complex of temples in Egypt, built in the ancient city of Thebes.

TEMPLE OF HATSHEPSUT
Hatshepsut was the first female pharaoh. She dressed as a man in order to rule.

ABU SIMBEL
Two temples are cut into the rock at Abu Simbel: one dedicated to Pharaoh Ramesses II, the other to the gods Ra, Ptah and Amun.

CROSSING THE DESERT

Few people lived in the deserts. Most people lived close to the River Nile, where they could farm. However, dotted throughout the deserts, there were oases: places with water where travellers could rest. Men would cross the desert using groups of camels to trade with the people who lived beyond the dry sands.

The Indus Civilization

Like the ancient civilizations of Mesopotamia and Egypt, civilization in India developed along the banks of a river: the Indus. The river flows from the highlands down to the Arabian Sea, crossing the 3,000-kilometre-long Indian plains. The Indus Valley has large stretches of fertile land, which allowed people to settle and farm the area.

AGRICULTURE

The main crops grown in the Indus Valley were wheat, barley, root vegetables and dates.

1922

The year British archaeologists discovered one of the civilization's main cities: Mohenjo Daro.

TERRACOTTA FIGURES

In 1946, British archaeologist Sir Mortimer Wheeler discovered many small terracotta statuettes in Harappa. The statues were of women. They were thought to be goddesses of fertility. Some of them were encrusted with precious metals. As there were so many of these statues, they were probably made to be traded.

THE INDUS WRITING SYSTEM

The Indus Civilization had its own writing system, made up of at least 20 characters and more than 200 symbols. They used writing in business and also probably in places of worship. They spoke a language related to Tamil, which is still spoken in southern India.

The meaning of the symbols in the Indus writing system is not known.

PRIEST-KING

No temple buildings have been identified in the ruins of the Indus Valley. Small statues of goddesses have been found and the cities may have practised a form of religion in which the king was both a military and a spiritual leader. This sculpture is thought to be of one of these 'priest-kings'.

The birth of China

The very first Chinese dynasty recorded in history was the Shang, which ruled for seven centuries. It was followed by the Zhou Dynasty, which ruled from 1027 BC to 221 BC. In this period, a single Chinese culture developed. The great thinker Confucius lived during the Zhou Dynasty.

CONFUCIUS

The philosopher Confucius, who lived from 551–479 BC, is one of the most important people in Chinese history. He developed a moral code that is still followed by many people today.

JADE

From the end of the Neolithic Age (New Stone Age), objects made of jade were very important in Chinese culture. Jade objects were thought of as lucky charms. Jade was also used to make tools and weapons.

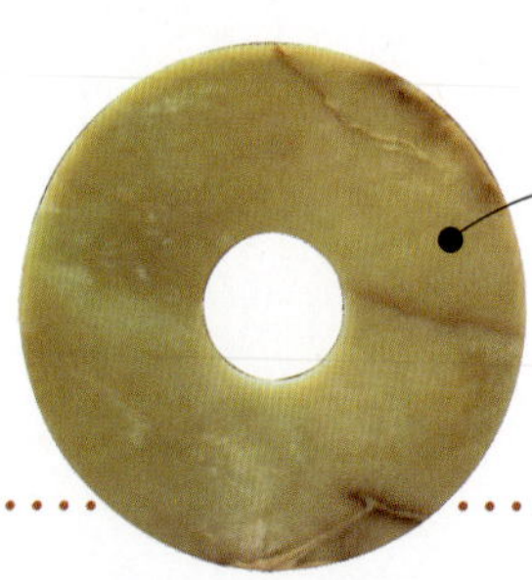

CIRCULAR PIECE
This piece of jade dates from the late Neolithic Age.

OXEN
This jade figure was made in the Zhou Period. The oxen is one of the 12 animals in the Chinese Zodiac.

BRONZE

The Zhou Period marked the height of the Chinese Bronze Age, which had started during the Shang Period. The bronze foundries were kept very busy making enough metal to be worked into statues or tools.

RITUAL VESSEL

During the Shang and Zhou dynasties, cups and vases that were used in rituals were decorated in a special way. Often, the pieces were covered with fierce animals that were thought of as guardians or protectors, such as the tiger on this vessel.

39

The number of emperors who ruled during the Zhou Period.

BRONZE BELLS

Bells were made from bronze. They were carved using knives and decorated with religious symbols.

The Aztecs

A group of people known as the Aztecs lived in the area that is now central Mexico between the 13th and 16th centuries. The Aztecs built a huge, highly organized empire. Their capital city was at Tenochtitlan, on the site of present-day Mexico City. The remains of this city show that it had magnificent buildings. They built tall temples to allow their priests to come closer to the gods that were thought to live in the sky.

TEMPLO MAYOR
This was the main temple. The steps led to two smaller temples where blood sacrifices were made to the gods Tlaloc and Huitzilopochtli.

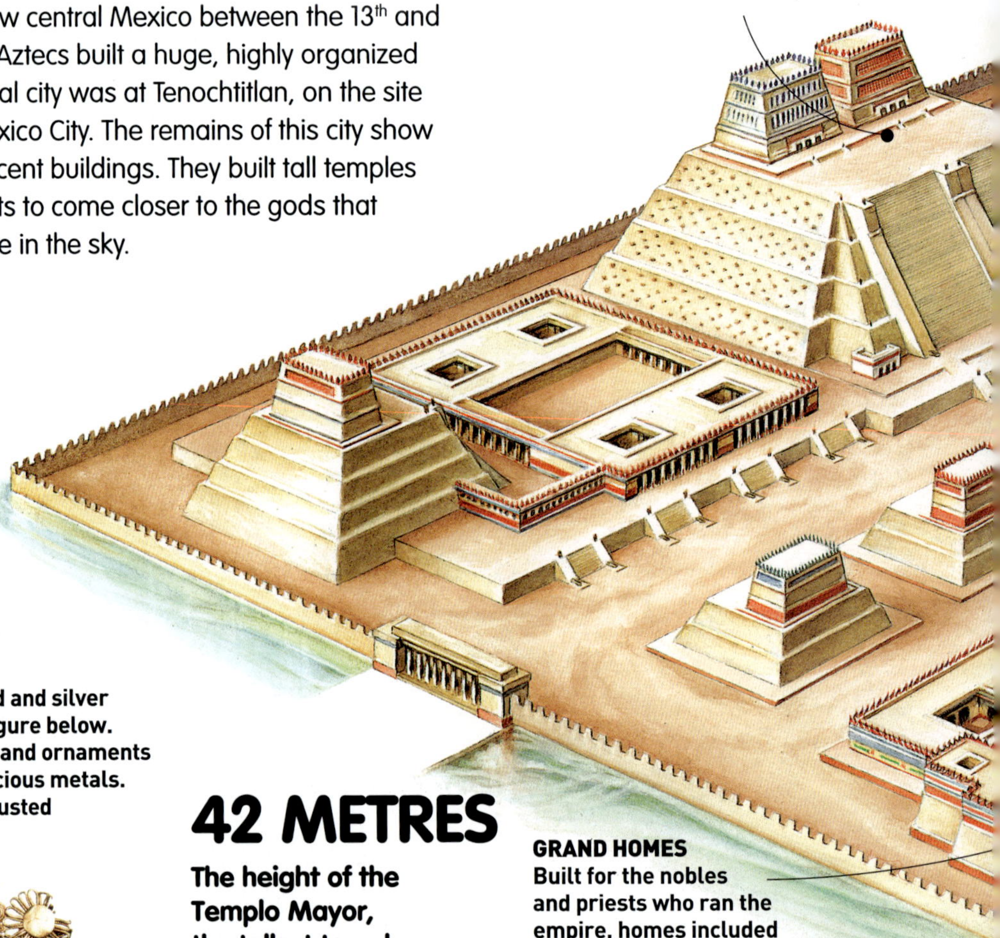

WORKING IN METAL

The Aztecs made gold and silver objects such as the figure below. Necklaces, pendants and ornaments were made from precious metals. Often they were encrusted with stones.

42 METRES

The height of the Templo Mayor, the tallest temple in the city.

GRAND HOMES
Built for the nobles and priests who ran the empire, homes included classrooms where astronomy and religion were taught.

JEWELLERY

The Aztecs wore finely made gold jewellery. Ornate jewellery showed that its owner was important.

TZOMPANTLI
This building for storing bones was filled with spears. The skulls of enemy soldiers killed in battles were put on the spears.

TEMPLE OF THE SUN
The solar calendar, which was important to Aztec religion, was kept here.

TENOCHTITLAN

The city was divided into four sections, symbolizing the four directions of the world. It was founded on an island in the middle of Lake Texcoco in the Valley of Mexico. The Aztecs hunted the birds that lived on the lake, fished, and developed chinampas – gardens on artificial islands. At its peak, Tenochtitlan had more than 200,000 inhabitants, making it one of the largest cities in the world at the time.

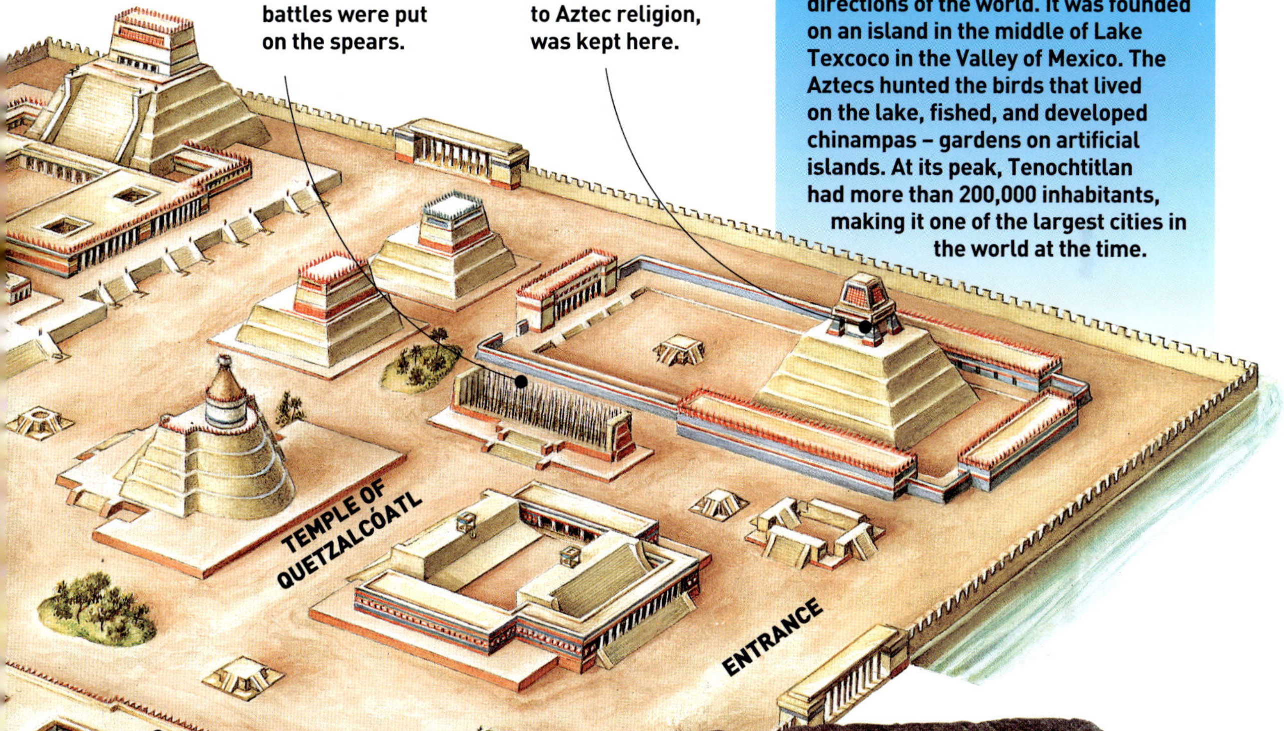

THE GOD TLALOC

In Aztec mythology, Tlaloc was the god of rain. He ruled the thunder and lightning, and made the water in mountain springs flow. He was represented as a man with large round eyes. Snakes were sometimes shown coming out of his mouth.

The Persian Empire

Around 2,600 years ago, the Persians, a people from South-West Asia, built an enormous empire. It stretched from the Mediterranean Sea in the west to the border with India in the east. The Persian Empire was different from the empires that had come before: it allowed the people it conquered to practise their own customs and religions. However, there were often rebellions, and wars with the Greeks eventually destroyed the Empire.

PAYING TRIBUTE

The chiefs of the lands the Persians conquered sent people to pay tribute to the Persian king.

PRESENTS
The people brought presents for the king, including food, drink, jewellery and animals.

CLOTHING
The different styles of clothing that appear in Persian art show the different cultures within the Empire.

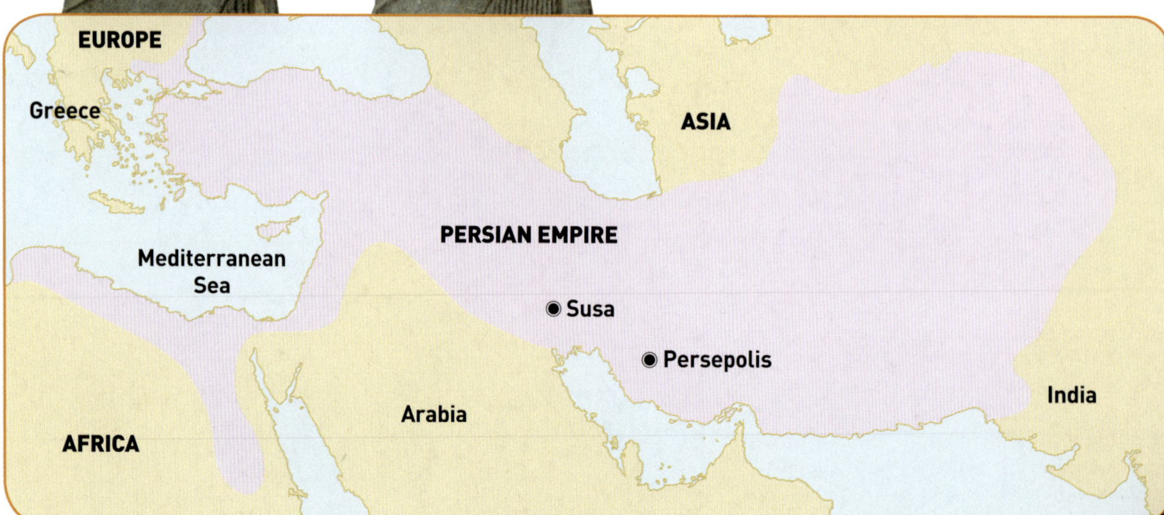

CYRUS THE GREAT

King Cyrus II, later named 'the Great', was the first to expand Persia. He rebelled against the Medes, who had ruled the Persians, then extended his Empire with several conquests.

THE BATTLES OF CYRUS THE GREAT

After overthrowing the Medes, Cyrus looked to expand his empire. He defeated Babylon and the Greek cities in Asia Minor (Turkey). He also joined forces with the Phoenicians, who allowed him to use their ships in the Mediterranean Sea. He was finally killed in a battle with the Massagetae, a tribe to the northeast of Persia.

3 MILLION SQ KM

The size of the Persian Empire when it was at the height of its power.

SPIES

The king sent spies all over the Empire to keep an eye on its people and to look for signs of rebellion.

Greek city-states

When the Mycenaean civilization in Greece disappeared in about 1100 BC, it left behind a series of small towns. In time, these towns developed into wealthy cities. Each city-state was run like a small country. Although great rivals, the different cities all shared the same language and the same religion. Athens and Sparta were the most powerful city-states, and they fought many wars against each other. Athens was known as a centre of learning and culture, and Sparta for its fearless warriors.

SOME CITY-STATES

MEGARA
This rich city competed with its neighbour Athens. Megara founded several colonies around the Black Sea.

ARGOS
This city-state fought a long struggle with Sparta for control of the southern Peloponnese Peninsula.

COLONIES

Each city-state founded smaller towns along the Mediterranean coast. They used these for trade.

OLYMPIC GAMES

Every four years, in the western city of Olympia, the city-states came together to honour their gods with a series of sporting contests. Any wars were stopped during the Olympic Games.

HELLAS

Hellas is the name for the culture that all the Greek city-states had in common.

EPHESUS

Ephesus was a centre for trade. The Temple of Artemis in the city, today in ruins, was one of the Seven Wonders of the World.

MILETUS

This city-state founded some colonies and was home to many outstanding philosophers, such as Thales.

THEBES

Sworn enemy of Athens, Thebes was one of the oldest city-states. It reached the height of its power 2,400 years ago.

Alexander the Great

In the 5th and 4th centuries BC, the Greek city-states lost their power and the neighbouring kingdom of Macedonia went from strength to strength. The Macedonian king Philip II invaded Greece. In 10 years, from 336–327 BC, his son, Alexander, conquered the Persians and almost all of the known world. His great empire reached from Greece in the west to India in the east and Egypt to the south.

BUCEPHALUS
Alexander rode into many battles on his horse Bucephalus.

CONQUEST

First, Alexander conquered Asia Minor. Next, he took Phoenicia, Egypt and Mesopotamia. He defeated the Persians in many battles, eventually taking their capital city, Persepolis. From there, he continued eastwards, and defeated the Indian king Porus.

ARISTOTLE

When Alexander was young, the great Greek philosopher Aristotle was his teacher.

THE BATTLE OF ISSUS

Shocked by news of Alexander's conquests, the Persian king Darius III decided to face up to him on the Issus plain in Syria in 333 BC. Darius suffered a disastrous defeat.

BATTLE STRATEGY

In battle, the Macedonians formed groups of soldiers lined up with no gap between them. The first line carried long lances. They formed a solid barrier that enemies could not break through.

1. A smaller group formed on the right, next to the cavalry.

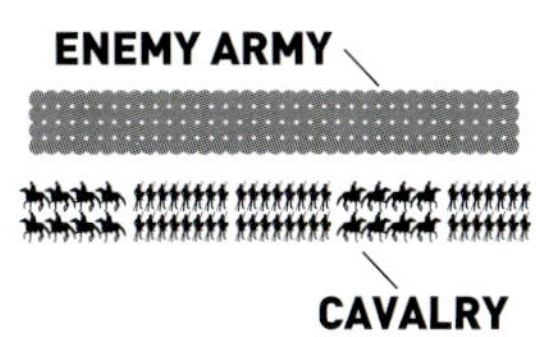

2. This group started the attack, breaking through the enemy lines.

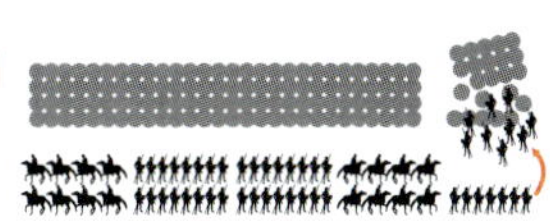

3. The cavalry rode through the gap that opened up.

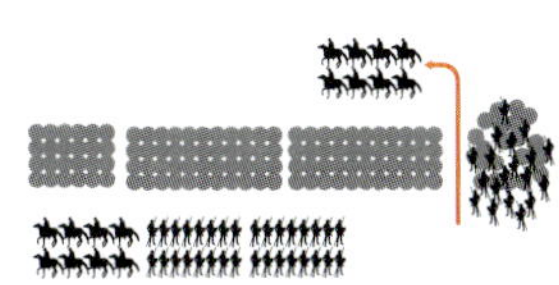

70
CITIES
Founded by Alexander during his conquests.

The Roman Empire

At its peak in the first century AD, the Roman Empire controlled the entire Mediterranean Sea. The Empire had developed from the Roman Republic. The late Republic suffered a bitter civil war, which the first emperor, Augustus, brought to an end. The Emperor Augustus and his successors created one of the most powerful empires in history.

A VAST EMPIRE

More than 50 million people lived under Roman rule.

NERO
Emperor Nero ordered the burning of Rome, then blamed it on the Christians, a group that he hated. He was called a public enemy by the Roman Senate, and killed himself.

AUGUSTUS
Under the rule of its first emperor, Roman armies conquered new lands to increase the size and wealth of the Empire.

TRAJAN

The Roman Empire reached its greatest size during the rule of Emperor Trajan (AD 96–117). In his honour, Trajan's Column was erected in Rome. It tells the story of the conquest of Dacia (modern-day Romania).

5 CENTURIES

The length of time that the Roman Empire lasted.

TRIUMPHAL ARCHES
These monuments (below) were built to mark victories by the Roman armies.

PAX ROMANA

The name for the period of peace that the Roman Empire brought with it.

Fall of the Roman Empire

Many things caused the fall of the Roman Empire, including an economic crisis, power struggles, a religious crisis, and invasions from the north. Eventually, the empire could not repel the invaders. About 1,500 years ago, this vast Empire was divided into two parts.

COLONIES

The Empire was forced to leave many of its colonies, such as the one at Volubilis in North Africa, which was later occupied by Arabs.

MIDDLE AGES

The fall of the Roman Empire marked the start of the Middle Ages.

CHRISTIANITY

Christianity began to spread in the centuries after the death of Jesus. At first, Christians were treated badly because they questioned the god-status of the emperor. However, in 337 Emperor Constantine became a Christian just before he died. Soon afterwards, Christianity became the official religion of the Empire.

INVASIONS

Tribes from northern Europe – the Goths, Vandals, Franks and Huns – attacked the Roman Empire more and more often. These invasions were the reason that the last emperor was overthrown.

AD 476

The year that the Roman Empire ended in the west.

DIVISION

As the Empire stopped growing, there were no new sources of materials and slaves. It became vulnerable to economic crisis: the growing army could not be paid and the costs of administering the Empire could not be met. In time, the Empire split into two: a western empire based around Rome, and an eastern empire based around Constantinople. Emperor Theodosius (right), who died in AD 395, was the last emperor to rule both halves of the Empire.

The Papacy of Rome

By the end of the Roman Empire, Christianity had become a widespread religion. Throughout the Middle Ages, the power of Christian leaders grew and grew. The Catholic Church became very powerful. Its highest authority was the Pope, who was the Bishop of Rome.

BISHOPS

Bishops are in charge of areas called dioceses.

ST PETER'S BASILICA
St Peter's is found in the Vatican City in Rome. The first building was erected in the 4th century. The current building dates from the 16th century.

266

The number of popes in the 2,000-year history of Christianity.

POLITICAL POWER

The power of the Catholic Church grew throughout the Middle Ages. The Pope became one of the most powerful men in Europe.

THE VATICAN

In the 4th century, the Roman emperor Constantine gave his summer residence, the Lateran in Rome, to the city's bishop. After this, the Church's power grew until it controlled areas called the Papal States, based around the Vatican.

VATICAN PALACES
The home to several popes, the oldest palaces were built in the 9th century. The largest date from the 15th and 16th centuries.

THE CHURCH DIVIDES INTO TWO

In the early years of the Church, there were many different ideas about how Christianity should be practised. Eight councils were called together with the aim of unifying the Church. However, these efforts failed. The Eastern Church, based around Constantinople, finally split from the Western Church, based in Rome, in the 11th century.

ST PETER
Considered to be the first pope, St Peter was one of Jesus' apostles. He was buried in Rome.

The Vikings

The Vikings were a Scandinavian people who, from the 8th century, began a series of daring sea voyages. For the next three centuries, they invaded countries to the south and west. They reached as far as Russia, invaded France, conquered parts of Ireland and northern Britain, and plundered the Mediterranean. They even reached the coast of North America.

COINS
Sailing was important to Viking life. Ships appear often on Viking tombs, jewellery and coins.

WEAPONRY
A Viking's sword was his most precious possession.

POSITIVE CONTRIBUTION

Despite the terror that their attacks held, the Vikings made positive contributions to trade. They often adopted the customs of the lands they conquered.

VIKING SOCIETY

From the 9th century, the people of Scandinavia were organized into independent kingdoms. At the top of the power structure was a king, who was surrounded by a court of nobles. Viking warriors dedicated themselves to war and exploration. At the bottom of the structure were the peasants and thralls (slaves).

BELIEFS

Viking beliefs were based around a series of myths that explained how the world began. They had many gods. Odin – the god of war, wisdom, poetry and music was the most important. His son Thor was the god of thunder and protector of people.

LEIF ERIKSSON
Leif landed on Newfoundland, off the coast of Canada, in around the year 1000.

EXPLORATIONS

The Vikings were great explorers. They colonized Greenland and Iceland. The Vikings are also the first Europeans known to have set foot in America. The Icelandic Sagas tell the story of some ships that were sailing from Iceland to Greenland when they were blown off course by a storm. In this way, they arrived by accident at the coast of North America.

793

The year of the first Viking raid, which took place in Lindisfarne, off the coast of England.

THE END

By 1100, when Sweden converted to Christianity, the Viking raids were at an end.

The Islamic world

The religion of Islam appeared in Arabia at the start of the 7th century. It was founded by the prophet Mohammed. He set out the ideas behind the new religion and also built a state based on these ideas. After just 50 years, Islam had expanded from the Arabian Peninsula to the Atlantic in the west and India in the east.

AL-ANDALUS
Conquered by the Arabs in the 8th century, it became a wealthy state ruled separately from the Abbasid and Fatimid Caliphates in the east.

ORGANIZATION

Followers of Islam were united by a religious leader called a caliph. Under the caliph came local emirs and princes.

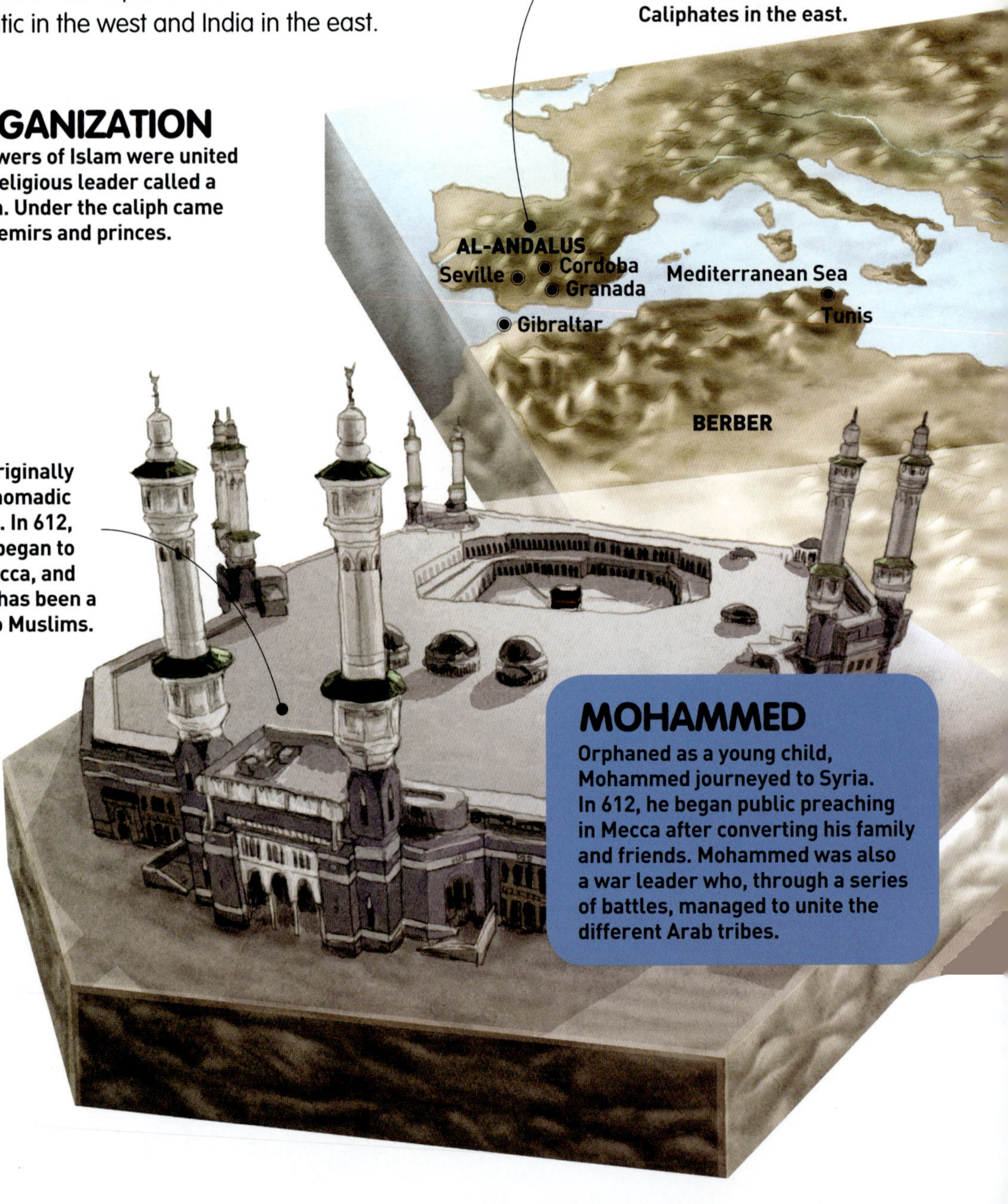

MECCA
Mecca was originally a shrine for nomadic desert tribes. In 612, Mohammed began to preach at Mecca, and since then it has been a sacred city to Muslims.

MOHAMMED

Orphaned as a young child, Mohammed journeyed to Syria. In 612, he began public preaching in Mecca after converting his family and friends. Mohammed was also a war leader who, through a series of battles, managed to unite the different Arab tribes.

BAGHDAD
Baghdad was capital of the Abbasid Caliphate from the 8th century, under which Islam reached the height of its power.

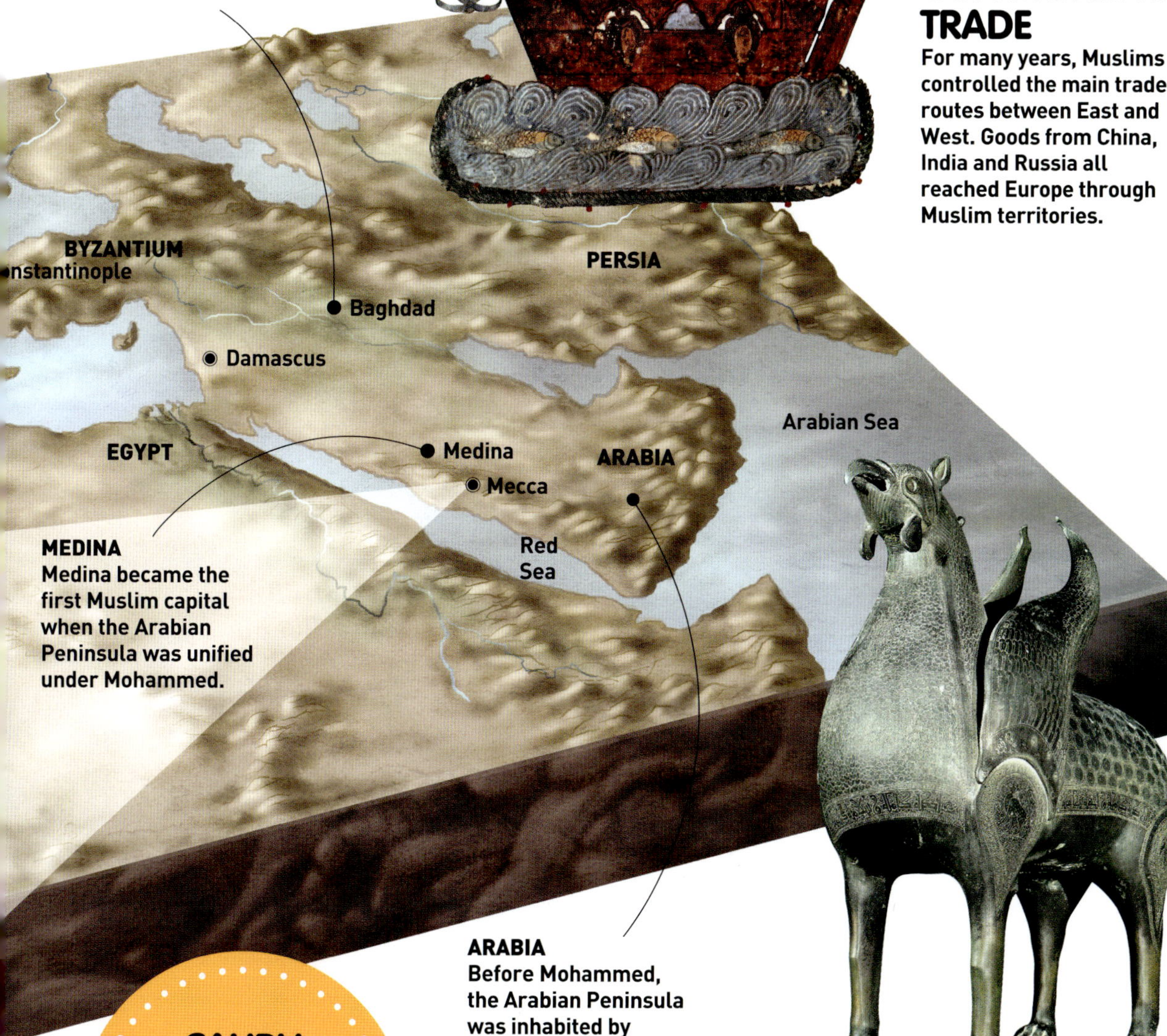

CONTROLLING TRADE

For many years, Muslims controlled the main trade routes between East and West. Goods from China, India and Russia all reached Europe through Muslim territories.

MEDINA
Medina became the first Muslim capital when the Arabian Peninsula was unified under Mohammed.

ARABIA
Before Mohammed, the Arabian Peninsula was inhabited by nomadic tribes. Many trade routes crossed the desert, which was claimed by both the Persians and the Byzantines.

CALIPH
The political and spiritual leader of a community of Muslims.

CULTURE AND SCIENCE

The arts and science flourished under Arab influence. The Arabs took texts from Ancient Greece and China and built on the knowledge they contained.

Science and Islam

In the Middle Ages, the Muslim world achieved great scientific advances. Works from Ancient Greece and Rome were translated and studied by Muslim scholars, who built on this knowledge. Universities were founded in Muslim cities and became centres of scientific study. Arab scholars made advances in many different fields, especially mathematics, astronomy and medicine.

MATHEMATICS

One of the biggest achievements of the Arab world was to spread the use of the base-10 number system that was used in India. This system also included the concept of zero for the first time.

MECHANICS
The Arabs made many fine machines, such as this water clock.

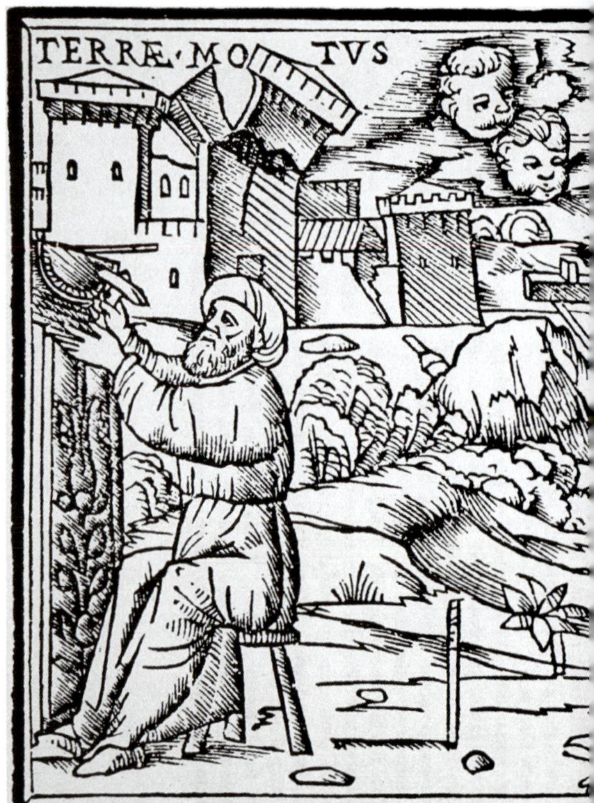

ASTRONOMY

The Arabs developed new ways to study the stars. They made accurate calendars and maps of the planets, and invented new instruments for measuring the positions of the stars.

EXCHANGE

Muslims' tolerance of other cultures allowed them to learn new things from them.

ASTROLABE
This instrument allowed sailors to navigate by measuring the positions of the stars.

MEDICINE

Medicine developed with advances in chemistry, the use of medicinal plants and the study of the human anatomy. Arab doctors were thought to be the best in the world and were often called for by Christian kings and princes.

450

The number of books written by Avicenna.

AVICENNA
A Persian doctor, naturalist and philosopher, Avicenna worked at the court of Baghdad in the 10th century. His book *Canon of Medicine* provided a complete system of medicine for doctors to follow.

Genghis Khan and the Mongol Empire

In the 13th century, Genghis Khan brought together the different Mongol tribes and established a strong new Mongolian state. With the help of a skilful and ruthless army, he went on to create the largest continental empire in history.

MESSENGERS

The Mongol emperors used 10,000 messengers, who travelled by horse to every part of the Empire.

MONGOL FEDERATION
Genghis Khan's first achievement was to unite the Mongol tribes into one federation.

GENGHIS KHAN

Born in around 1162 to an aristocratic family in a small Mongol tribe, Genghis Khan's original name was Temujin. After fighting with several different tribes, he rose to lead the new confederation of Mongol tribes. In 1206, he was elected supreme leader of the mongols and given the name Genghis Khan. He died in 1227 while on a military campaign.

GREAT EMPIRE

In little more than 20 years, Genghis Khan conquered the whole of Central Asia. His empire reached from the Caspian Sea to the Pacific Ocean as he conquered Persia, Afghanistan, part of Russia and the north of China.

5,800 KM

The span of the Mongol Empire at the time of Genghis Khan's death.

MONGOL ARMY

The Mongols' military successes were made possible by the efficient way their army was organized. It was a people's army and men trained for war from childhood. They were known for cruelty because they often killed their prisoners.

EQUIPMENT
Mongol soldiers wore leather armour, steel helmets and fur coats. They carried a bow or a lance, a shield, an axe and several spears.

HORSEMANSHIP
The Mongols were excellent horsemen. They used stirrups, which had been invented in China, allowing them to fire their weapons while they were galloping.

THE LAST GREAT KHAN

Just 30 years after the death of Genghis Khan, the Mongol Empire collapsed. The last great emperor of the Mongols was Genghis Khan's grandson, Kublai Khan. He completed the conquest of China and transferred the Mongol capital to Beijing. Under the Yuan Dynasty, founded by Kublai Khan, China reached its modern-day borders.

The Renaissance and Humanism

Between the 14th and 16th centuries, Western Europe experienced an explosion in cultural and scientific achievement known as the Renaissance. A new movement, Humanism, stressed the importance of education. These movements restored the values of the ancient Greeks and Romans, breaking with the religious restrictions of the Middle Ages.

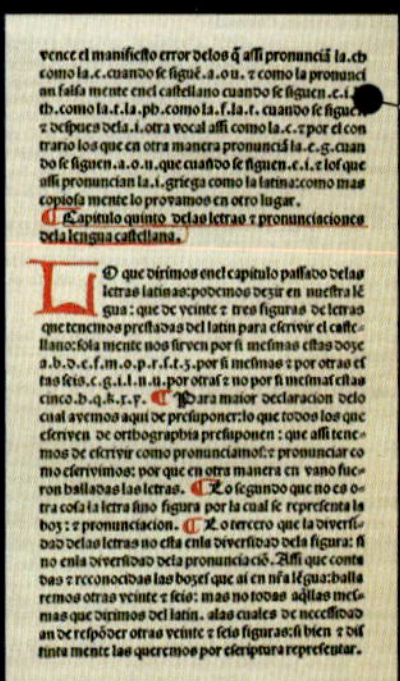

vence el manifiesto error delos q̃ assi pronunciã la.ch como la.c.cuando se siguẽ.a.o.u. z como la pronunciã falsa mente enel castellano cuando se siguen.e.i. ch.como la.t.la.ph.como la.f.la.t. cuando se siguen z despues dela.i.otra vocal assi como la.c.z por el contrario los que en otra manera pronunciã la.c.g.cuando se siguen.a.o.u.que cuãdo se siguen.e.i.z los que assi pronuncian la.i.griega como la latina:como mas copiosa mente lo provamos en otro lugar.
¶ Capitulo quinto delas letras z pronunciaciones dela lengua castellana.

LO que diximos enel capitulo passado delas letras latinas:podemos dezir en nuestra lẽgua: que de veinte z tres figuras de letras que tenemos prestadas del latin para escrivir el castellano:sola mente nos sirven por si mesmas estas doze a.b.d.e.f.m.o.p.r.s.t.z.por si mesmas z por otras estas seis.c.g.i.l.n.u.por otras z no por si mesmas estas cinco.h.q.k.x.y. ¶ Para maior declaracion delo cual avemos aqui de presuponer:lo que todos los que escriven de orthographia presuponen : que assi tenemos de escrivir como pronunciamos:z pronunciar como escrivimos: por que en otra manera en vano fueron halladas las letras. ¶ Lo segundo que no es otra cosa la letra sino figura por la cual se representa la boz:z pronunciacion. ¶ Lo tercero que la diversidad delas letras no esta enla diversidad dela figura: si no enla diversidad dela pronunciaciõ. Assi que contadas z reconocidas las bozes que ai en nr̃a lẽgua:hallaremos otras veinte z seis: mas no todas aq̃llas mesmas que diximos del latin. alas cuales de necessidad an de respõder otras veinte z seis figuras:si bien z distinta mente las queremos por escriptura representar.

HUMANISM

Humanists stressed the importance of the individual and questioned the authority of the Church.

PRINTING PRESS
Invented by Johannes Gutenberg in around 1450, the printing press helped to spread new ideas more quickly.

MEN OF SCIENCE

During the Renaissance, scientists started to base their studies on experiments. This new way of studying science soon paid off.

LEONARDO DA VINCI
As well as being a painter, Leonardo da Vinci was also an inventor and a physicist.

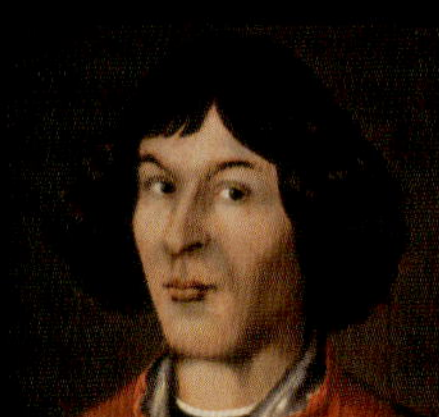

NICOLAUS COPERNICUS
Copernicus suggested that the Earth revolved around the Sun. Before this, people believed that the Sun revolved around the Earth.

PARACELSUS
Paracelsus was a doctor who first studied the link between symptoms and illnesses.

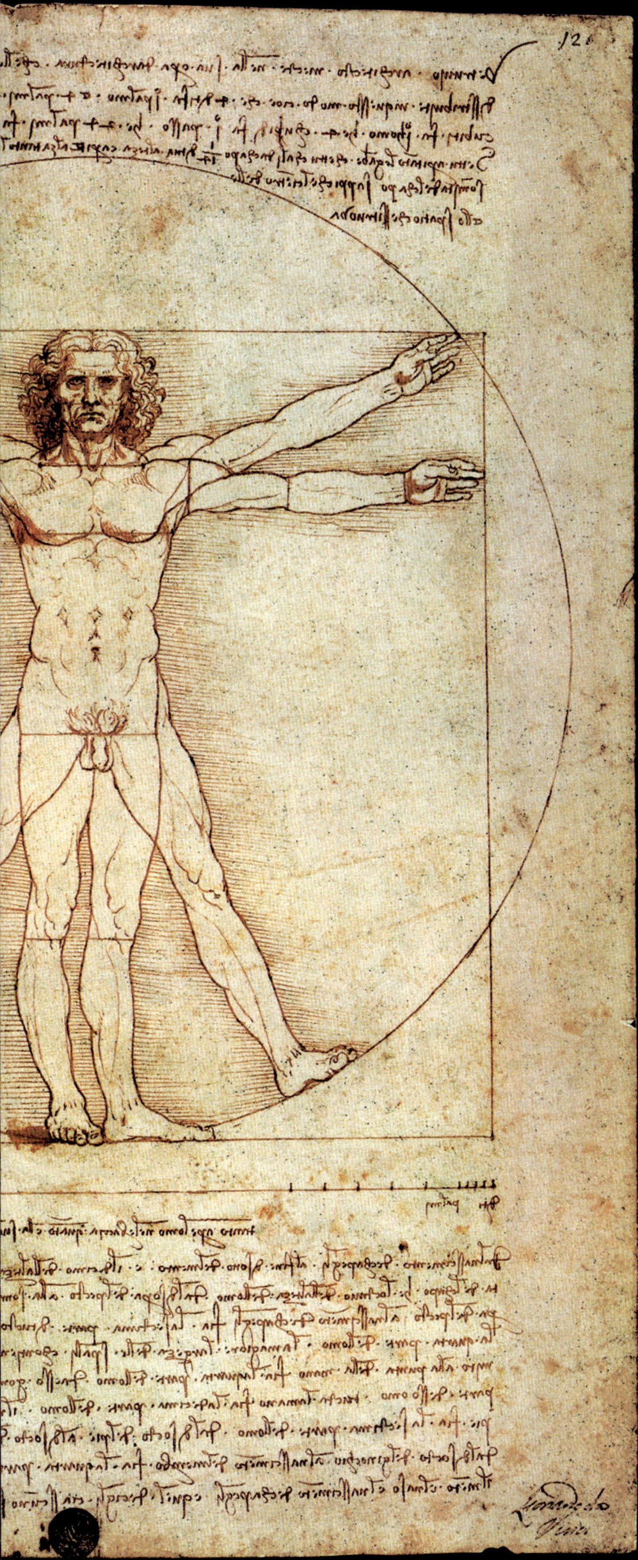

A NEW VISION OF MAN

[illegible]

FLORENCE CATHEDRAL
The Duomo, as it is commonly called, after its magnificent dome, is one of the finest churches of the Renaissance. It was designed by Filippo Brunelleschi.

ITALY, THE HEART OF THE RENAISSANCE

The Renaissance started in the prosperous city-states of Italy. Rich Italian princes used their wealth to support the new thinkers and artists.

The conquest of America

On 3 August 1492, Christopher Columbus set sail from Europe, reaching a continent that was unknown to him on 12 October: America. Soon afterwards, a series of expeditions set off from Europe for these newly discovered lands and conquered them. European powers imposed themselves on the native people and a long period of colonization began.

33

The number of days Columbus sailed before seeing land.

ACCIDENTAL DISCOVERER

Christopher Columbus was a sailor from Genoa, Italy. He set off from Spain to find a new route to Asia. Instead, he discovered the Bahamas in the Caribbean. He made three more voyages to the Americas, always believing that he had sailed to Asia.

RELIGION

As well as military conquest, Europeans wanted to convert the people of the Americas to Christianity.

CONQUEST OF THE NATIVE PEOPLES
The newly arrived Spanish *conquistadors* (conquerors) found two advanced cultures, the Aztecs of Mexico and the Incas of Peru, and defeated them both.

CONQUISTADORS
The *conquistadors* had more powerful armour and weapons than the people they found in the Americas. They also carried new illnesses such as influenza, which killed millions of the native people.

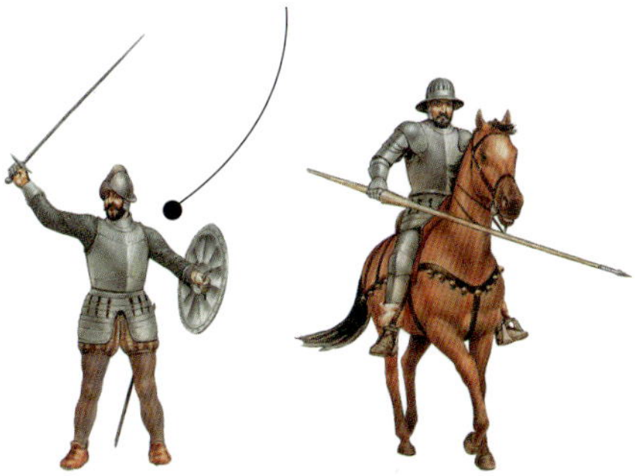

CONQUEST

The conquest of the native people of the Americas was bloody. The Spanish conquered the Caribbean and Central America and went on to defeat the Aztecs of Mexico and the Incas of Peru. The Portuguese conquered Brazil, while the French and the English established themselves in the north.

SLAVES
The Portuguese brought slaves with them to work in their plantations in Brazil. The scale of deaths from disease among the native populations meant that slaves from outside were needed to run the plantations.

COLONIAL ERA

In the centuries following the conquest, the European powers established many colonies in the Americas. Gold and silver were brought back from America, and plantations were established to grow coffee, sugar and tobacco.

The French Revolution

In 1789, the powerful French monarchy was overthrown, and King Louis XVI and Queen Marie Antoinette were executed, making way for a new era in which politics and justice were to be decided by the people. This was the French Revolution, which was fought under the slogan 'Liberty, Equality, Fraternity', and the Modern Age began.

JACOBINS

This group of revolutionaries were very radical and led the bloodiest years of the Revolution.

CAUSES

1. A monarchy was very rigid in a world that was changing.
2. The development of a powerful new class of people, called the bourgeoisie, who traded and became wealthy.
3. The unhappiness of the ordinary people.
4. The spread of new ideas about freedom.
5. The economic crisis that France suffered after a series of bad harvests.

THE FACES OF THE REVOLUTION

JOSEPH SIEYÈS

GEORGES JACQUES DANTON

JEAN-PAUL MARAT

THE RIGHTS OF MAN AND OF THE CITIZEN

This document was published on 26 August 1789. It laid out rights to liberty and to property, and stated that all citizens were equal before the law.

THE STORMING OF THE BASTILLE

On 14 July 1789, the people of Paris broke into the Bastille and set its prisoners free. This was an important event in the French Revolution.

A DECISIVE DECADE

The old regime was declared dead and the country was now ruled by the 'Third Estate': the bourgeoisie and the common people. This happened on 17 June 1789. The Revolution was ended by a coup that brought Napoleon Bonaparte to power in 1799.

MAXIMILIEN ROBESPIERRE

CAMILLE DESMOULIN

MARQUIS DE LAFAYETTE

LOUIS SAINT-JUST

The Industrial Revolution

Between the second half of the 18th century and the start of the 19th century, the Industrial Revolution transformed how people lived and worked. It began in Britain, then spread to the rest of Europe. Countries moved away from old ways of working and introduced factories and machines to make goods. In the 19th century, this process was made faster by the arrival of the railways. They could carry goods and people from place to place much more quickly and in larger numbers than ever before.

14 HOURS

The length of the working day during the Industrial Revolution.

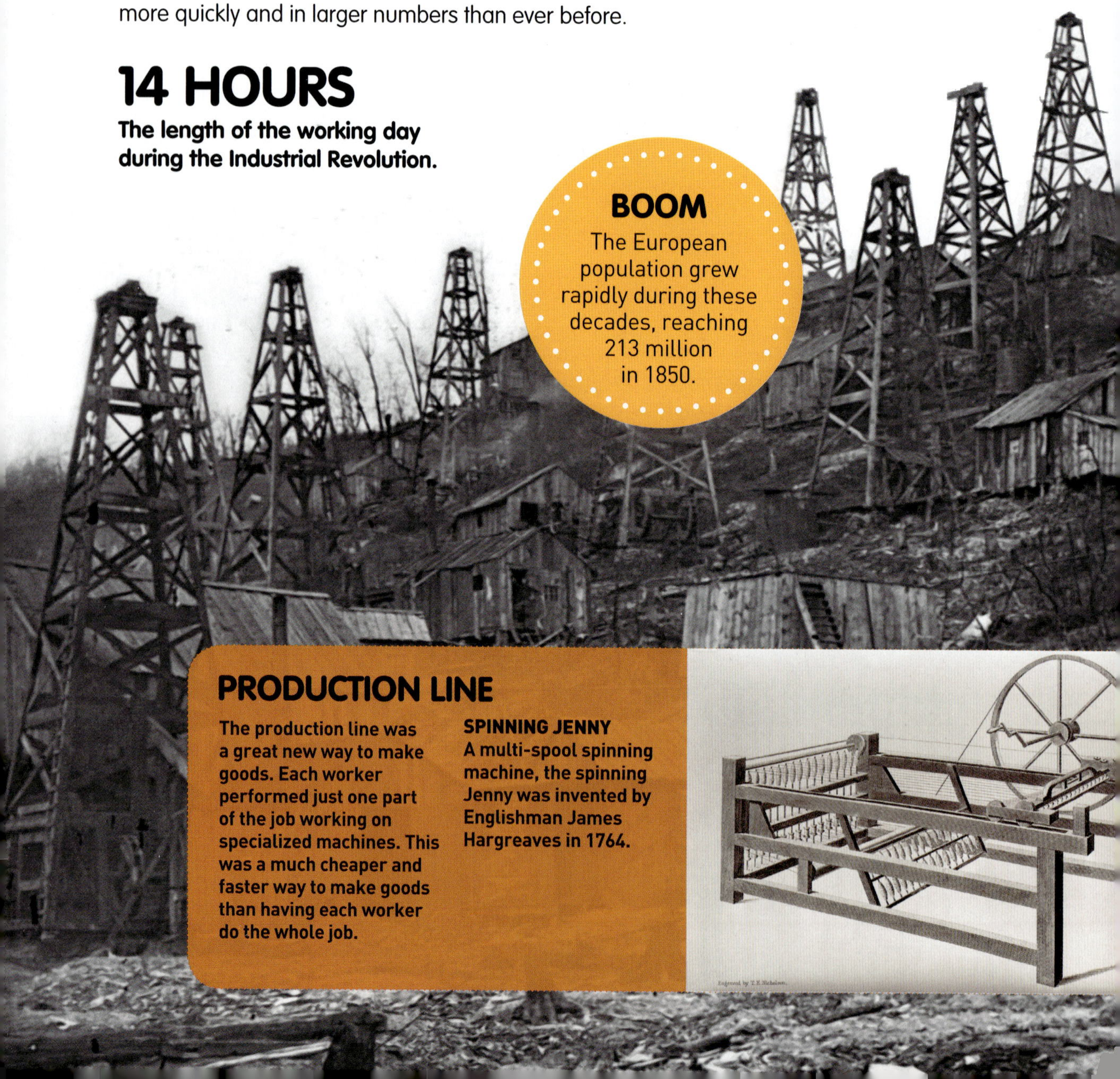

BOOM

The European population grew rapidly during these decades, reaching 213 million in 1850.

PRODUCTION LINE

The production line was a great new way to make goods. Each worker performed just one part of the job working on specialized machines. This was a much cheaper and faster way to make goods than having each worker do the whole job.

SPINNING JENNY
A multi-spool spinning machine, the spinning Jenny was invented by Englishman James Hargreaves in 1764.

FUEL

At first, coal was the main fuel of the Industrial Age. Later, petrol became more important.

TAYLORISM

Taylor's principles were:

1. Training workers to give them specialized skills.
2. Controlling workers' time.
3. Using machines to do work where at all possible.
4. The scientific study of 'time and motion' to work out the best way to organize workers.

STEPHENSON'S ROCKET This locomotive was powered by a new, improved steam engine. All later steam trains followed this design.

FREDERICK TAYLOR An American engineer who came up with a system for making work more efficient.

The American Revolution

By the mid 1700s, there were 13 British colonies in North America (excluding Canada). Britain taxed the people living there, but did not let them have a say in how they were governed. The colonists complained about this and the British government sent soldiers to quell any protests. An armed confrontation took place in April 1775 at Lexington, Massachusetts, sparking the Revolutionary War.

REVOLUTIONARY ARMY

The first major battle took place at Bunker Hill, near Boston, on June 17, 1775. The Revolutionary forces were led by George Washington, shown below crossing the Delaware River on Christmas night, 1776.

TIMELINE

1775 The American Revolutionary War begins.

1776 On July 4, the Continental Congress (the governing body of the 13 colonies) adopts the Declaration of Independence.

1777 The British are defeated at Saratoga, New York. France sides with America. The British capture Philadelphia, Pennsylvania.

1778 The British capture Savannah, Georgia.

1779 Spain joins the war on America's side.

1780 The Dutch join the war on America's side. British victory at Charleston, South Carolina.

1781 After a siege at Yorktown, Virginia, the British surrender.

THE DECLARATION OF INDEPENDENCE

Signed on July 4, 1776, the Declaration of Independence declared that the American colonies were no longer under British rule. Among the signatures are those of future presidents Thomas Jefferson and John Adams, as well as John Hancock and Benjamin Franklin.

1781

The year that British forces surrendered after defeat at Yorktown, marking the end of the war.

ALLIES

Other countries joined the fight on America's side. These included France, Spain and the Netherlands.

PAUL REVERE

Paul Revere was a silversmith from Boston who is famous for an overnight ride to warn American forces about approaching British troops before the battles of Lexington and Concord in April 1775.

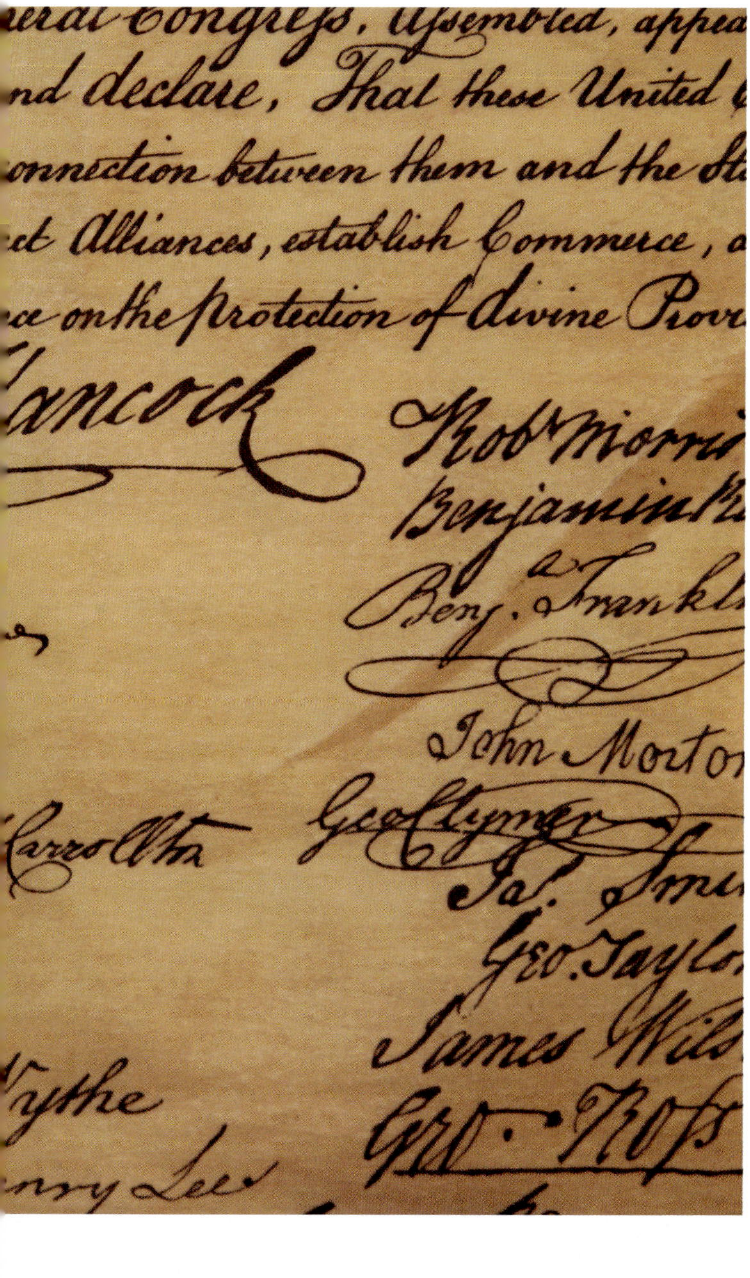

THE LIBERATORS

In the decades after the American Revolutionary War, the colonies of Latin America fought to gain their independence from Spain and Portugal. Two famous leaders of this campaign were Simon Bolivar and José de San Martin (shown here).

The Scramble for Africa

In the 1880s, European powers, particularly Great Britain and France, Germany and Portugal began to colonize large parts of Africa. As their wealth grew with industrialization, they were looking for new sources of raw materials, and hoped to set up plantations in Africa to supply them with goods such as coffee, sugar and timber. In just 20 years, almost all of Africa was under European control.

EXPLORATION AND CONQUEST

Throughout the 19th century, European geographical societies paid for expeditions into Africa. Many of these expeditions had peaceful scientific aims. However, they paved the way for the later military conquest of Africa.

THE DECLINE OF THE ZULUS

In the 1870s, the Zulu Kingdom dominated Southern Africa. However, the Zulus were defeated in conflicts with the British and the Boers, and their dreams of establishing an empire were dashed.

ZULU WARRIORS
This is a print from the 19th century.

BOERS

Dutch colonists who rebelled against British rule in South Africa and were defeated in the Boer Wars (1899-1902)

SUEZ CANAL

The Suez Canal provided a route from Europe to India. In 1875, Egypt sold its shares in this important canal. The British prime minister, Benjamin Disraeli, bought the shares, giving Britain's presence in Africa a major boost.

BENJAMIN DISRAELI
This is a caricature of the British prime minister published in the *London Sketch Book*.

MISSIONARY

The British missionary David Livingstone believed in spreading the 'Three Cs': Christianity, Commerce and Civilization. He explored Africa from 1841 until he died in 1873.

A French missionary school in Africa.

World War I

World War I was fought from 1914 to 1918. More than 60 million soldiers fought in the war, and 10 million men lost their lives. The conflict eventually involved 32 countries, as the 'Allies' – including Great Britain, France, Russia and the United States – fought the 'Central Powers' – Germany, Austria-Hungary and the Ottoman Empire. The war started after a period of tension in Europe, and also involved European colonies around the world. It was fought using new technology, which led to many more soldiers being killed than in any previous war.

ALLIANCES IN THE WAR

July-August 1914
War is declared between the Central Powers and the Allies.

August 1914
Japan declares war on Germany in a move to take over Germany's Chinese colonies.

October 1914
Turkey (the Ottomans) joins the war on the side of the Central Powers.

May 1915
Italy joins the war on the side of the Allies.

October 1915
Bulgaria joins the Central Powers.

March 1916
Portugal joins the Allies.

August 1916
Romania joins the Allies.

April 1917
The United States declares war on the Central Powers.

November 1918
Germany signs the Armistice with the Allies, admitting defeat and ending the war.

WESTERN FRONT

In 1914, the German army advanced to within 25 kilometres of Paris. The French and the British Expeditionary Force held their advance at the Battle of the Marne. Throughout the following four years of bloody battles, these positions held until the end of the war. Trenches gave soldiers some protection from the enemy, but they could be cold, wet and muddy. These French soldiers are at the Somme in 1916, in which neither side won a huge advantage but the German army never fully recovered.

MAIN BATTLES

The war showed the power of the new industrialized warfare. Machine guns, tanks and other new equipment made old ideas about warfare outdated. The war lasted much longer than either side thought it would, as neither side could break through the other's lines.

1 Marne

Two million men took part in this battle in September 1914. Nearly 200,000 men were killed.

2 Gallipoli

In 1915, Allied troops fought for control of the Dardanelles, a sea route to Russia. They were defeated by the Turks, and 156,000 Allied troops were killed.

3 Tannenburg

Fought in August 1914, the German army defeated the Russians. This was the first in a series of victories for Germany on the Eastern Front.

4 Jutland

This naval battle between Great Britain and Germany was for control of the North Sea. The British suffered great losses, but they won the battle in May 1916.

5 Verdun

This battle was fought between February and December in 1916. More than 700,000 soldiers died.

6 Somme

Fought between June and November in 1916, there were more than 1 million casualties at Somme. Tanks were used in this battle for the first time by the British.

The Russian Revolution

As World War I raged across Europe, in 1917 a revolution took place in Russia. The land and factories were taken from their owners and turned over to the peasants and workers. The Revolution was led by a communist group called the Bolsheviks, led by Vladimir Lenin. It was the first communist revolution in the world.

NICHOLAS II

The last Tsar (monarch) of Russia, Nicholas, and his family were executed by the Bolsheviks in 1918. His rule had been full of conflict, and he was a weak leader. The terrible loss of life of World War I was the final decisive factor that led to his downfall.

AGAINST THE TSAR

In February 1917, there had been demonstrations against the Tsar, which included burning tsarist symbols (below). In October, the Winter Palace, the symbol of the monarch's power, was stormed.

POWER TO THE PEOPLE

In his book *State and Revolution*, Lenin laid out his plans for a new society, in which ordinary working people – the proletariat – held political power.

LENIN

Lenin led Russia from 1917 until 1922, when he suffered a stroke. He died in 1924 at just 53 years old.

The rise of Fascism

In the period between the two world wars, a number of totalitarian regimes took power in Europe. In 1922, Benito Mussolini's fascists took power in Italy. Then in 1933, Adolf Hitler's Nazis came to power in Germany. These two leaders became allies. Hitler launched a series of invasions of Germany's neighbours, which eventually led to World War II.

MEDIA

The totalitarian regimes used cinema and the radio to share their ideas.

IDEOLOGY

German Nazis and Italian fascists shared many ideas and beliefs. They promoted a strong nationalism and were against communism and liberal democracy. They killed and imprisoned anyone who was against their rule. Hitler also began a campaign against Jews that led to the Holocaust in which 6 million people were killed.

This is a poster advertising a Nazi film from 1936.

IL DUCE
This was the name given to Benito Mussolini, meaning 'The Leader'. He wanted to return Italy to the glory of ancient Roman times and used many symbols from Italy's Roman past.

THE FÜHRER
Born in Austria, Adolf Hitler became the führer, or leader, of Germany. All Germans were expected to obey him without question.

SHOCK FORCES OF ITALIAN FASCISM

The Italian Fascist Party ran a paramilitary group called the 'Blackshirts'. This group of about 30,000 men fought opponents of Mussolini in street battles.

BENITO MUSSOLINI
Mussolini was a teacher, journalist and militant socialist. After fighting in World War I, he became a militant nationalist.

SPANISH CIVIL WAR

In 1936, a nationalist general in the Spanish army, Francisco Franco, led a revolt against the elected Spanish government. This began a three-year civil war in which 500,000 people were killed. Franco won the war with the help of the Italians and Germans. He remained dictator of Spain until his death in 1975.

FRANCISCO FRANCO
General Franco ruled Spain with a form of strict Catholic nationalism. Those who opposed his rule were punished.

HITLER AND GERMAN NAZISM

Hitler came to power in 1933 with a message that was anti-Jewish, anti-communist and anti-democratic. He soon established a totalitarian system based on the concept of 'National Socialism' (abbreviated to 'Nazi'). The Nazis believed that there was a superior European race called the 'Arians', and persecuted anybody who they believed did not belong to this race.

World War II

In 1939, Germany invaded Poland. This started World War II. The Axis Powers – Germany, Italy and Japan – fought the Allies of France, Great Britain and, later, the Soviet Union and the United States. In total, more than 70 countries took part in the war, which lasted until 1945. After initial successes in which the Axis armies occupied much of Europe, Germany invaded Russia in June 1941. They almost reached Moscow, but were then pushed back both there and in North Africa and Italy. By 1944, the Axis armies were on the defensive, fighting to hold back the Allies.

VICTIMS

About 60 million people – two percent of the world's population – died in the war.

PEARL HARBOR

On 7 December 1941, the Japanese launched a surprise attack on Pearl Harbor, a US military base in Hawaii in the Pacific Ocean. They destroyed 18 warships and 188 aircraft, and killed more than 2,000 people. After the attack, the United States joined the war on the side of the Allies.

FALL OF BERLIN

On 30 April 1945, the Red Army of the Soviet Union entered the German capital Berlin. A few days later, the German leader Adolf Hitler committed suicide, signalling victory to the Allies in Europe. Victory in Asia followed later in the year, finally bringing the war to an end.

ANGELS OF DEATH

New aeroplanes were developed during World War II. Light fighter planes had a key role in supporting troops on the ground.

STUKAS
These German planes were used in attacks on ground forces.

D-DAY

In the early morning of 6 June 1944, 156,000 British, Canadian and American troops landed on the shores of Normandy in northern France, which was occupied by the Germans. The landings signalled the end of German control in Europe.

The Cold War

The period between the end of World War II in 1945 and the fall of the Berlin Wall in 1989 was known as the Cold War. Two large blocks of countries opposed each other. On one side was the communist Soviet Union and its allies. On the other was a block of capitalist countries led by the United States. The Cold War led to an arms race as both sides developed new weapons, but the two sides never fought each other directly.

H-BOMB

In 1952, the United States destroyed a Pacific island testing a new nuclear weapon. It was the first hydrogen bomb.

AGREEMENT TO DISARM

In the 1980s, the leader of the Soviet Union, Mikhail Gorbachev (left) and the president of the United States, Ronald Reagan (right), began a series of talks aimed at ending the Cold War. They agreed to reduce the size of their forces and to get rid of all their nuclear weapons. However, both countries, along with several others, still have nuclear weapons today.

CUBAN MISSILE CRISIS

When, in 1962, the United States discovered proof that the Soviet Union planned to send nuclear missiles to Cuba (see photograph right), 150 kilometres from US land, they threatened war. In the end, the Soviet leader Nikita Khrushchev, backed down and did not send the missiles. This was the closest the two sides came to starting a war against each other.

THE BERLIN WALL

Erected in 1961 to separate communist East Berlin from capitalist West Berlin, the wall stopped East Germans from escaping to the West. The wall was 166 kilometres long. Many people were killed trying to cross into West Berlin. The wall finally came down on 9 November 1989.

THE ORIGIN OF THE TERM 'COLD WAR'

The phrase 'Cold War' was first used by the American adviser to the president, Bernard Baruch (right). In 1947, he said in a speech: 'Let us not be deceived, we are today in the midst of a cold war.' The term became popular after a book called Cold War was published by Walter Lippmann in the same year.

The United States

During the 20th century, the United States rose to become a superpower. After the Second World War, it became the leader of the capitalist world in opposition to the communist block headed by the Soviet Union. After the Soviet Union collapsed in 1991, the United States was left as the only world superpower. In recent years, U.S. foreign policy has been led by its response to the terrorist attack on 11 September 2001, known as the 9/11 attacks.

ATTACK ON THE TWIN TOWERS

On 11 September 2001, the United States suffered a series of suicide attacks by the terrorist group Al-Qaeda. Two hijacked planes flew into the Twin Towers in New York City and a third was crashed into the Pentagon, a US government building. In addition to the 19 hijackers, 2,973 people were killed and another 24 people remain missing. As a result of these attacks, the United States and its allies invaded Afghanistan, where Al-Qaeda leaders were thought to be hiding. They also responded with a series of new laws that affected civil liberties.

160,000

The number of people in the area who survived the attack.

INDEPENDENCE

The United States won its independence from Great Britain in a war that lasted from 1776 to 1783.

NIXON RESIGNS

Richard Nixon was the first American president to be forced to resign. He was found to have ordered illegal spying on his rivals. Here, Nixon and his wife are shown leaving the White House, the residence of the American president, after his resignation in 1974.

THE KENNEDY ASSASSINATION

John F. Kennedy, elected president in 1961, was shot dead in 1963 in Dallas, Texas, while riding with his wife in an open-top car. The assassin, Lee Harvey Oswald, was himself assassinated before he could be brought to trial.

GEORGE W. BUSH

President from 2001 to 2009, Bush was leader when the 9/11 attacks took place. His response included the starting of wars in Afghanistan and Iraq.

BARACK OBAMA

Elected in 2008, Barack Obama is the first African American to be president of the United States. At the time of his birth in 1961, the marriage between his black father and white mother would have been illegal in parts of the United States. His election was made possible only by the struggle for civil rights of the 1960s, which won African Americans equal legal rights.

China, a rising power

In 1949, after a long civil war, Mao Zedong took power and declared the creation of the People's Republic of China, a communist state. This massive Asian country grew to become a major power. Recently, a series of economic reforms have led to a great deal of capitalist development and economic growth, but the Communist Party remains in charge.

ECONOMIC REFORMS

From the late 1980s, Chinese leader Deng Xiaoping began a series of economic reforms, opening China to foreign investment. This led to huge growth in Chinese industry, and now China is the biggest manufacturer in the world.

SUMMIT
Chinese leader Deng Xiaoping meets U.S. president Jimmy Carter in 1979.

LAND REFORM IN CHINA

Ownership of the land was collectivized under Mao Zedong, China's leader. Peasants were organized into cooperatives, which were responsible for arranging the work and distributing food.

ACCUSATIONS
This painting shows peasants attacking a former landowner.

1979

The year the United States officially recognized the government of Beijing.

MAO ZEDONG

Mao followed a kind of communism that came to be known as Maoism. One of the main differences between China's communism and that of the Soviet Union was the leading role that the peasants and the countryside played in Mao's China. In 1966, Mao began a process that came to be known as the Cultural Revolution. This period caused chaos as people from the cities were forced to move to the countryside.

SCIENCE AND CULTURE

Most places in the world have people living there. Different groups of people have developed their own ways of living, or cultures, thinking up new ideas and inventing the technology that shapes our modern lives.

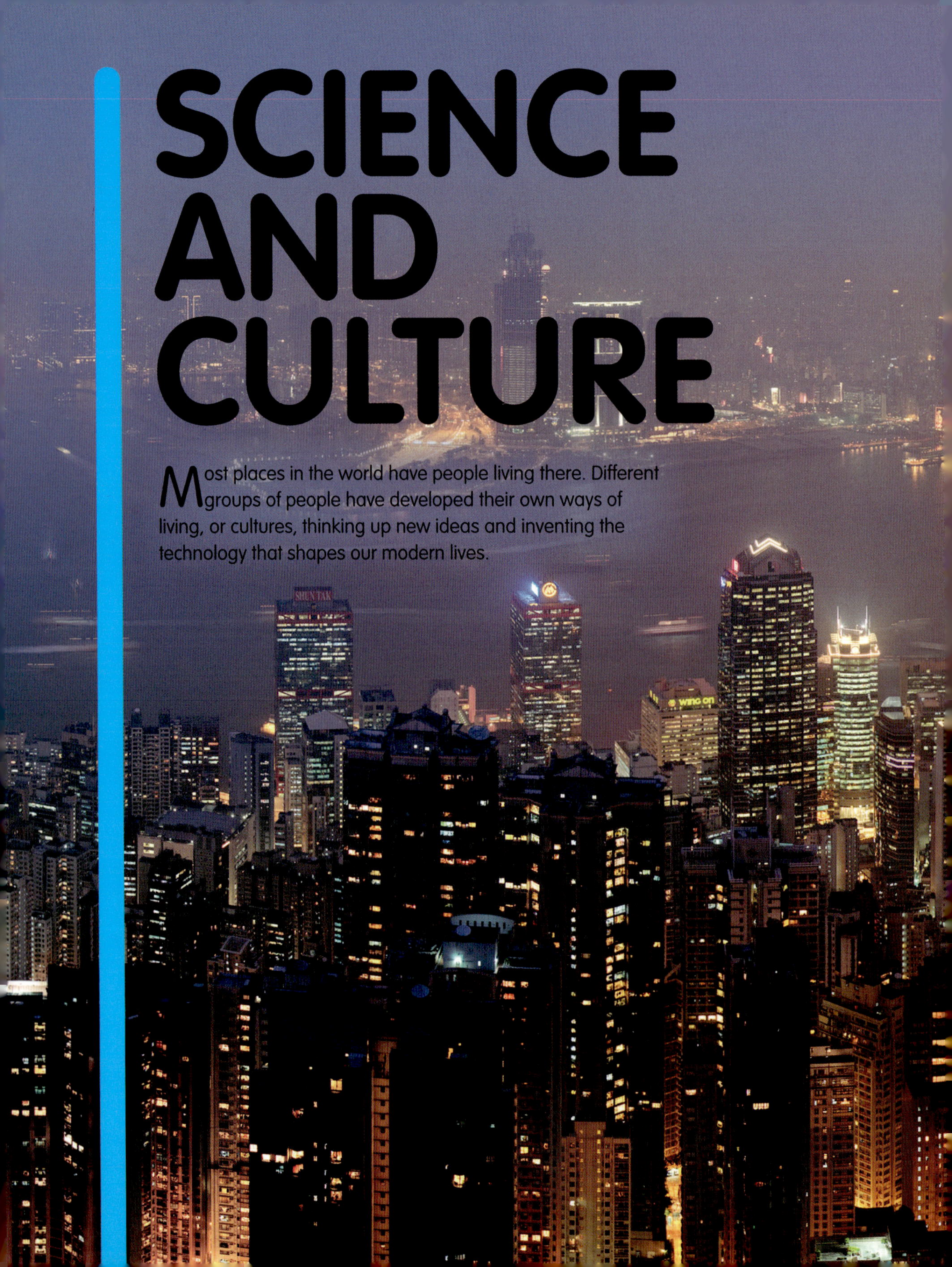

CITY AT NIGHT
Today, half the world's population lives in cities such as Hong Kong (below).

Science

Throughout the ages, humans have tried to figure out how things work. Modern science uses experiments to learn more about the world and to test new ideas.

EXPERIMENTS

A hypothesis is a statement that makes predictions about how things work. Experiments test hypotheses.

WHAT IS SCIENCE?

Scientific knowledge is based on evidence. The evidence comes from experiments that test whether or not a hypothesis is correct. If the evidence shows that a hypothesis is not correct, then scientists try to come up with a new one. A hypothesis may become a theory when there is sufficient evidence to prove it is true. It becomes the model, or theory, for the way things work.

SCIENTIFIC KNOWLEDGE

Scientists try to come up with laws to explain the way that the world works. These laws can be used to make predictions about the future. Science is:

1. **Fact-based:** Science deals with facts and events.
2. **Rational:** It is based on reason and logic, not on feelings or opinions.
3. **Verifiable:** It can be checked against data.
4. **Objective:** Scientific knowledge changes when new data is found.
5. **Systematic:** It builds on a body of knowledge, and each area of science can be tested for accuracy against this knowledge.
6. **Explanatory:** Science tries to explain how the world works.

BIOTECHNOLOGY

One of the most important branches of science is biotechnology. It uses living organisms to solve problems.

METHOD

1. **Observation:** Can be direct or indirect, and provides data.
2. **Comparison:** Tests the data you have collected against current theories and previous tests.

ADDING TO SCIENTIFIC KNOWLEDGE

According to the Austrian philosopher, Karl Popper, if you cannot test an idea in a way that might show it to be false, it does not add to scientific knowledge. This idea is called Popper's Falsification Principle.

Great scientists

Scientific discovery has been made through the hard work, intelligence and talents of many men and women. Science involves teamwork, but throughout history, brilliant individuals have come up with brand new ideas that have shaped what we know. Here are some of the most important scientists.

ALBERT EINSTEIN
(1879-1955)

Possibly the most famous scientist ever, Albert Einstein's ideas have changed the way we think of the Universe. His new ways of looking at space and time led to many new discoveries. His theories explain the force of gravity and the way that light behaves. His ideas have made many inventions possible, including the laser (which is widely used in surgery), nuclear energy and computers.

MARIE CURIE
(1867-1934)

A French-Polish mathematician, physicist and chemist, Curie worked with her husband Pierre investigating radioactivity. Curie discovered the radioactive elements radium and polonium. Her discoveries led to new treatments for cancer. Thousands of lives have been saved using treatments made possible by Curie's work. She was the first woman to receive a Nobel Prize – the top award for scientists.

DIMITRY MENDELEYEV
(1834-1907)

The Russian scientist Mendeleyev worked out how to group chemical elements. To do this, he worked out the Periodic Table, which was first published in 1869. The way he arranged the elements led to predictions that other unknown elements might exist. Years after his death, many of these elements have been found.

ISAAC NEWTON
(1642-1727)

An English mathematician, physicist, astronomer and philosopher, Newton contributed new ideas to many different areas of science. His theory of gravity lasted until Einstein came up with a new theory. Newton also developed a new branch of mathematics called calculus.

Archimedes
(287-212 BC)
A brilliant mechanic, Archimedes explained how levers work and invented many different machines.

Johannes Kepler
(1571-1630)
Kepler, a German astronomer, discovered laws that explained the movement of the planets around the Sun.

Robert Boyle
(1627-1691)
An Englishman who is considered the father of modern chemistry, Boyle carried out many experiments with gases. He came up with new laws to explain their behaviour.

Thomas Edison
(1847-1931)
A US physicist and inventor, Edison, developed the telegraph, a form of long-distance communication. In total, he came up with more than 1,000 inventions.

Max Planck
(1858-1947)
The German physicist Max Planck made the first discoveries in quantum physics. Planck discovered that subatomic particles behave in a very different way from the large things that we can see.

Ernest Rutherford
(1871-1937)
Rutherford, a physicist from New Zealand, studied the atom. He discovered that atoms all have a small nucleus at their centre surrounded by orbiting electrons.

Railways

The first trains appeared nearly 200 years ago. They travelled at speeds of under 20 km/h. Modern trains can reach much higher speeds. The fastest of all is the Alstom V150, which runs between Paris and Strasbourg in France. It reached a top speed of nearly 600 km/h in 2007, when it broke the world record for speed of a train running on ordinary tracks.

574.83 KM/H

The top speed of the world's fastest train.

ALSTOM V150

The locomotive of the Alstom V150 is fitted with powerful electric motors. There is one locomotive at either end of the train. When the train reaches the end of its journey, it does not need to be turned around to go back in the other direction.

EMERGENCY EXIT
This allows the driver to leave the train if something goes wrong.

POWER

The locomotives are powered by electricity. This is supplied through the line that runs above the tracks.

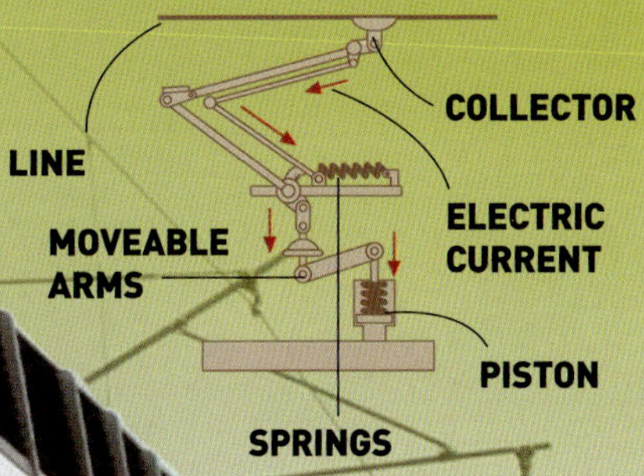

WHEELS AND RAILS

Each wheel on the train is powered by its own electric motor (below, left). The system of rails on which trains run (below, right) has remained largely unchanged for the last 150 years.

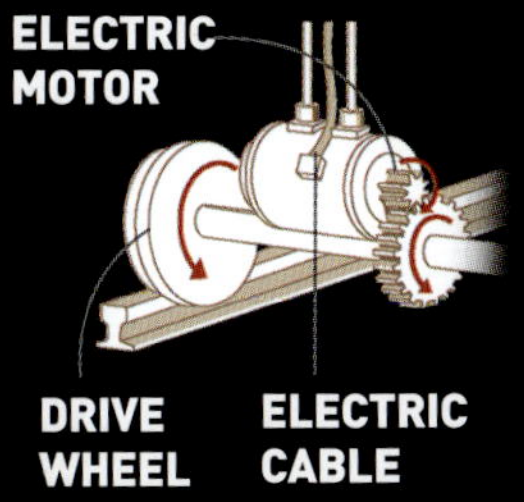

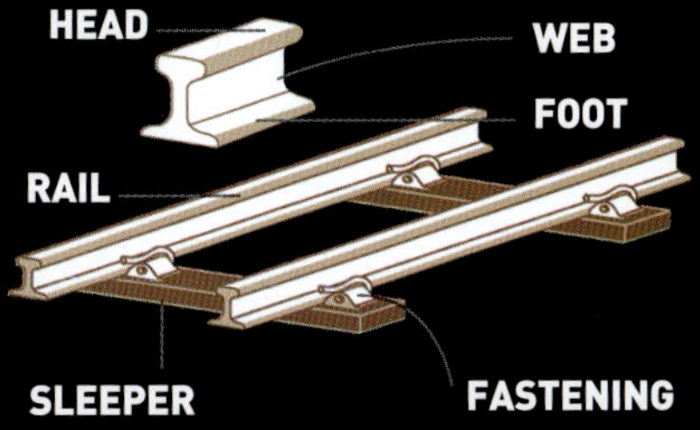

Aeroplanes

In 1903, the brothers Wilbur and Orville Wright made the first ever sustained powered flight in an aeroplane. Since then, aeroplanes have become a major means of transport. The first planes were made of wood, canvas and steel, and were small and light. Modern jet planes are large and heavy. However, all planes are able to fly because of the same basic rules of physics.

GIANT IN THE SKY

The Airbus 380 is the largest passenger jet in the world. It can carry up to 850 passengers. This giant aircraft can fly 15,200 km without stopping – the distance from New York to Hong Kong, at a speed of mach 0.85, or 945 km/h.

HOW DO THEY FLY?

The secret to flight is in the shape of the wings. This shape is called an aerofoil. Air passing over the aerofoil has to travel further than the air passing underneath it. This means that the air above the wing is travelling faster than the air underneath it. This causes lower air pressure above the wing than under it, which produces a force called lift. Lift pushes the wing upwards.

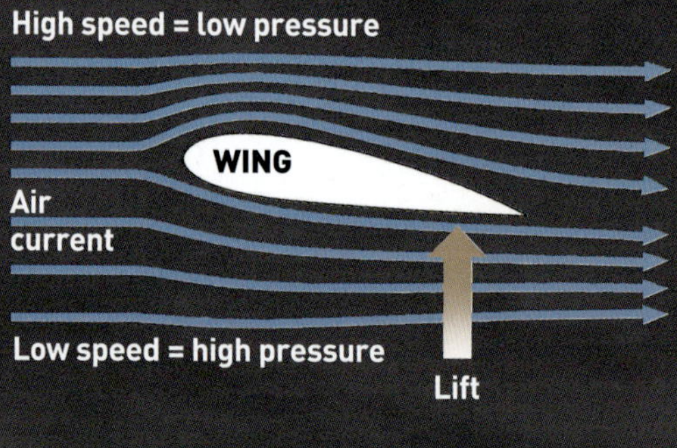

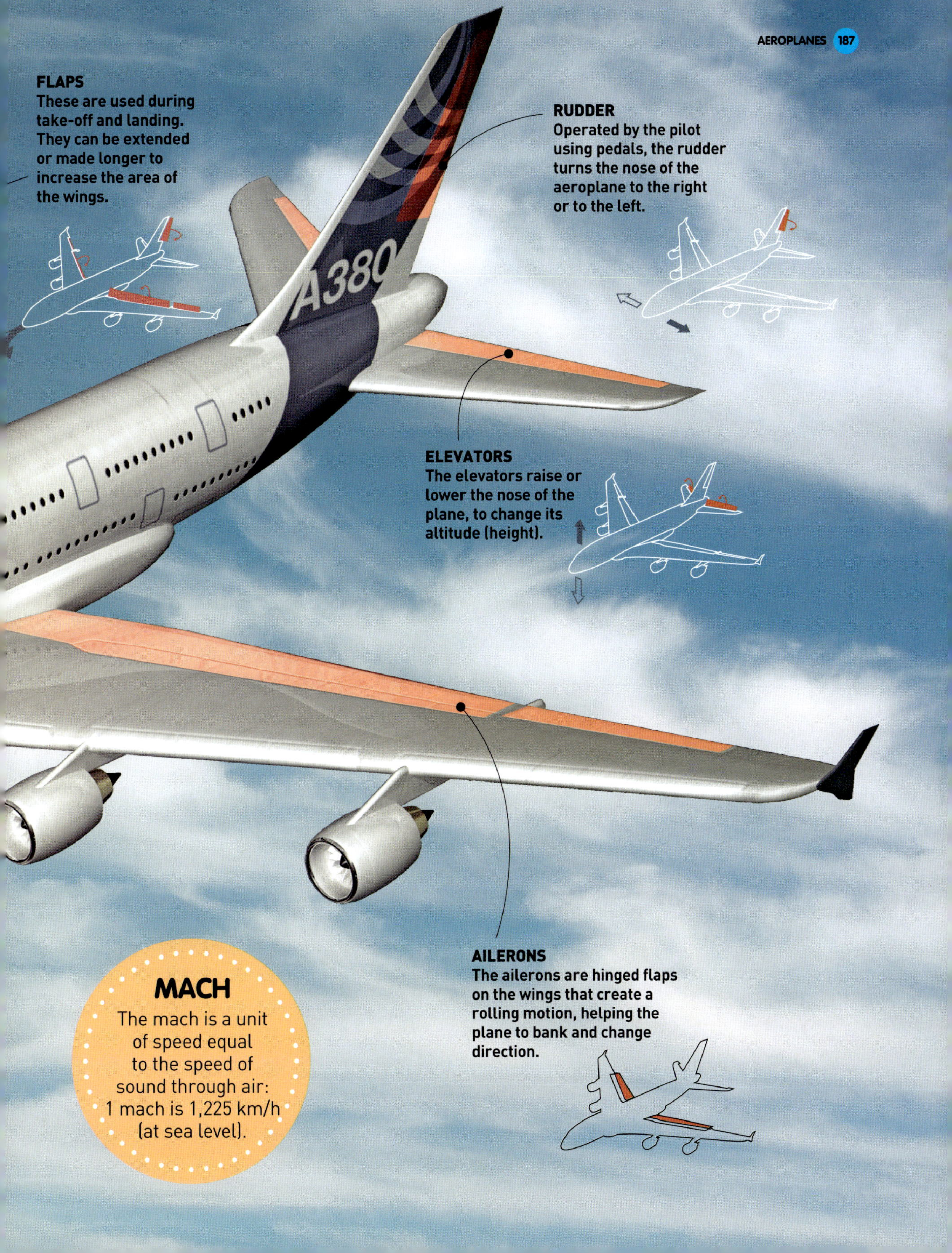

FLAPS
These are used during take-off and landing. They can be extended or made longer to increase the area of the wings.

RUDDER
Operated by the pilot using pedals, the rudder turns the nose of the aeroplane to the right or to the left.

ELEVATORS
The elevators raise or lower the nose of the plane, to change its altitude (height).

AILERONS
The ailerons are hinged flaps on the wings that create a rolling motion, helping the plane to bank and change direction.

MACH

The mach is a unit of speed equal to the speed of sound through air: 1 mach is 1,225 km/h (at sea level).

The conquest of space

In 1957, humans sent the first artificial satellite into space. Since then, there have been many expeditions into space. Some have been manned expeditions, but most have been unmanned, sending spacecraft far out into the Solar System, or satellites to orbit the Earth. We have learned a great deal about our Universe through these voyages of discovery.

RIVALRY
The United States and Russia have been the two main countries to explore space and are great rivals.

SATELLITES

Satellites are spacecraft that orbit the Earth. They are launched into space on rockets. Many different types of satellite are now orbiting the planet. They carry out jobs such as providing telecommunications, satellite television, information about the weather and information for military uses. They send the information they gather back to Earth using radio waves.

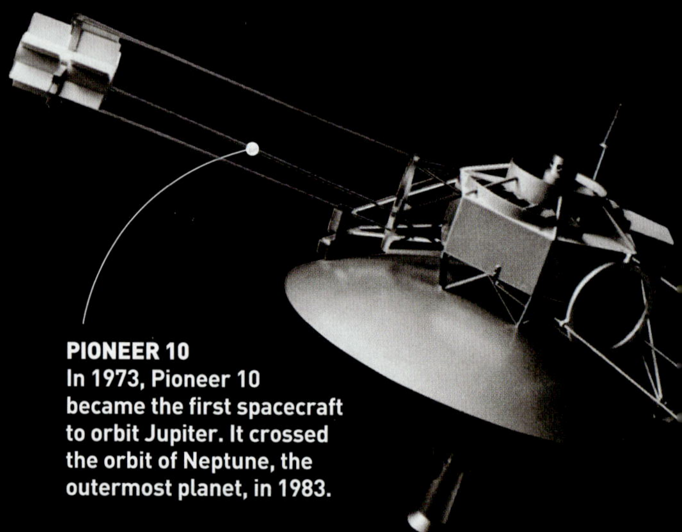

PIONEER 10
In 1973, Pioneer 10 became the first spacecraft to orbit Jupiter. It crossed the orbit of Neptune, the outermost planet, in 1983.

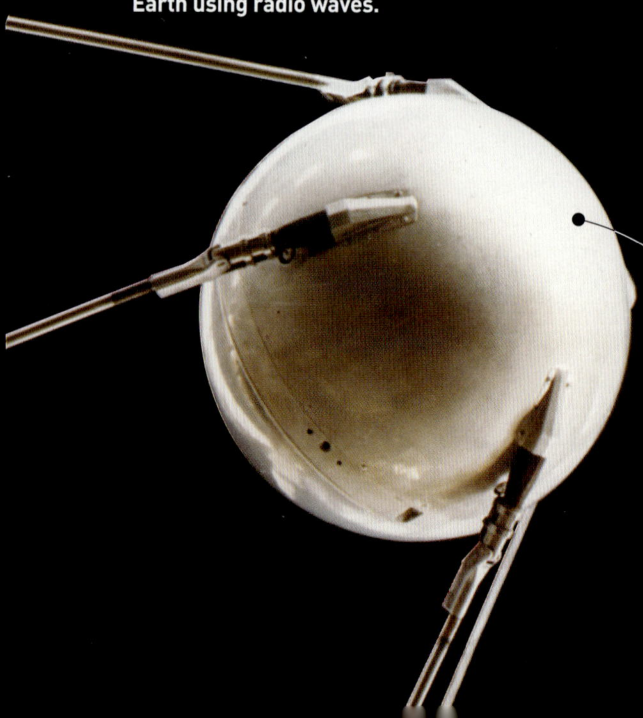

SPUTNIK I
The first ever satellite was launched into space by the Soviet Union in 1957.

SPACE PROBES

Space probes are unmanned spacecraft that explore space. They are sent to study natural objects such as planets and send back information about them. They are equipped with cameras, radios to send information to Earth, and solar panels, which produce the electricity that powers them.

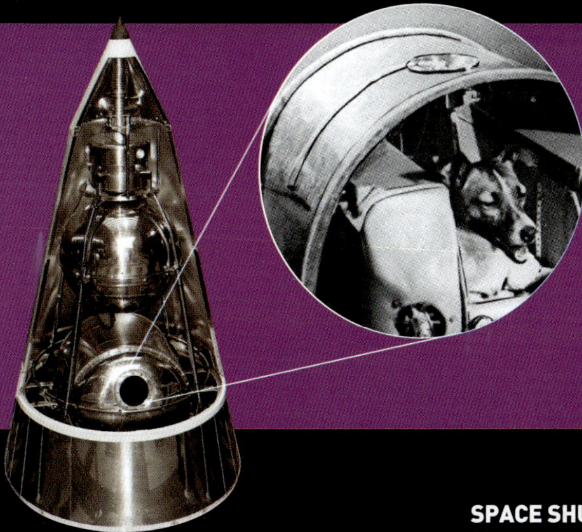

THE FIRST ANIMAL IN SPACE

For its second space flight, the Soviet Union launched a satellite called Sputnik II into orbit. This was the first space flight to carry a living being – a dog called Laika. The dog was connected to a machine that monitored its health. Since then, other animals, including monkeys, have been sent into space.

SPACE SHUTTLE
The space shuttle was a special kind of spacecraft that could return to Earth and fly many missions. After 135 missions, the Space Shuttle Program ended in 2011.

MANNED SPACE FLIGHT

Manned spacecraft carry equipment that provides air, water and food for the astronauts on board. They are also fitted out with areas for astronauts to relax. This equipment makes manned spaceflight very expensive. The first man in space was Yuri Gagarin, who orbited the Earth at a maximum height of 315 kilometres in 1961.

DISCOVERY
This space shuttle belongs to the United States and has completed many missions.

THOUSANDS

The number of artificial satellites that orbit the Earth.

Man and the Moon

In the 'Space Race' between the Soviet Union and the United States, the Soviets put the first man in space in 1961. Eight years later, the United States put the first man on the Moon. On 20 July 1969, the Apollo 11 mission reached the Moon and two of its astronauts took the first human steps on its surface. Five more Apollo missions reached the Moon, the last one in 1972.

THE JOURNEY

Apollo 11 took four days to travel from the Earth to the Moon. The astronauts stayed on the surface of the Moon for 21 hours 37 minutes.

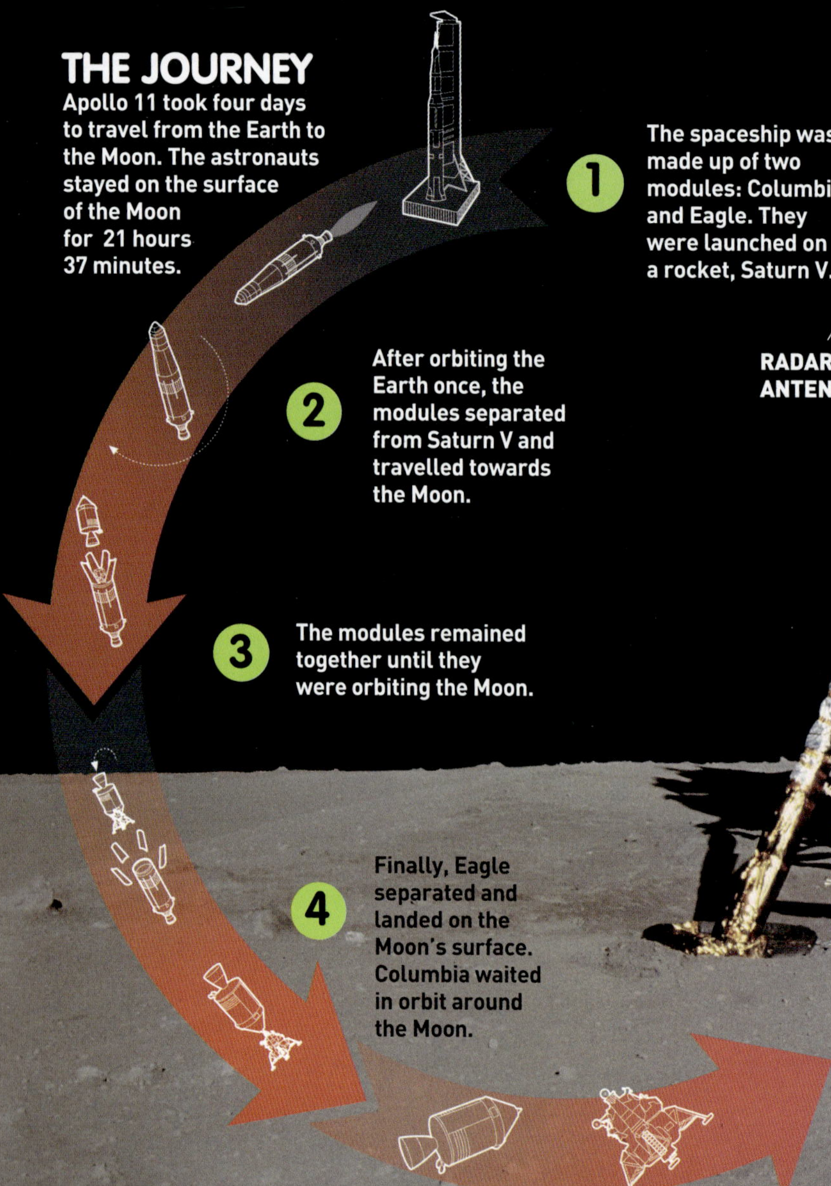

LATER MISSIONS

Apollo 11 was the first of six American missions to reach the Moon. Between 1969 and 1972, Apollos 12, 14, 15, 16 and 17 were all successful. Only Apollo 13 failed to make it, being forced to return to the Earth after an oxygen tank exploded. After six successful Moon landings, the Apollo program ended, and nobody has been back to the Moon since.

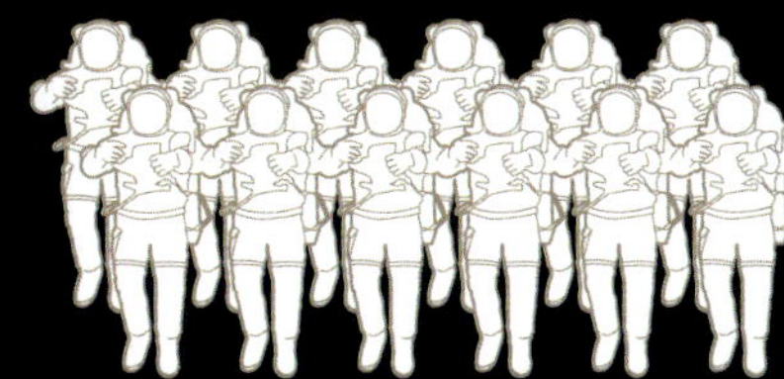

12 ASTRONAUTS HAVE WALKED ON THE MOON.

384,400 KILOMETRES

The average distance from the Earth to the Moon.

CREW

Three highly-experienced astronauts made up the crew. All three had taken part in previous missions.

NEIL ARMSTRONG
The first human being to set foot on the Moon.

MICHAEL COLLINS
Remained in Columbia while his two colleagues landed on the Moon.

EDWIN ALDRIN
The second human being to set foot on the Moon.

SMALL STEP

As he stepped onto the Moon, Amstrong said: 'That's one small step for a man, one giant leap for mankind.'

Computers

In the past few decades, computers have come a long way – from huge calculating machines that took up a whole room, to the home computers and laptops of today. Today, computers are important to our everyday lives at school, at work and at home. Research is now being done using DNA to build new computers that could be even more powerful than those we have today.

INSIDE THE TOWER

The tower of a computer contains many cables, boards and circuits. Each component, or part, has its own job to do.

POWER
Electricity comes from an outside source. A fan stops the computer from overheating.

CPU
This is the computer's 'brain', where it processes data.

VIDEO CARD
This processes data sent from the CPU so that it can be displayed on a monitor.

HARD DRIVE
This stores information on a magnetic recording device.

TOWER
A protective case.

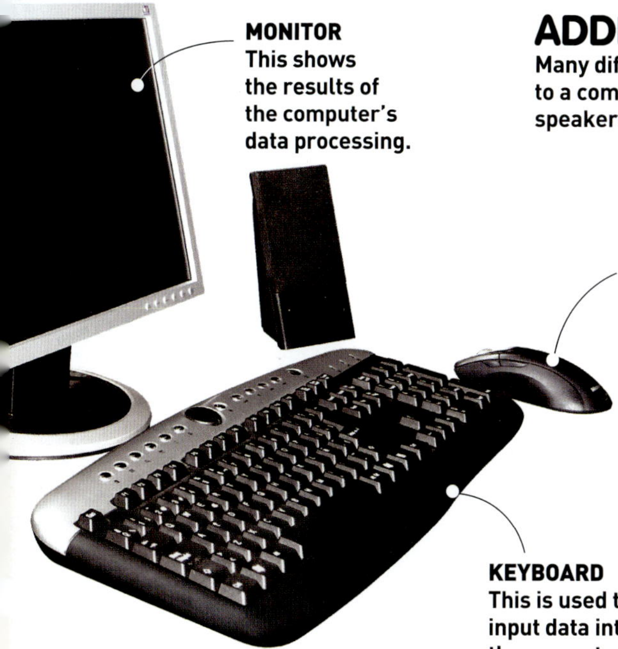

ADDED VALUE

Many different devices can be connected to a computer, including monitors, speakers, scanners and printers.

1970

The year the microprocessor was invented, making computers much cheaper to produce.

PIXEL

A pixel is the smallest or most basic unit of a digital image on a computer monitor.

MOTHERBOARD

The motherboard is a central board to which all the other parts of a computer are connected. The parts communicate with each other via the motherboard.

226,800 KG

The weight of one of the fastest computers ever made, IBM's 'Roadrunner'.

The Internet

The Internet is a computer network that extends across the globe. To access the Internet from our homes, our computers connect with another far more powerful computer called a server. The server then sends our request along routes across the entire world. Finally, the reply arrives back at our computer. The whole process can take just a fraction of a second to complete.

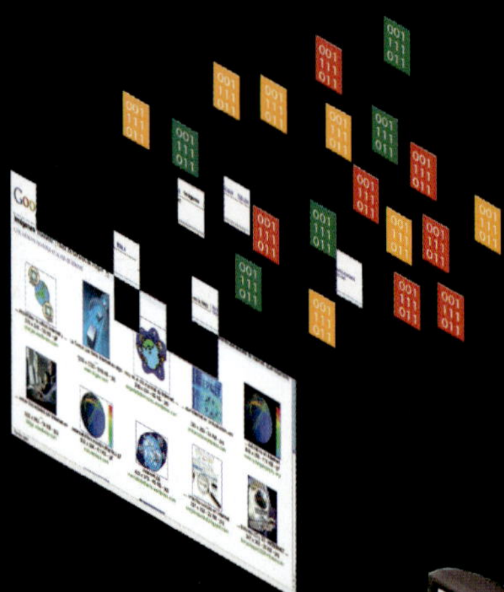

1 COMPUTER

The computer sends its request for information to the server in 'packets'.

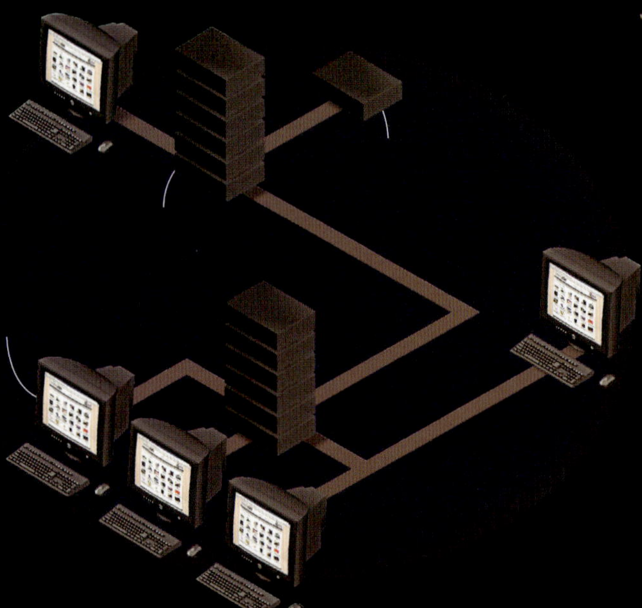

2 SOURCE SERVER

This reads the requests from many different computers and sends them on to the target servers.

3 ROUTES

Different networks are connected to each other by routes. A router decides which is the best route to send the information along.

4

TARGET SERVER

Sends information back to the server that requested it.

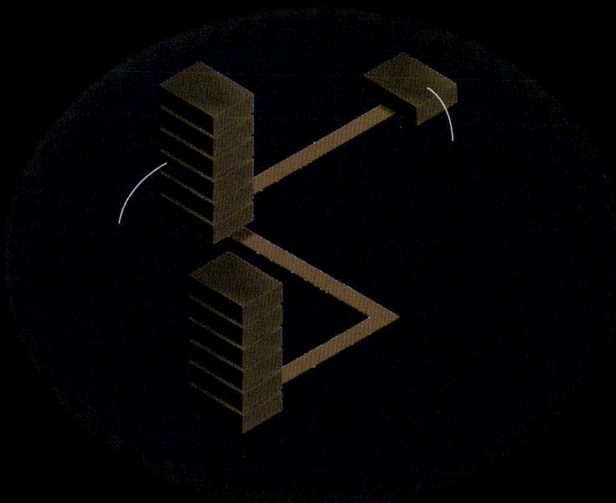

56%

The proportion of websites that are written in English, the most common language on the Internet.

5

RECEIVING THE INFORMATION

When the information reaches the computer, it is used to display the results of the request.

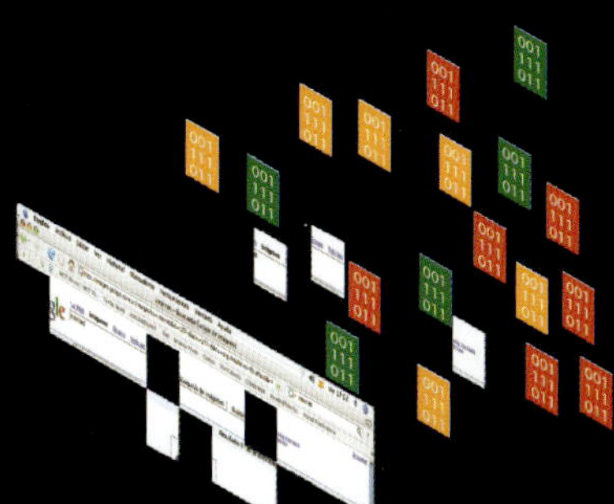

2.3 BILLION

The number of Internet users at the beginning of 2009. The number is constantly growing.

ASIA

The continent with the greatest number of Internet users. (45%), followed by the United States (23%) and Europe (22%).

Sources of energy

Ever since the invention of the steam engine, the world has kept moving using energy made from sources that cannot be renewed. Fossil fuels, such as oil and gas, will probably start to run out over the next few decades. Other sources of energy, such as the force of rivers, will never run out, but can cause damage to the environment. One of the biggest challenges facing us today is to find a way to produce energy that is cheap, clean and from a source that will not run out.

RECYCLING RUBBISH
Much of the waste that we produce can be treated in biodigesters, producing heat, electricity and fertilizers.

GROUND HEAT
In volcanic areas, geothermal power stations use heat deep under the Earth's crust to make electricity.

WIND POWER
One of the most promising energy sources comes from windmills. They produce a good supply of electricity in windy areas. Some people object to the windmills because of their noise and how they look.

10%

The percentage of the world's oil that comes from Saudi Arabia, the largest producer of all.

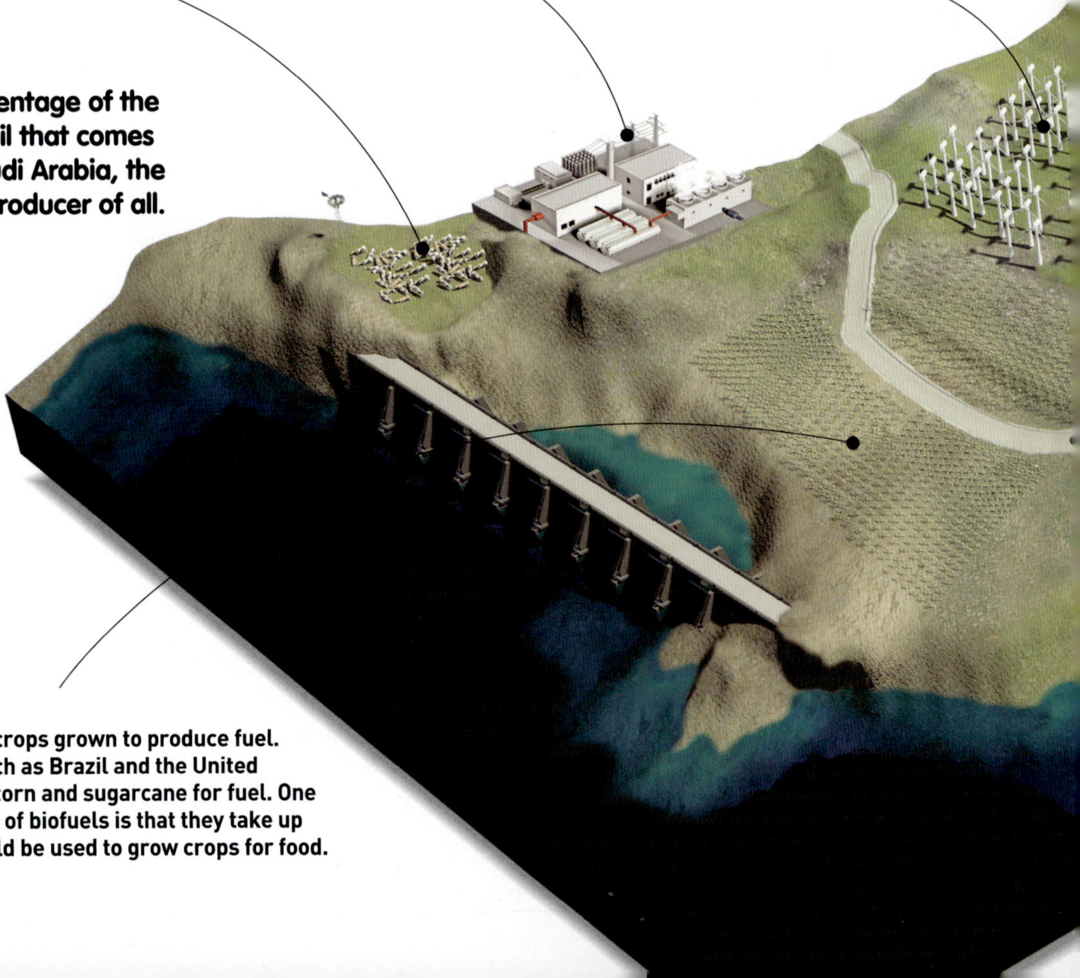

BIOFUELS
Biofuels are crops grown to produce fuel. Countries such as Brazil and the United States grow corn and sugarcane for fuel. One disadvantage of biofuels is that they take up land that could be used to grow crops for food.

CLEAN FUELS

As well as its ease of use, what an energy source does to the environment is a very important factor when deciding whether or not to use it.

THE GIFT OF THE SUN

The Sun is a clean source of energy that can provide heat and electricity, using, for example, solar panels. However, several problems need to be solved to make it a good source of energy on a large scale.

WATER POWER

The energy of rivers can be converted into electricity cheaply and cleanly in hydroelectric plants. However, building dams on rivers in order to convert this energy can cause flooding.

OIL AND GAS

Oil and gas are very good sources of energy. However, reserves are starting to run out. Burning oil and gas gives off carbon dioxide, which causes global warming.

NUCLEAR POWER

A clean, powerful source of energy that will not run out, nuclear power can also be extremely dangerous. The technology it needs is very complex and if it goes wrong, accidents can lead to the release of deadly radioactivity into the environment.

Seven wonders of the ancient world

These seven pieces of architecture were thought by the ancient Greeks to be the most spectacular in the world. They were proof of how creative people could be. This list is taken from a short poem by Antipater of Sidon, written around 125 BC, but earlier lists were written by the historian Herodotus and the engineer Philo of Byzantium.

2 HANGING GARDENS OF BABYLON The Hanging Gardens were built during the sixth century BC. At the time, Babylon, on the banks of the River Euphrates, was a powerful city.

3 TEMPLE OF ARTEMIS The temple was built in the city of Ephesus, Turkey, and dedicated to the goddess Artemis, called Diana by the Romans. King Croesus of Lydia had it built.

4 STATUE OF ZEUS AT OLYMPIA Made of marble and gold, this huge statue of the god Zeus was 12 metres high. It was made by the Greek sculptor Phidias in about 432 BC.

2,300,000

The number of stone blocks that were used to make the Great Pyramid of Giza.

1 GREAT PYRAMID OF GIZA

Of all the seven wonders, the Great Pyramid is the oldest and the only one still standing. It was made for the ancient Egyptian pharaoh Khufu (also known by his Greek name, Cheops). The architect Hemiunu designed the pyramid. It was finished in about 2540 BC, and is just outside the Egyptian capital city, Cairo.

IRAQ

The Hanging Gardens of Babylon were in an area that now forms part of the country Iraq.

5 TOMB OF MAUSOLUS

Made of white marble, this enormous tomb was built in the city of Halicarnassus in Turkey. It was made for Mausolus, the ruler of Caria, on his death in 353 BC.

6 COLOSSUS OF RHODES

This giant statue of the Greek god Helios was built on the island of Rhodes in the third century BC. It was made of bronze plates placed over an iron frame.

7 LIGHTHOUSE OF ALEXANDRIA

This lighthouse was built in the third century BC, on the island of Pharos near Alexandria in Egypt. It was a tower nearly 120 metres high.

Great Wall of China

The Great Wall is made up of hundreds of smaller walls that were built to defend China from invasion. It stretches thousands of kilometres across the north of the country. Walkways and corridors allowed troops to move quickly in the event of an attack.

LEGEND
The wall was called 'the stone dragon' because it resembled a dragon looking to the west.

TOWERS
Placed every 500 metres, the towers were used to keep watch. When enemy troops were spotted, smoke would be sent up from the towers.

SMOKE SIGNALS
One column of smoke from a tower signalled fewer than 500 enemies. Two columns meant a larger force. At night, fires were used instead.

WALLS
The walls are an average height of 6.5 metres, going up to 10 metres in places. The base of the walls is about 6.5 metres wide.

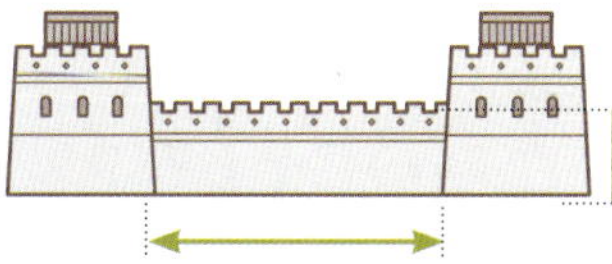

The distance from one tower to the next is about 500 metres.

SIGNALS
Enemy attacks were communicated from tower to tower.

FACT FILE

LOCATION China
TYPE Defensive construction
WHEN BUILT
From 221 BC to AD 1644
SIZE
6,400 kilometres long; 6–10 metres high, 6 metres wide

BUILDING
The sections built during the Ming Dynasty, which are now a tourist attraction, are made of stone and covered with bricks. Other sections are made of clay or limestone.

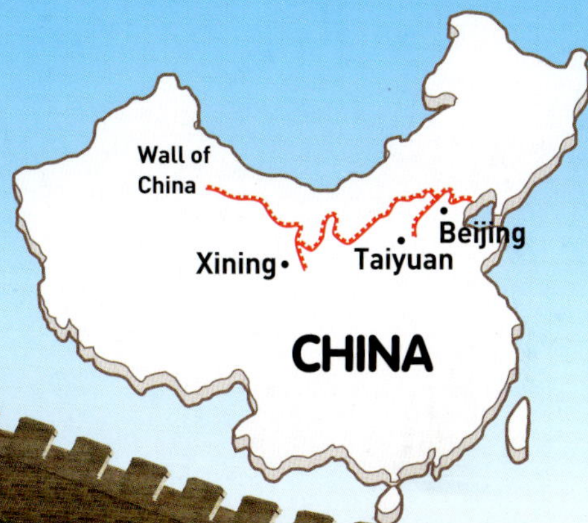

BUILDING TECHNIQUES

The work was carried out during the Qin, Han and Ming dynasties. The oldest part of the wall dates from the fifth century BC. The emperor Qin Shi Huang joined up the different sections. During the Ming dynasty, it was rebuilt using a layer of mud bricks.

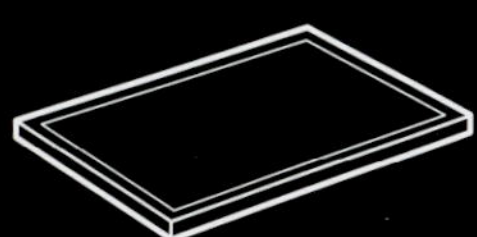

QIN DYNASTY
The first walls were made of earth and stone.

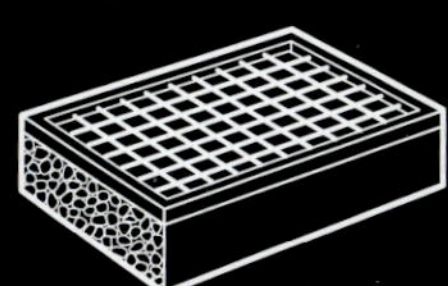

HAN DYNASTY
Wooden frames were filled with a mix of water and fine gravel.

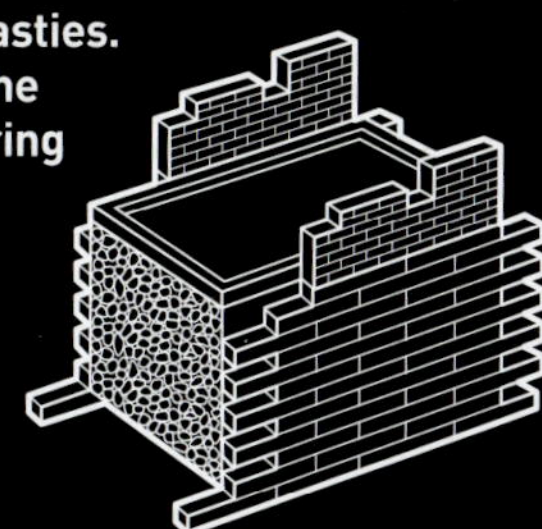

MING DYNASTY
A mix of stone and earth was used, covered with a layer of mud bricks.

6,400 KM
The length of the wall, from the border with Korea to the Gobi Desert.

Machu Picchu

The abandoned city of Machu Picchu sits high up in the Andes Mountains in southern Peru. This masterpiece of architecture and engineering was built during the 15th century, probably on the orders of the Sapa Inca (king) Pachacuti. It was largely forgotten until the beginning of the 20th century.

FACT FILE

LOCATION 112 km northwest of Cuzco
ALTITUDE 2,430 m above sea level
AREA 32,592 hectares

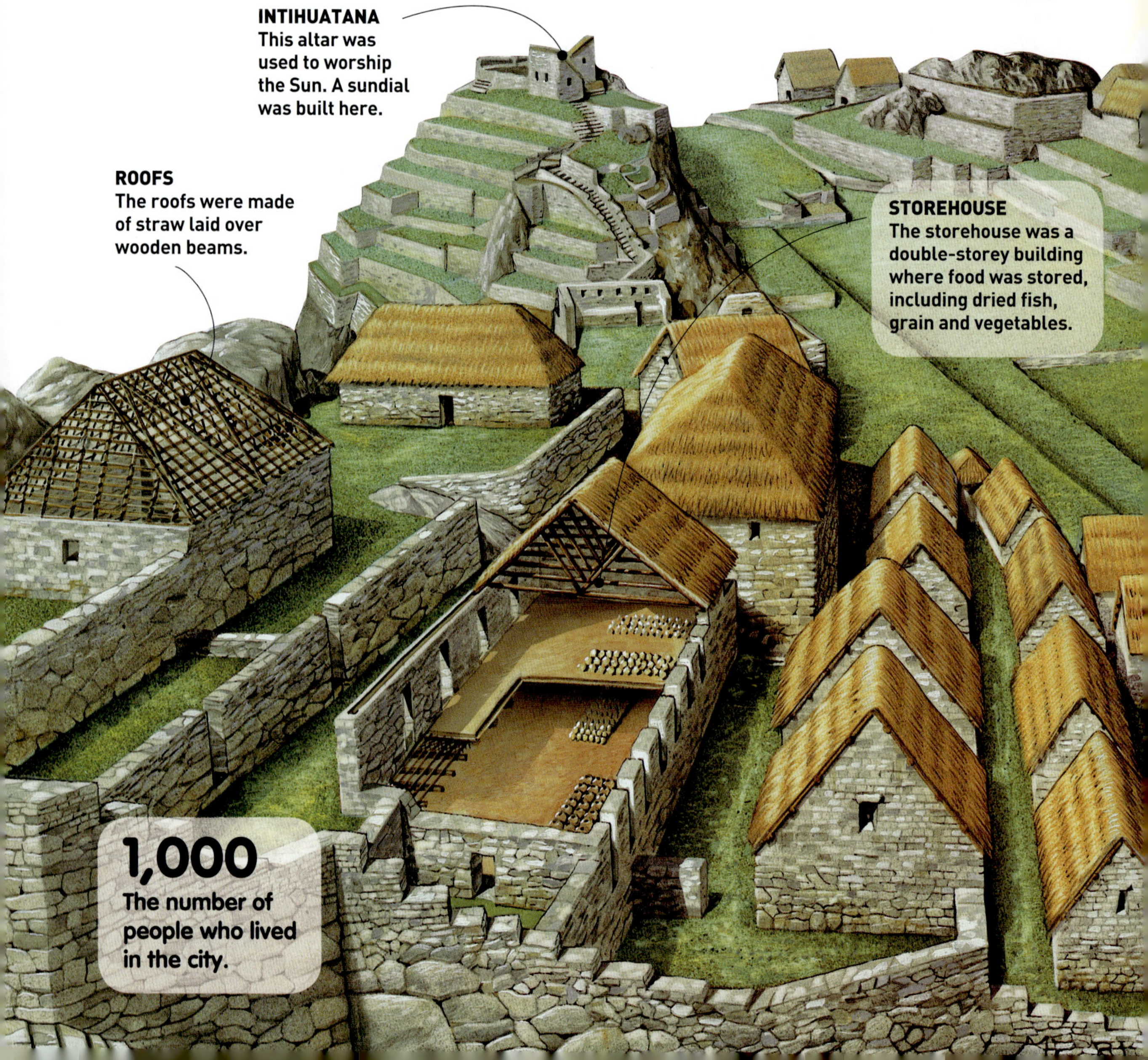

GRANITE

All the buildings that are still standing are made of a stone called granite.

HOUSES OF THE NUSTA (PRINCESSES)
The grandest houses were situated in the royal quarter and had stone carved beds, their own bathroom and a private terrace.

TEMPLE OF THE SUN
The temple was a large building that only the Sapa Inca and his priests were allowed to enter.

THE NATURAL SETTING

The city was built between two steep peaks, overlooking the raging Urubamba River. A 400-metre-long wall separated the city from the farmland. The city was entered along the Inca Way and the Inca Bridge.

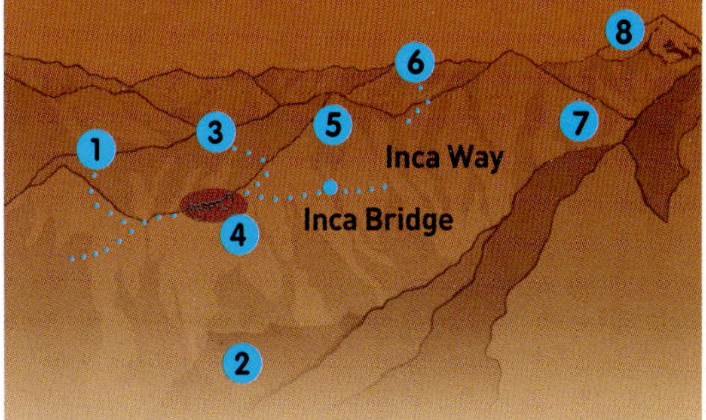

1. Wayna Picchu Peak
2. Urubamba River
3. Intipunku
4. Machu Picchu
5. Machu Picchu Peak
6. Phuyupatamarca
7. Aobamba River
8. Salkantay mountain

CROPS
The city was surrounded by terraces for growing crops.

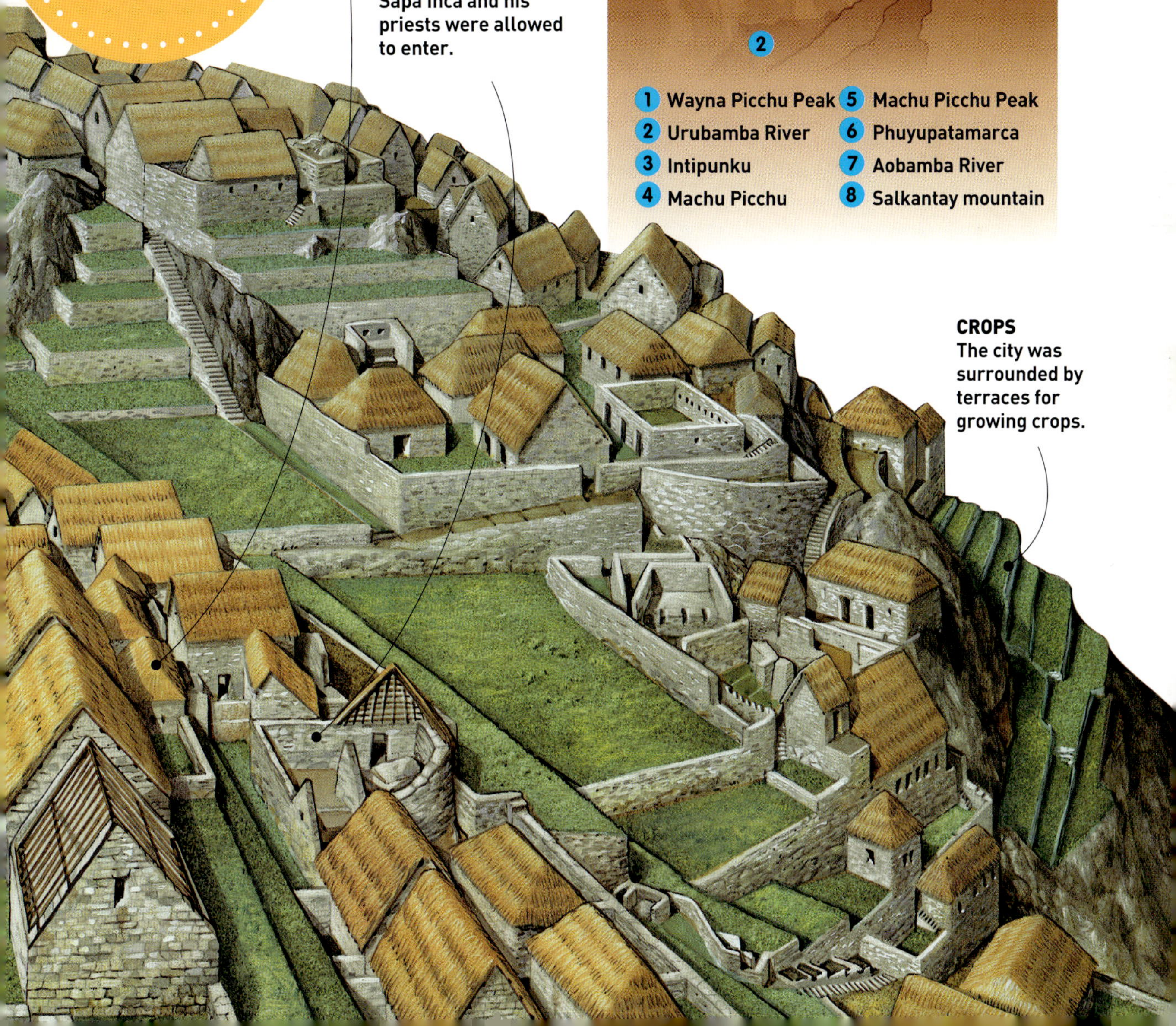

Taj Mahal

The Taj Mahal is a beautiful mausoleum, or tomb, next to the River Yamuna in the Indian city of Agra. It was built in the 17th century by the Mogul emperor Shah Jahan to honour his wife Mumtaz Mahal, who had died in childbirth. They are now both buried in this sparkling mausoleum built of white marble with precious stones laid into it.

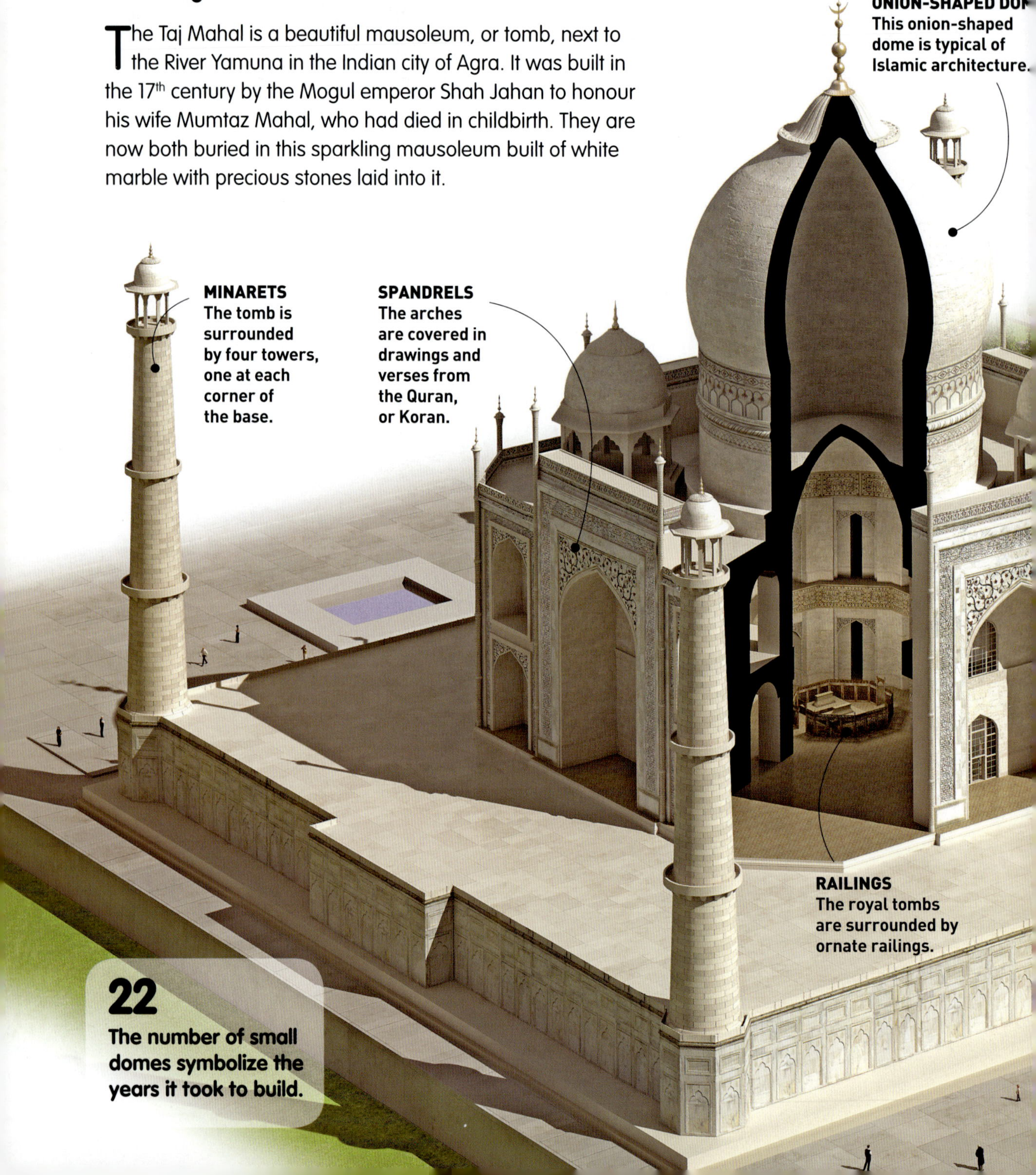

LIGHT

Light enters the central palace through the precious stones encrusted into the marble.

GARDENS
The gardens are divided into 16 sections, with many beds of flowers, raised paths, rows of trees, fountains, streams and wide ponds. The water reflects the majestic palace.

PLINTH
The mausoleum sits on a rectangular base, or plinth. It adds height to the building, making it look more impressive.

THE TOMBS

Made of marble decorated with rhinestones, the tombs are found in the main building. They are decorated by a ring of lotus flowers.

AN UNINTERRUPTED VIEW
The palace is at the back, with fountains and gardens at the front. This gives visitors an uninterrupted view of the mausoleum, allowing them to see how large it is.

The Statue of Liberty

Overlooking the mouth of the Hudson River, to the south of Manhattan Island, New York, the Statue of Liberty is one of the most famous monuments in the world. The full name of the colossal statue is 'Liberty Enlightening the World'. It was a gift from France to the United States in 1886, to mark 100 years of American independence.

FACT FILE

STRUCTURE
The statue is given its strength by an internal tower. A skeleton around the tower keeps the outer layer of copper in place.

PLAQUE
On the pedestal, there was a plaque with the poem 'The New Colossus' by Emma Lazarus written on it. This plaque is now on show inside the statue.

BASE
The base is square and rests on a star-shaped plinth. It weighs 27,000 tonnes.

MUSEUMS
There are two museums at the foot of the statue.

THE DESIGN

The design is reminiscent of the famous Colossus of Rhodes. It was the work of French sculptor Frédéric Auguste Bartholdi. The engineer Gustave Eiffel designed the internal structure. The architect Eugène Viollet-le-Duc chose the copper used in the construction.

Frédéric Auguste Bartholdi

TORCH
The torch was originally made of copper. In 1916, the copper was swapped for 600 pieces of yellow glass, making it glow. The flame is covered in sheets of gold.

CROWN
There are seven rays on the crown. They symbolize the seven seas and seven continents of the world.

FIRST SIGHT

The statue was the first thing European immigrants saw when they arrived in the United States by boat.

HEAD
It is five metres from the chin to the forehead. To reach the head, visitors must climb 354 stairs.

LIFT
Visitors can reach the tenth floor by lift. The last 12 floors must be climbed on foot.

92.99 M

The height of the statue from the base to the torch.

TABLET
The tablet has the date of American independence written on it and represents the law, or rights.

TUNIC
The long tunic is in the manner of classical Greek goddesses.

Modern architecture

At the start of the 20th century, artists of all kinds were inventing new ways to express themselves. In architecture, new styles were used to design buildings. These included Rationalism, whose main architect was Le Corbusier, and Organic Architecture, whose most famous figure was Frank Lloyd Wright. Many more new styles of architecture were developed as the century continued.

FALLINGWATER

Designed by Frank Lloyd Wright, this is an example of Organic Architecture. The building is made to fit in with the landscape in which it is built, including the waterfalls, rocks and plants.

SYDNEY OPERA HOUSE

Built in the harbour of the Australian city of Sydney, the opera house is made in the shape of a huge sail. Designed by architect Jørn Utzon, it was completed in 1973.

COUNTRY VILLA
La Villa Savoye near Paris was designed by Le Corbusier and built in 1931. It has recently been renovated and is now open to the public.

FACADES
Each outside wall (facade) is different. Large windows let in plenty of light.

COLUMNS
The first floor and the terrace are supported by columns leaving a large open space beneath.

STAIRWAY
Stairs lead from the ground floor to the first floor and a terrace on the second floor.

MACHINES
Le Corbusier described houses as 'machines for living in'.

COLOURS
The stark white outside is very different from the brightly coloured walls on the inside of the building.

LE CORBUSIER
Swiss architect Le Corbusier was a pioneer of modern architecture. He designed buildings (right) with sharp lines, plain colours, and no decoration.

Tower block, Marseilles, France, 1947–1952

Notre Dame de Haut, Ronchamp, France, 1954

Prehistoric art

Humans have made art for thousands of years, drawing and making objects that come from their imaginations. The first drawings that we know of were made on cave walls more than 30,000 years ago. These and other early works of art often show what their makers were thinking about life and death.

ALTAMIRA
The cave of Altamira, Spain, was painted about 15,000 years ago. It is one of the finest examples of ancient cave paintings in the world.

SCULPTURES

The first sculptures were of animals that have been found on the ends of tools. Another common type of early sculpture is called a Venus figure. This takes the form of a rounded female figure, and symbolizes Mother Earth, who was believed to be the source of all life.

ARCHITECTURE

The oldest buildings are those made of huge slabs of stone. These buildings often had religious or ritual importance to the people who built them.

STONEHENGE
A circle of stones in southern England, Stonehenge is believed to have been a place for religious ceremonies, but nobody knows for sure.

CAVE PAINTINGS

Drawings of people and animals were made on the rocky sides of caves thousands of years ago.

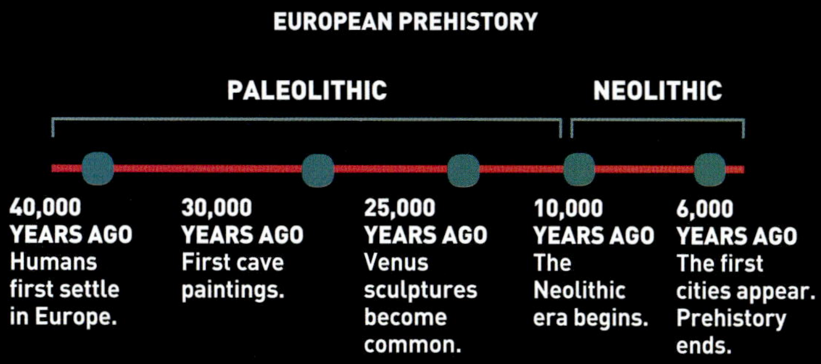

FIGURES
The most common figures in cave paintings are animals such as mammoths, bison, hyenas and horses.

REALISM
Animals are drawn very realistically. Humans appear very rarely, and are drawn in much less detail.

COLOURS
The paints were made of natural substances. Black, made from carbon, and red, made from iron oxide, were the most used colours.

Modern art

In the 19th and 20th centuries, painting changed a lot. With the invention of the camera, painters no longer felt they had to paint as things were in real life – this could be recorded by photographs. Artists began to try different approaches with colours and shapes. New schools such as Impressionism, Expressionism and Cubism were started by painters exploring new ideas. Many of these new schools first appeared in Europe.

COLOURS
Painters began to use bright colours to capture the light of a specific time of day.

***The Luncheon on the Grass*, Edouard Manet, 1863**

SHOCKING IMAGES

The most revolutionary paintings of the 19th century appeared in France. Many people were shocked by works that showed naked people doing everyday things. Edouard Manet's '*The Luncheon on the Grass*' showed a naked woman sitting in a park. Before then, only mythical figures had been shown naked. Manet was an important artist in the school called Impressionism.

***Cruel Tales*, Paul Gauguin, 1902**

AFRICAN INFLUENCES

Along with Paul Cézanne and Vincent Van Gogh, French painter Paul Gauguin was one of the most important artists of the 19th century. He was inspired by art that was once thought to be 'primitive'. He was also influenced by African art.

REVOLUTION

French painter Paul Cézanne revolutionized painting by drawing a scene containing lots of points of view. To Cézanne, any object could be painted as one of three shapes: cylinder, cone or sphere. One of the most important movements of the 20th century, Cubism developed from Cézanne's work.

SPACE
Instead of seeing the whole scene as one image, Cézanne painted each individual object as if it were a sculpture on its own.

Apples and Oranges, Paul Cézanne, 1899

AVANT-GARDE

In the early 20th century, new art schools developed that were called avant-gardes. They introduced new ways to look at art and new ideas about what art could be. The most important avant-garde movements include Expressionism, Futurism, Cubism, Surrealism and Dada. It was no longer the job of the artist to create an accurate representation of the visible world.

Guitar on a Chair, Juan Gris, 1913

FORMS
Cubists such as Spanish painter Juan Gris tried to represent objects as they might appear in our imaginations rather than in real life.

The Modern Olympic Games

In Ancient Greece, athletic events called Olympic Games were held at festivals to honour the god Zeus. In the late 19th century, Pierre de Coubertin was inspired by the Anicent Greeks to start the modern Olympic Games. The first Modern Olympics took place in Athens in 1896, and now takes place every four years.

GAMES OF PEACE

In ancient Greece, treaties were signed so that wars were not fought during the Olympics. De Coubertin hoped that his modern Olympics would also allow nations to come together peacefully, and would help people to have a better understanding of each other.

SILVER MEDAL
This silver medal is from the 1908 London Olympics.

PIERRE DE COUBERTIN
Frenchman Pierre de Coubertin (1863–1937) founded the Modern Olympic Games.

MEN ONLY

As in the ancient Games, women were not allowed to compete at Athens in 1896.

MARATHON TROPHY
Frenchman Michel Bréal donated this cup for the winner of the Olympic marathon.

43

The number of events at Athens in 1896, including various athletics events, gymnastics, swimming, shooting and wrestling.

ATHLETICS CHAMPION

Greek shepherd Spyridon Louis won the first Olympic marathon in front of his home crowd. The marathon is a road race over a distance of 42.195 kilometres. In addition to running events, the sport of athletics included field events such as the discus, the javelin and the long jump.

OLYMPIC PARTICIPATION

YEAR	HOST	COUNTRIES	ATHLETES
1896	Athens	12	280
1900	Paris	24	997
1904	St Louis	12	645
1908	London	22	2,008
1912	Stockholm	28	2,407
1920	Antwerp	29	2,626
1924	Paris	44	3,100
1928	Amsterdam	46	2,833
1932	Los Angeles	37	1,332
1936	Berlin	49	3,963
1948	London	59	4,104
1952	Helsinki	69	4,955
1956	Melbourne	67	3,314
1960	Rome	83	5,338
1964	Tokyo	93	5,151
1968	Mexico City	112	5,516
1972	Munich	122	7,134
1976	Montreal	92	6,084
1980	Moscow	81	5,179
1984	Los Angeles	140	6,829
1988	Seoul	159	8,391
1992	Barcelona	169	9,356
1996	Atlanta	197	10,318
2000	Sydney	199	10,651
2004	Athens	201	10,625
2008	Beijing	204	11,028

Religious belief

For thousands of years, humans have asked questions about life, death and how the universe began. Many religions try to answer these questions. Religions also teach people right from wrong and try to help people to live peacefully with each other. Religious ceremonies and rituals, such as prayer, allow people to come together to share their faith.

LIFE AND DEATH

Many religions answer questions about dying. Some religions teach that we have a soul that keeps on living after our bodies have died.

NO GOD
Buddhism does not have a god. Instead, Buddhists live in a way that is inspired by the life of the Buddha.

CHRISTIANITY
Like Judaism and Islam, Christianity teaches there is one God.

MANY GODS OR ONE GOD

Some religions teach that there are many different gods, each of which is in charge of a particular aspect of life. Other religions teach that there is just one God.

HINDUISM
Hindus worship many different gods.

GROUP WORSHIP

Religious ceremonies often involve large gatherings of people, who come together to pray. In some religions, the faithful are expected to undertake a religious journey, called a pilgrimage. Muslims, for example, should visit the holy city of Mecca at least once. Several million pilgrims visit Mecca every year.

TEMPLES
Many religions hold their ceremonies in special buildings, called temples, churches, synagogues, gurdwaras or mosques.

PRAYER
Prayer is a ritual in which the faithful believe that they are communicating with their god. People pray in groups or in private.

RITUALS

In every religion, believers take part in rituals. Many rituals are linked to important events, such as birth, marriage and death. The rituals are normally led by a religious leader, such as a priest or an imam. In some religions, a person called a shaman acts as a link between the living and the dead.

FAITH

Many of the answers provided by religions cannot be proved to be correct. They are believed through an act of faith.

World religions

There are many religions in the world, from those followed by a very small number of people to others, such as Christianity and Islam, which have hundreds of millions of believers worldwide. Buddhism and Hinduism are very important religions in Asia. Many people follow traditional animist religions which hold that there are spirits living with us.

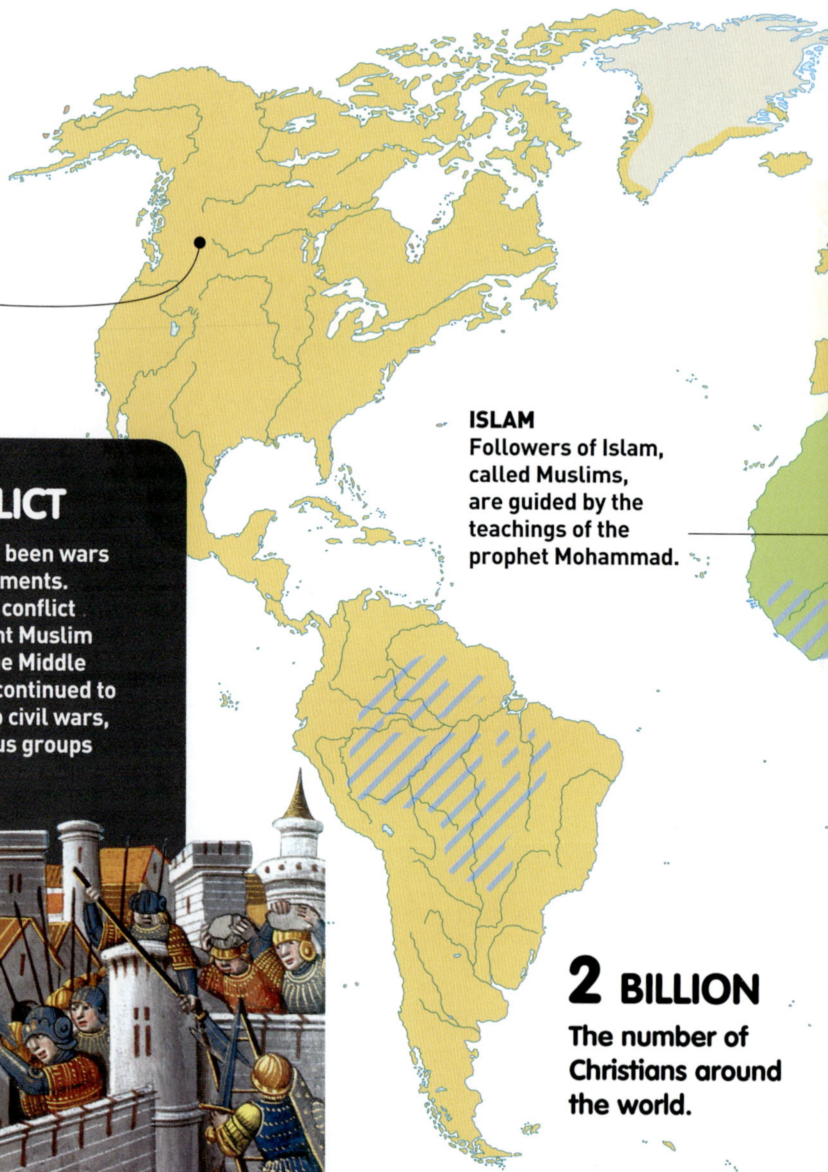

CHRISTIANITY
The largest religion in the world, Christianity is divided into many different churches, such as Catholic, Protestant and Orthodox.

ISLAM
Followers of Islam, called Muslims, are guided by the teachings of the prophet Mohammad.

RELIGIOUS CONFLICT

Throughout history, there have been wars started over religious disagreements. The Crusades were a medieval conflict in which Christian armies fought Muslim forces over the Holy Land (in the Middle East). Religious conflicts have continued to the present day, contributing to civil wars, persecution of minority religious groups and terrorism.

2 BILLION
The number of Christians around the world.

EAST-ASIAN RELIGIONS

A large number of religions began in East Asia, including Taoism and Confucianism, which are followed by more than 500 million people between them. In Japan, Shintoism is the major religion – its followers believe in honouring their ancestors.

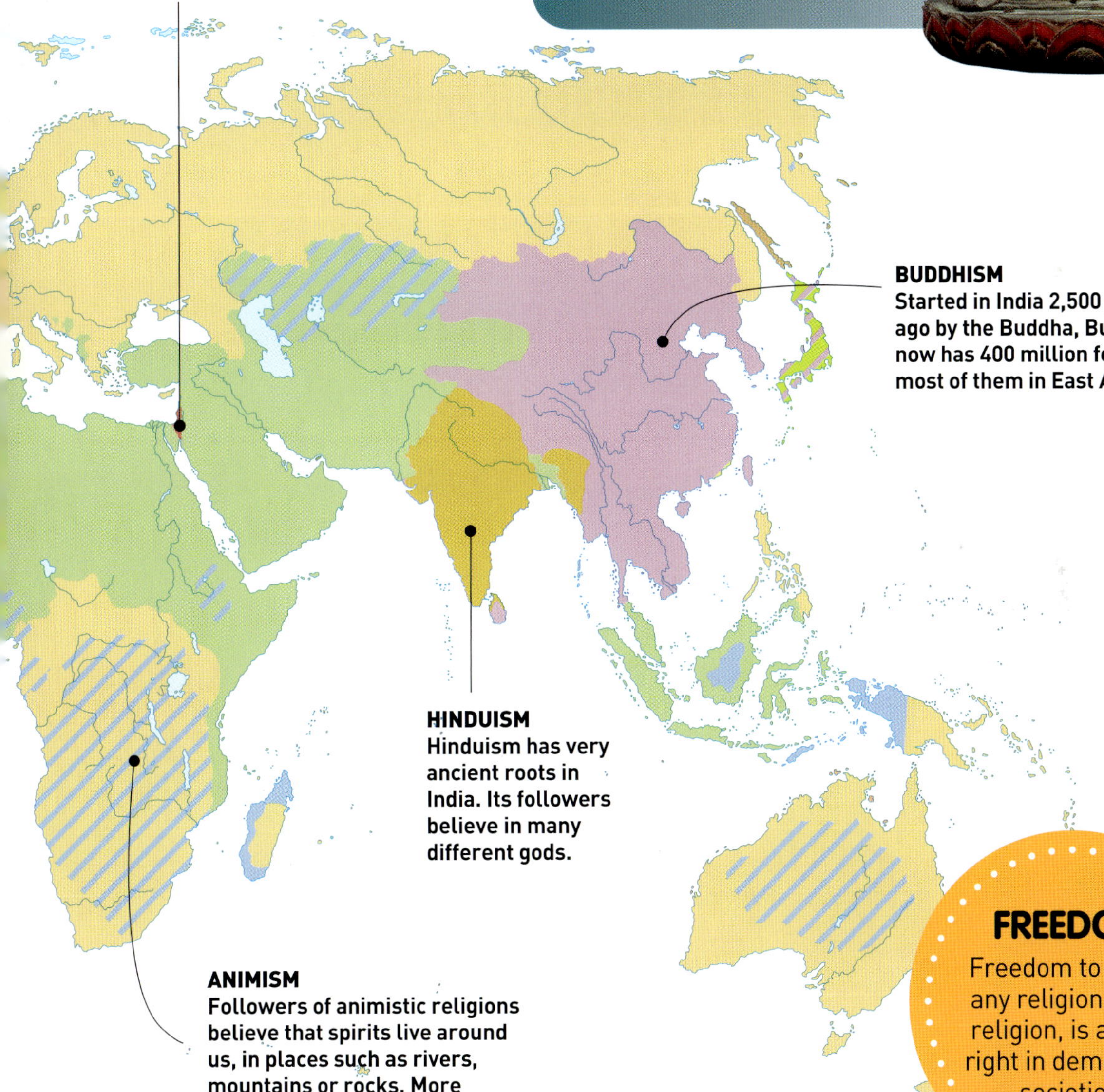

JUDAISM
Although it is a small religion, Christianity and Islam have their roots in Judaism. Its 16 million followers live mostly in Israel and the United States.

BUDDHISM
Started in India 2,500 years ago by the Buddha, Buddhism now has 400 million followers, most of them in East Asia.

HINDUISM
Hinduism has very ancient roots in India. Its followers believe in many different gods.

ANIMISM
Followers of animistic religions believe that spirits live around us, in places such as rivers, mountains or rocks. More than 100 million people follow animistic religions.

FREEDOM

Freedom to follow any religion, or no religion, is a basic right in democratic societies.

GLOSSARY

ARISTOCRATIC
Describes someone who is of a high social standing, such as a nobleman.

ATMOSPHERE
The air around the Earth. The Earth's atmosphere is made up mostly of oxygen and nitrogen.

AXIS
A line through the centre of a spinning object. For example, the Earth spins on its own axis.

BACTERIA
Tiny organisms, some of which can cause disease.

BLOOD PRESSURE
A measure of the pressure at which blood flows through the body.

CALCIUM
A silvery white metal that is found in minerals such as limestone. Leaves, bones and shells all contain calcium.

CAMOUFLAGED
Something that is well-hidden. For example, the spots on a leopard help it to blend in with the tall grass so that it can sneak up on its prey.

CANAL
An artificial channel for boats and ships to sail through. In the body, a channel along which substances are passed.

CAPITALIST
Someone who supports capitalism. Capitalism is when the wealth of a country is owned by private individuals rather than by the state.

CARBON DIOXIDE
A colourless gas. Carbon dioxide is given off when humans and other animals breathe. It is also a greenhouse gas.

CELLS
The basic structural unit of all living organisms. Some animals are made up of a single cell, while others are made up of many. Cells perform all the processes to sustain life.

CIVIL RIGHTS
The rights of all of a country's citizens or people to have freedom and to be equal to each other.

COLD-BLOODED
Describes a creature that has a body temperature that changes depending on the surrounding temperature. Fish, amphibians and reptiles are cold-blooded.

COLONIZE
To control another country and make it a colony.

COMMUNIST
Someone who supports communism. Communism is a political system in which the state controls everything.

CONDENSE
To change into water, for example water vapour condenses into liquid water.

COUP
A takeover.

DEFEAT
To beat someone in a battle.

DESTINY
What is intended or meant for someone in the future.

DIET
The food a person or animal eats regularly.

DIGEST
To soften food in the stomach and intestine so that the body can absorb it.

DISSOLVED
When something has been mixed into a liquid so that it becomes part of the liquid.

DYNASTY
A series of kings or queens who come from the same family, for example, the Ming Dynasty.

EMIR
A Muslim commander or local chief.

EVAPORATION
The process of a liquid changing into a gas or vapour, for example, water evaporates to become water vapour.

EVOLUTION
The process where animals and plants develop from earlier or simpler forms of life.

FASCIST
Supporting of facism – a system of politics that is led by a dictator or person with total control or power.

FOREIGN POLICY
The way a country deals with other countries.

GALAXY
A collection of stars and dust. Our galaxy is the Milky Way.

GRAVITY
The force that pulls all objects in the Universe towards each other.

HABITAT
The natural living place of an animal or plant, for example, a lion's natural habitat is grassland or savanna.

HORMONE
A substance made in the glands of the body that is transported by the blood to stimulate organs in the body.

HUMIDITY
The amount of moisture in the air.

HYMNS
Religious songs.

HYDROGEN
A very light gas. Hydrogen has also been used to make deadly bombs.

IDEOGRAM
A character that symbolizes the idea of a thing without using the sounds used to say it. Examples are written numbers and the characters in Chinese writing.

ILLEGAL
Something that is against the law, for example, some animals are hunted illegally.

INDUSTRIALIZATION
The large-scale development of industries in a country or region.

INFINITE
Something that has no definite beginning or end.

INFLATE
To fill something with air or another gas.

LIFE CYCLE
The series of changes that an animal or plant goes through during its life.

MAGMA
A molten (melted) substance that is found beneath the Earth's crust.

MEMBRANE
A thin layer of skin, or a covering, which usually protects something else.

MILK TEETH
The first set of teeth that a human has. The milk teeth fall out and permanent adult teeth grow in their place.

MINERALS
An inorganic (non-living) substance needed by the human body for good health, such as calcium.

MOLECULES
A group of two or more atoms that are linked together in a chemical bond.

NEBULAE
Thinly spread clouds of dusts and gases.

ORBIT
To move around something, for example the Earth orbits the Sun.

ORGANISMS
A living animal or plant.

ORGANS
Parts of the body with particular functions, for example the stomach is an organ in the digestive system that helps the body to digest food.

OXYGEN
A gas found in the atmosphere that people and other animals need to stay alive. Something with oxygen is described as being oxygenated.

PREDATOR
An animal that hunts other animals. Lions and crocodiles are predators that hunt smaller animals such as antelope.

PREY
An animal that is hunted or killed by another animal, for example antelope are hunted by lions.

PROTEINS
Substances that are necessary for growth and good health. Animal proteins come from animals.

RADIATION
Heat, light or another energy source that is given out by something, for example the Sun.

REBELLION
A rise in opposition or armed resistance to an established government or leader.

REFLECT
To send something back from a surface, for example, heat, light and sound can be reflected.

REIGN
To rule a country or region, usually by a king or queen.

REPRODUCE
To make more of something, for example, humans reproduce to make children.

RITUAL
A series of actions or ceremonies, which are often religious, and take place regularly.

ROTATE
To turn around.

SHRINE
A sacred or holy place such as a temple or chapel.

SPECIES
A group of plants or animals that have the same characteristics.

SPORES
Minute, usually single-celled, reproductive units such as fungi.

TIDE
The regular rising (high tide) and falling (low tide) of the sea, which usually happens twice a day.

TOTALITARIAN
Describes a form of government that has just one political party.

TRADE
Business dealings such as the buying and selling of goods.

WARM-BLOODED
Describes a creature that has a warm body temperature that stays about the same regardless of the changes in temperature of the surroundings. Birds and mammals are warm-blooded.

INDEX

T

UV

WYZ

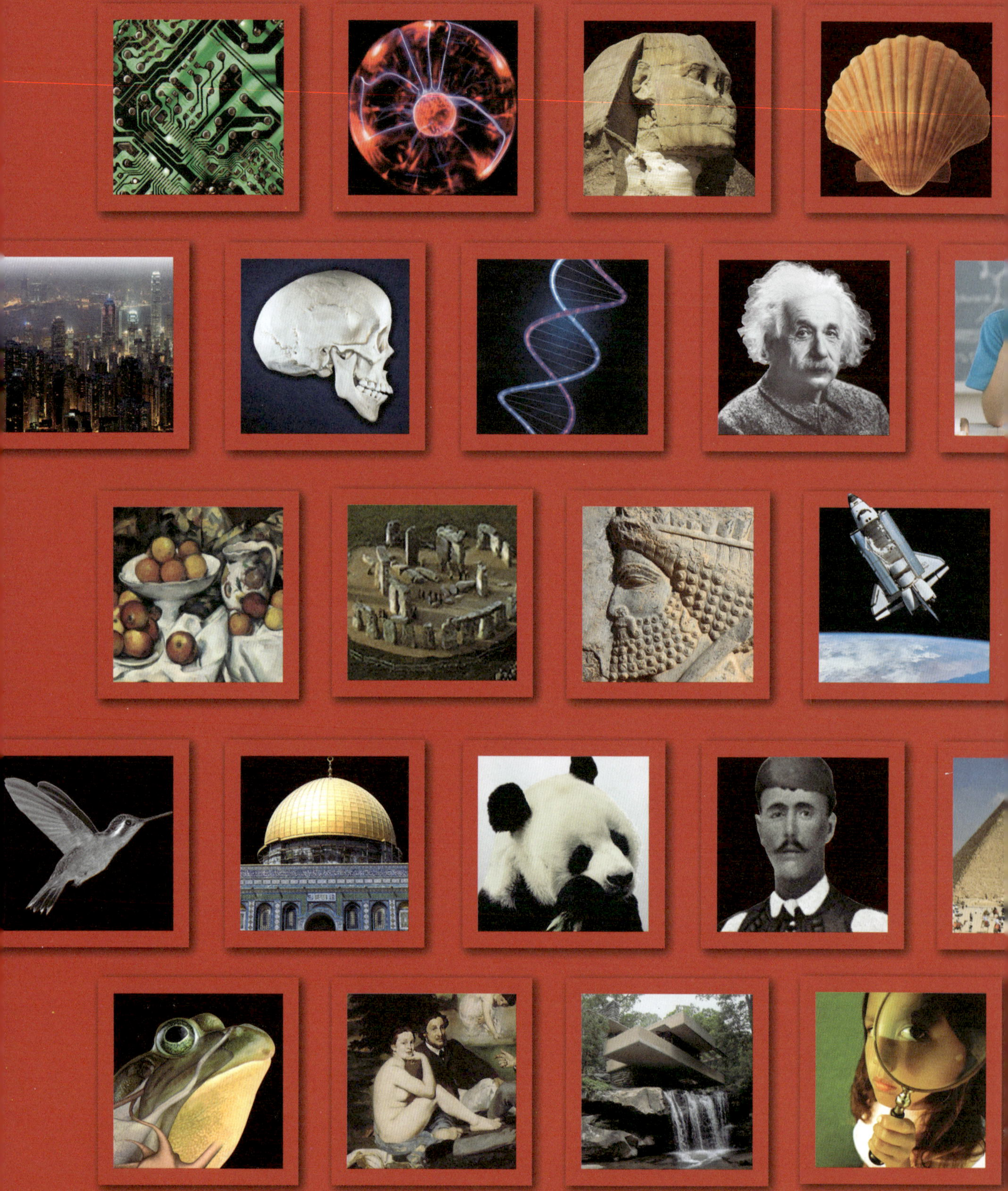